The Long Road to Freedom

The Story of Wang Mingdao

Stephen Wang

Sovereign World Ltd

Sovereign World Ltd
PO Box 777
Tonbridge
Kent TN11 0ZS
England

ISBN 1 85240 314 4

The publishers aim to produce books which will help to extend and
build up the Kingdom of God. We do not necessarily agree with every
view expressed by the author, or with every interpretation of Scripture
expressed. We expect each reader to make his/her judgement in the
light of their own understanding of God's Word and in an attitude of
Christian love and fellowship.

Cover design by CCD, www.ccdgroup.co.uk
Typeset by CRB Associates, Reepham, Norfolk
Printed in England by Clays Ltd, St Ives plc

Contents

About the Author

Stephen Wang was converted through the ministry of Wang Mingdao while he was away from his North China hometown studying at a middle school in Peking. Later he became a member of Wang Mingdao's church.

In 1945 Stephen entered Yenching University in Szechuan. Here he joined the evangelical fellowship on campus and began to learn to serve the Lord. Aware of God's call to full-time service, upon graduation he went to Shanghai to join Inter-Varsity Christian Fellowship's literature ministry for a brief period, then devoted himself to the translation of the Henry Halley Bible Handbook into Chinese. In 1950 he married Elizabeth Lu, secretary to Leslie Lyall of the China Inland Mission's literature department in Shanghai.

After the withdrawal of foreign missionaries from China, the Wangs returned to Peking and taught in middle schools for one year. In August 1955 Stephen was arrested along with Wang Mingdao as a key member of his so-called 'counter-revolutionary clique'. After one year and eight months in prison, Stephen spent the next twenty-one years in labour camps. Only in 1979, after the Party changed its policy, was he released and invited to teach English in a medical school. Two-and-a-half years later he came to North America as a visiting scholar and joined OMF the following year. After a further two years he moved to Toronto, Canada and later planted a church – the Toronto China Bible Church – pastoring it until he retired in 1996.

Stephen and Elizabeth have three children – twin daughters and a son. All were converted during the Cultural Revolution, when their father was dragged out of their home to be publicly criticised and denounced by the authorities and paraded through the streets. They are all engaged in full-time service for the Lord.

About the Translator

Ma Min was born in Chengdu in 1962 in an old church building occupied by the Railway Hospital and grew up in Southwest China. In the 1970s he studied English at a teacher's college and gained much language experience by spending time talking to American tourists in Xi'an. After college he pursued a career in teaching. Through some of his students he was introduced to other foreigners who 'kept talking about Jesus'. Ma Min desperately wanted to visit England, but it was impossible at that time to obtain a passport to do so. His Christian friends prayed for him and very soon his passport application was granted. He gave his life to Christ in response to this miracle.

Foreword

In the many visits to China I have made over the past twenty-five years, one man's name stands out over and above all other names in regard to house church leaders. His name is Wang Mingdao, the spiritual father of the modern-day Church in China.

Born at the turn of the twentieth century, during the infamous Boxer Rebellion, Wang Mingdao dominates the past century in the history of the Church in China. Though a contemporary of Watchman Nee, John Sung, Allen Yuan and other church leaders, he is best known inside China as a compassionate pastor, a biblically-based preacher and an absolutely resolute partisan of the cause of Christ.

Pastor Wang's prison testimony is perhaps what westerners have heard the most about. Who can erase from his or her memory that incredible comment regarding his more than twenty-three years in China's prisons: 'They were my honeymoon with Jesus!'

In the decade of the 1980s, after his release from prison and before his death, many missionaries and leading churchmen from around the world trekked to Shanghai for a personal visit with this man of God and his wife Deborah. But of all the commentaries on these visits, none is as insightful as my good friend Alex Buchan, a journalist for Compass Direct.

Alex quotes Pastor Wang as saying, 'When I was put in jail I was devastated. I was an evangelist – I wanted to hold crusades all over China. I was an author – I wanted to write books. I was a preacher – I wanted to study my Bible and write sermons. But I had no Bible, no pulpit, no audience, no pen and paper. I could do nothing – nothing except get to know God. And for more than twenty years that was the greatest relationship I have ever known. But the cell was the means.' His parting advice was, 'I was pushed into a cell, but you will have to push yourself into one. Simplify your life, so you have time to know God.' No wonder his favourite hymn was 'All the way my Saviour leads me.'

Author Stephen Wang was a close friend and colleague of Wang Mingdao for many years in China. Thus he is in the best position to pen the details of this excellent volume about this great man of faith. I have known Stephen as a friend since he emigrated to Canada and am so thankful that he has taken the time to painstakingly document this biography, *The Long Road to Freedom*, in his native language as well as supervise the translation into English.

Though Wang Mingdao went to his heavenly reward just over ten years ago, his heritage continues today in the fast-growing Church in China. He would be so proud of his spiritual successors as they cry 'Make China the largest sending nation of missionaries in the world!'

Paul Estabrooks
Minister-at-large
Open Doors International

Chapter 1

A Peaceful Year

The 1940s saw sweeping changes in China. Following the unconditional surrender of the Japanese in 1945, marking the end of their occupation of Mainland China, the Nationalist government desperately sought to re-establish control. But four years later, the Communists won their decisive victory and the government once again changed hands. The founding of the People's Republic of China in 1949 turned a brand new page of Chinese history.

For Wang Mingdao, too, this was an extraordinary time. Living under the harsh conditions and cruel realities of Japanese occupation, he had fought a fierce spiritual battle between life and death and had won a glorious victory. Brothers and sisters who deeply loved the Lord offered their heartfelt thanksgiving for him and the precious lessons they learned from his struggle and victory. But soon, a new and tougher battle was to dawn for him.

In 1949, when Wang Mingdao was forty-nine years of age, the Chinese people entered a new China. With his own eyes, he witnessed the triumphal march of the People's Liberation Army into the capital city on 3 February 1949, prompting this entry in his diary for that day:

'The People's Liberation Army entered the city today ... I walked to the city centre and saw the parade of the horse-drawn cannons followed by foot soldiers. Military bands led the parade with loud and joyful music from trumpets and drums, demonstrating their power and strength. Soldiers marched through in perfect unison with tidy uniforms and synchronised steps. Such a grand parade was never seen in China before.'

These first impressions of the Communists seem to have been positive, although he clearly found the new government of the people rather strange. Yet within the churches in Beijing there was much doubt, if not fear. On 31 January, before the arrival of the People's Liberation Army, the churches had already begun to prepare for change. Wang Mingdao lamented the pitiful lack of faith and vision of those pastors who changed constantly, tossed and blown about by the wind of changing circumstance. On 8 February, in a sermon entitled 'The Rolling Sea and the One who Calmed the Sea', he urged Christians 'to face change with the unchangeable, to prepare for ordinary times as extraordinary days, and to live in extraordinary days as in ordinary times.'

On 23 February, Beijing United Church was formed. The immediate agenda was how to adapt to the changing situation: the purpose was practical survival. The time resembled the early days of the Japanese occupation after the breakout of the Pacific War on 8 December 1941. The Church knew too well what had happened in Russian after the October Revolution in 1917 when churches were closed, pastors arrested and Christians persecuted. It is easy to understand their concerns and fears.

Following the liberation of Tianjin, Wang Mingdao went to the city on a week-long preaching trip. Every time he passed by the old French Concession as he made his way across the city by rickshaw, he read the bold white letters painted on a dark convent wall: 'FREEDOM OF RELIGION', which were visible for two or three years. Whenever he saw them he believed that the Communists would protect freedom of religion, and for the first year after liberation, he had no reason to doubt it: he travelled widely across China on many preaching trips, visiting, among other places, Hankou, Wuchang and Changsha to preach God's Word. No one stopped him, no one interrupted his preaching, and many came to listen to him. He began to believe that the Communists would indeed guarantee religious freedom. In this year, churches in China enjoyed much freedom.

Chapter 2

The Destiny of Chinese Christianity

After claiming victory all over mainland China, the Communists shifted their attention to the ideological front. 'Common Guidelines' were passed on 29 September 1949 which spelt out the principle that all citizens of the People's Republic of China were entitled to freedom of religion. But how these written words would actually be realised remained to be seen.

In the spring of 1950, Mr Wu Yaozong led a delegation to visit churches in Guangzhou, Changsha, Hankou, Tianjin and Beijing. The delegation consisted of leading figures in the religious groups and representatives from the national councils of the All China Christian Progressive Association, China Christian Association, China YMCA and China YWCA. Full of fear that the Chinese Church would suffer in the same way that the Russian Church had done, churches in different cities competed against one another to extend an invitation to the delegation. Wu Yaozong used the visit to call for major reform to rid the Chinese Church of the exploitation of imperialism. According to him, war ships and cannons had brought Christianity into China, and the Church had always been the instrument of Anglo-American imperialism. This was the reason why the Chinese people resented Christianity so deeply. As he represented the government, few dared to oppose him; in fact, many willingly followed his lead.

After touring around China, the delegation returned to Beijing where they were received three times by Premier

Zhou Enlai of the Central People's Government. Wu Yaozong summarised the message he received from Zhou Enlai in this one sentence: 'Christians must voluntarily fight imperialistic power and eliminate its influence.' On 23 September, the Proclamation of Reform subtitled 'Chinese Christianity in the Reconstruction of New China' was published. A Three-Self concept of self-governing, self-sustaining and self-propagation was conceived with the purpose of curbing imperialistic influence. On the same day, the national newspaper *People's Daily* featured an editorial entitled 'The Christian Patriotic Movement', lending strong support to the proclamation. The future direction of the Chinese Church was now clearly set.

On 26 May, on a visit to Changsha, Wang Mingdao heard from local church leaders that he belonged to the official delegation. He answered their inquiries about the Church in the North by saying that he had no idea of the situation in other churches, but everything was all right in his church. It was not until his return to Beijing that he realised that things had changed dramatically.

On 25 June 1950, war broke out in Korea between the North and the South and, two days later, the United States entered the conflict. On the same day, the UN passed a resolution to send troops to the aid of South Korea. On 25 October, the Chinese People's Volunteer Army crossed the Yalu River to fight with North Korea against the US. The Korean War suddenly became headline news in China.

These events proved decisive in shaping the fate of the Church in China. The Proclamation of Reform, which was a letter of allegiance from the Chinese Church to the new government, had been published before China became involved in the Korean War. In the face of war, the government was able to exert influence on Christians to choose between supporting American imperialism and helping the Chinese government. Naturally, Chinese Christians chose the latter, and in this way the Korean War promoted 'Three-Self reform' within the Church. On 29 December, the sixty-fifth meeting of the State Council of the Central People's Government published 'Guidelines for the Reform of

Cultural, Educational, Charitable and Religious Organisations Sponsored by the US', to which twenty-six national and local Christian leaders in Shanghai added their support. This set the tone for a national conference on its implementation.

Chapter 3

Reflections on His Fiftieth Birthday

In May that year, while on a preaching trip to Wuchang, Wang Mingdao's thoughts as he had reflected on his imminent fiftieth birthday had overwhelmed him. His diary includes the following confession to the Lord:

> 'In July, I will be fifty years old. As I remember, it has been over twenty-five years since the door opened for service when I was twenty-five; God has used me for His good work. Yet my spiritual life was full of weakness and failure: love that was insufficient, thoughts that were impure, words and actions that were careless, service and work that were unfaithful. I owe much to the grace of God. As I approach my fiftieth year, I cry out before God for revival. May my remaining years be spent not only on working for God but living a life pleasing to Him. (8.30 a.m.)'

God heard and accepted the deep longings and aspirations of Wang Mingdao's heart. He was preparing him to face the greatest spiritual battle of his life which would require all his spiritual maturity and test his relationship with God to the limit.

The day after he returned to Beijing from his trip, Wang Mingdao preached a message on courage. On 25 July, despite the fact that over twenty people came to congratulate him on his fiftieth birthday, he made time to write seven thousand words for the preface of his autobiography entitled *Over Fifty Years*. At a special service in the evening, he preached on the early part of his life from birth to new birth at fourteen, taking as his title 'A Piece of Burning Wood Plucked from the Fire'.

In August, while in Tianjin preaching, the Spirit brought home to Wang Mingdao the importance of his church, Beijing Christian Tabernacle. He wrote in his diary:

'As hundreds of people face this crisis, the work of the Church is very important. Churches all over the country are concerned. Yet I have lacked care and diligence in my work. I have not prayed for it unceasingly. Neither have I served faithfully. I have treated God's house and His work as a game. I have seriously disregarded the grace which God has entrusted to me. As I think about it this afternoon my heart is mixed with regret and fear. After my return to Beijing, I must serve God with vigour and vitality from a renewed heart. (5.10 p.m.)'

Wang Mingdao's words clearly indicate his awareness of the battle ahead of him. Beijing Christian Tabernacle must stand up for God's name and witness for Him. He was full of remorse over his proud attitude, but he was encouraged and revitalised to complete the work God had for him.

On 30 September, Wang Mingdao's autobiography *Over Fifty Years* was published, the culmination of three years' work. The idea for the book had come from a young Christian who had suggested he write his life story. The work had started in May 1948 and by July 1950 seven chapters had been completed. With the addition of a chapter entitled 'In Memory of Mother', written in the winter of 1949, the book was finished. *Over Fifty Years* was Wang Mingdao's precious gift to the Chinese Church.

Chapter 4

Some Anecdotes

After the age of fifty, whatever experiences a person may go on to have, his character seldom changes. Wang Mingdao was no different. Few people were better qualified to talk about the characters of Wang Mingdao and his wife than their son Tianzhe. The 1947 New Year's edition of *Fu Yin Pao* carried an article he wrote on the subject of 'My Parents':

> 'Some people may be interested to know about my father's habits and temperament: here are some observations, including both the positive and the negative sides of his personality. Dad has never liked the idea of fathers and sons covering up for one another.
>
> His heart is not as open as he would like it to be. Sometimes small things can make him see red, even though they rarely affect his work. For example, at the funeral service of Dr John Sung, some people failed to arrive on time because of bad traffic. Dad was extremely annoyed. But when he got up to speak, it was one of the most touching sermons I ever heard. Of course, this is not a good example for others to follow. It is best not to lose our temper. Dad's temper has subsided quite a bit in recent years.
>
> Many people know my mother's support for my father. Yet "support" is probably not the best description. When it comes to habits and opinions, Mom and Dad are often poles apart. For example, Dad likes to be polite, but Mom thinks that it's more important to make others feel loved. Dad loves being clean and tidy, and sometimes he will sweep the courtyard before the service. But Mother feels keeping clean must not interfere with one's work. Dad

emphasises the daily life of the believers in his teaching. But Mom regards this as dealing with superficial problems. She stresses discipline, diligence and spiritual maturity. Dad likes reading. But Mom will go weeks without reading a newspaper or book. At first, Dad thought that the difference in their personalities was like ice meeting charcoal. But when he realised they could complement each other, he stopped complaining. Recently he pointed out some verses in Proverbs 31 to Mom, but she did not change.

Dad used to tell Mother she was ignorant because she did not like reading. But as the years have gone on he has realised that in some ways Mom is wiser than he is. Once he told her, "I have more knowledge but you have more wisdom." This sounds flattering but it shows how hard it is to know people.'

The following incident illustrates the spiritual wisdom and steadfast faith with which Mrs Wang approached even the most everyday of problems. Behind the tabernacle there was a large vat which was used to collect rainwater for bleaching white garments. Each winter, when the temperature dropped, the vat had to be emptied before the water froze, otherwise it would split. One year, Mrs Wang was so busy that she forgot all about it. As winter set in with heavy frost and snow, Wang Mingdao told her to use the water up or throw it away, and although she had every intention of doing so, she didn't get round to it. Seeing the vat had frozen up, Wang Mingdao was furious and picked up an axe: 'Seeing as it's going to break anyway, I might as well do it,' he fumed.

At times like this, Mrs Wang would rely on God to sort out the situation. She quietly prayed in her heart, 'Heavenly Father, if you think it doesn't matter if this vat gets broken, let him break it. That way it will not bother me.' As she prayed, she heard the axe drop to the ground followed by complete silence. Then Wang Mingdao walked off. After that, Mrs Wang asked a brother who often helped them around the house: 'Was it better to try to pull him away physically or to depend on the Lord? If I had tried to pull him away, he would have become even angrier and the vat would certainly have got broken. If you give the situation over to God, he may try to break it, but he won't be able to.' She smiled happily, 'You see, it is much better to depend on God!'

Mrs Wang's heart was filled with concern for the needs of other believers. When one brother's baby was just a month old, his wife had to return to work while he stayed at home with the baby. One day, when feeding time came he had no can opener for the milk. In the process of opening the can with a chopping knife he spilled all the milk. Not knowing what to do, he went out to try and find some help. In the street, he met Mrs Wang on her bicycle, who squeezed something into his hand and left without a word. It was a can opener. This touched him so much that he prayed to God, 'Lord, you know my need. I am willing to do the same to meet the needs of others.'

Someone once said eighty per cent of Wang Mingdao's achievement was due to his wife. This may have been a bit of an exaggeration but she did help many people with her work and hospitality produced by a loving heart. One day, a Mr Yu, who had come from a long distance away, needed somewhere to stay. He was suffering from a very infectious disease, which made it very difficult for him to live and dine with others. Should they open up their home to him? With love, Mrs Wang welcomed him, arranging for him to live and dine on his own. Even his own chopsticks and bowls had to be washed separately. She also asked one of the brothers to help look after him. After Mr Yu left, he wrote a long letter not to thank them for their hospitality but to complain that, by keeping him separate from everyone else, they had despised him and treated him worse than non-believers treated him. After the brother who had looked after Mr Yu read the letter, he was very upset. When Mrs Wang asked him why, he replied, 'Have you ever met anyone so ignorant and selfish? If you have a disease like that, you need to accept it. If others receive you with love, you should be grateful. How can you say they despise you? A person like that does not know right from wrong!' Hearing this, Mrs Wang said with a gentle smile, 'This way we will be rewarded.'

Chapter 5

Meetings on American Funding

On 14 March 1951 Wang Mingdao received a visit from Brother Yan, a fellow Christian leader in Beijing. In the past the two men had been on good terms but their relationship had been severed when Mr Yan had joined the Christian Assembly. This was their first meeting in six years. He had come to tell Wang Mingdao about a national meeting of Christians he had heard was being organised by the Religious Affairs Section of the Cultural and Educational Commission of the State Council to discuss how to deal with Christian groups that had received American aid. Wang Mingdao did not believe that the government would organise such a meeting, insisting, 'The government doesn't want to be accused of interfering with the Church. A meeting of that nature would definitely be interpreted as interfering – they won't do it.'

But two days later Mr Yan came to see Mr Wang again. 'It's true,' he said. 'My source from Shanghai has confirmed that the meeting is being held.' He had heard about it from Mr Watchman Nee. Mr Yan asked Wang Mingdao, 'If the meeting is held and you are invited, will you go? And if you are not invited, will you ask to go?' Wang Mingdao answered, 'It would be best if I am not invited. If they invite me, I won't go.' But he continued to insist, 'The government won't interfere with the Church. If they really are planning to hold a meeting for that purpose, it will be interfering, and I won't go.'

When Mr Yan urged him to participate, Wang Mingdao asked him why. 'Most of the participants will be from Modernist groups with no faith,' Mr Yan explained. 'If they make any decisions about what can or cannot be preached on, and we happen to preach on what they do not like, we would become anti-government reactionaries. I think you should participate in order to fight them.'

'I am just one person,' Wang Mingdao insisted. 'There are well over a hundred of them. Most of them are liberals. And those that aren't, won't want to be seen to be disagreeing. If I attend, I will have to accept the decision approved by the majority. If I don't, I won't have to. And they won't be able to interfere with what I decide.'

'You are right,' Mr Yan nodded his agreement. 'I won't attend either.'

Soon afterwards, Mr Watchman Nee arrived from Shanghai to attend this meeting. At the same time he put out a statement which he had published by the Beijing Union Press, asking all those belonging to the Christian Congregation to support the Three-Self Church. Mr Yan changed his position and attended. Wang Mingdao made this comment on the meeting:

> 'What the congregation is doing is totally different from what they are saying. Originally, they were against all other churches, saying that, whatever their organisation and name, they were all sects and that sects are sinful: therefore everyone must leave their sects. That's why anyone who attended their meetings was required to leave their own church immediately. But today Mr Ni has totally changed his position. Now he can sit in meetings alongside priests and even non-believers. What's more, if his church is not receiving any foreign aid, why is he in Beijing for this meeting to discuss what to do with American-assisted churches?'

Local church leaders were invited to the meeting, and on 13 April Wang Mingdao also received an invitation. It was not printed but handwritten, delivered specially to Family Shi Lane in the East City:

> 'The Cultural and Educational Commission of the State Council is to convene a meeting on 18 April to discuss

how to deal with churches receiving American financial aid. Please attend as invited.'

The Cultural and Educational Commission
of the State Council

As soon as Wang Mingdao received this invitation, he wrote the following reply:

'Since its founding, this church has never received any foreign financial aid. Therefore we will not attend a meeting of this nature.'

Beijing Christian Tabernacle

The reply was sent to the State Council. At the meeting, Mr Liu Liangmo made the following statement: 'Wang Mingdao refused the government's invitation to attend this meeting. What ideology is this if it is not anti-Soviet and anti-Communist!' When Wang Mingdao heard this, he commented, 'What does this have to do with anti-Soviet and anti-Communist ideology? We have never received any foreign aid, so what reason do I have to go to a meeting dealing with foreign aid? Am I not doing the right thing by not going?'

The meeting was attended by 154 delegates from different denominations and groups, including some that were not connected with American missions, such as Watchman Nee's Christian Assembly in Shanghai and Jing Dianying's Jesus Family in Shandong.

Not long after the meeting had got underway, Wang Mingdao received a telephone call. 'This is Chen Zonggui. Are you at home? I would like to come see you.' The two men used to know one another well.

'By all means,' Wang Mingdao replied. 'I will expect you.' When Chen arrived shortly afterwards, he asked Wang Mingdao directly if he had received the invitation. Wang Mingdao explained that he had received it but since his church had never received foreign aid he had no reason to go. Chen tried to find an excuse to explain his own presence at the meeting. 'I did not know what the meeting was about,' he hedged. 'They only gave me the invitation as I boarded the plane at the airport. It was only then that I discovered it had to do with foreign aid.' It was not until later that Wang Mingdao realised that Chen had lied to him. He had told him that the seminary in Chongqing, of which he was President, had been founded by Chinese, whereas in fact foreign missionaries had also been involved. That is why he had had to come to the meeting.

During the duration of the meeting, which was held over several days, many of those attending came to visit Wang Mingdao, including Wang Hengxin from Xuzhou and Li Rongru from Changchun. Some of those who knew Wang Mingdao came to his church for the Sunday service.

On the first day of the meeting, Mr Lu Dingyi, the Deputy Minister of the Cultural and Educational Commission of the State Council of the Central People's Government, made a speech, outlining the purpose of the meeting which he said was to fulfil the decision made by the State Council on 29 December 1950, to encourage the Three-Self Movement of Chinese Christians and to deal with American-aided churches so that Chinese Christians became independent of foreign influence. He emphasised patriotism and reminded everyone of how American imperialists had systematically used the Church to invade and undermine China. He ended by urging Chinese Christians to 'rally behind the banner of anti-imperialism and patriotism, unite with the people's government and follow its leadership to work together to build a new China.' He hoped that Chinese Christians would 'actively support and participate in the three movements in China: to fight America and support Korea, implement land reform and purge reactionaries.' He summarised his address by saying that he wanted Christians to throw themselves into politics.

After his speech, the programme included some denouncing sessions to condemn foreign missionaries and Chinese preachers, among them Zhu Youyu, Chen Wenyuan, Liang Xiaochu and Gu Reneng. In a passionate speech entitled 'I condemn the American imperialists who used religion to invade China', Chen Zonggui, the President of the Chongqing

Seminary, attacked foreign missionaries for their involvement with imperialism, accusing them of opening the gate for its invasion. He also denounced the interpretation of verses in Ezekiel 38 and 39 by some American pastors and missionaries, although he added that fortunately such interpretations were not widespread in China.[1]

Another vicious attack came from Cui Xianxiang, Director of the National Council of the Chinese Christian Church, who condemned Bi Fanyu's activities in the Chinese Christian Church.

One person who played quite a prominent role in the meeting was a Mr Wang from Qingdao. He denounced Gu Reneng, accusing him of lying and gossiping. Referring to the fact that he had been arrested, he even asked the audience, 'People like this, shouldn't they be killed?' One voice in the audience replied, 'Yes.' The next day, a report in the *People's Daily* described angry shouting from the audience with chants of 'Yes, he should be killed.' These denouncing sessions became models for nationwide accusation meetings which later became widespread.

This meeting produced a new national steering organisation for the Chinese Church, 'The Preparatory Committee of the Chinese Christian Anti-America Pro-Korea Three-Self Reform Movement Council'. Wu Yaozong was elected as its president and Liu Liangmo its secretary. Not even one person raised any opposition. The Three-Self Movement was thus established.

Afterwards, Wu Yaozong and Liu Liangmo published their reflections on the meeting in the weekly magazine *Tianfeng*. Wu Yaozong wrote, 'This meeting was an unprecedented union of patriotic Chinese Christians. Due to different denominations and differences in beliefs, Christian unity is not easy. But now, under the leadership of the government, different denominations and groups are united under the banner of patriotism.' He reported that the purpose of the meeting was 'finally, thoroughly, eternally and completely to eliminate the cultural invasion of American imperialism in China over one hundred years under the leadership of the Central People's Government.' On the achievement of socialism, he wrote,

'The first achievement of the meeting was that it gave all participants a new perspective: a clear understanding of the relationship between Christianity and imperialism. The second was the denouncing sessions which lasted two days. Denouncement has become a familiar weapon in the purging of reactionaries. But among Christians, condemning is still completely new. And not only is it new, but it is also problematic. In the gospel, Jesus taught, *"Do not judge, or you too will be judged."* Most Christians remember this teaching in their hearts. To denounce is not only to judge, but also to accuse, to condemn. This seems to go against what Jesus taught. Is this so? I don't think so. When Jesus taught us not to judge others, he was saying that we should not be looking out for one another's faults, out of our selfish motives, forgetting that our own failings are probably much worse. Denouncement totally complies with what Jesus taught. Matthew 23 records Jesus' most powerful denouncement of the teachers of the law and the Pharisees. He used not only his righteous voice to oppose evil, but took brave action to attack his enemies. With a whip he drove those who used religion to exploit people out of the temple.'[2]

Wang Mingdao rejected the points made in this article:

'The Bible never taught condemnation of this kind. The Lord Jesus' condemnation of the teachers of the law and the Pharisees is totally different because He was referring to a group of people in the society, not a particular person. What He hated was sin, not people. He wanted to separate people from sin completely. His work was to teach people to repent from sin and return to God. This is the purpose of religion. Accusation is totally the opposite. Accusation is aimed at people. Its purpose is to expose a person's shortcomings, mistakes, or sins to the public. It is to criticise and attack him. It is to produce hatred for him for political purposes. Therefore, at both the level of motivation and practice, the Lord's condemnation of the teachers of the law and the Pharisees is completely different from the accusation and condemnation proposed by Mr Wu. According to the teaching of Jesus, no matter what kind of sin a Christian commits, it must be dealt with according to Matthew 18. A brother's sin must not be treated with public condemnation, especially when the person in question is an elder of the church and a servant of God.'

Mr Liu Liangmo wrote under the title 'An epoch-making meeting':

'This was a historic meeting. Before the meeting was the time when the Chinese Church developed under the shadow of imperialism. It was the time when imperialism used the Church to invade China. After this meeting will be the time when the Chinese Church will self-govern, self-sustain and self-propagate. It will be the time when Chinese Christians can make great contributions to the peace of our motherland and the peace of the world. Lu Dingyi's speech at this meeting taught us how lovely our motherland is. It taught us how terrible imperialism is. In the past, many Christians did not recognise that the Church was deeply entrenched in imperialism. Now we have suddenly woken up. Let us begin our work of digging out the old roots of imperialism from the Church. Let us accuse those imperialists hidden in the Church. In accusation, we can begin to deeply re-evaluate and criticise our own attitudes. This is a painful process. Night after night many of our brothers have not been able to sleep – until suddenly a new joy filled their hearts. This is what we Christians believe to be experiencing the "new birth"! Let us obey Chairman Mao's teaching and apply the method of accusation in order to learn. Let us strive hard to rid our Church of imperialist influences, to take part in the Anti-America

Pro-Korea Movement, to build up the Three-Self Church. We must purify the temple of God. We must establish the Church of the Lord upon the rock.'

The author's beliefs are very clear. He equates this change in ideology with the Christian experience of new birth. In reality, of course, it has nothing to do with new birth in Jesus Christ. Both Wu Yaozong and Liu Liangmo belonged to the national council of the YMCA, Wu in charge of publications and Liu in charge of ministries. Wang Mingdao once said,

'Many people think the YMCA is a Christian organisation. It is not! It is out to destroy Christian faith. After the breakout of the Pacific War, the Japanese organised a North China Christian Council. At first they tried to set up a United Christian Council for North China. Its director Zhou Guanqing was the Secretary of the Beijing YMCA. After a few months, when they changed the United Council to the Christian Council, they replaced Zhou, having realised that the YMCA could no longer lead the Church. The purpose of this meeting was to deal with the Christian Church receiving American money. The YMCA was one of the organisations represented. If they were having a meeting for Christians, the YMCA should not have been included. Their name is very misleading.'

Mr Wu and Mr Liu were both liberal Modernists and they had taken on the role of leading the Chinese Church on the road of 'Three-Self'. Wang Mingdao once made this comment on Wu Yaozong's beliefs:

'Among the Chinese "Christians" who do not believe in God, two famous individuals particularly stand out. One is Feng Yuxiang, the other is Wu Yaozong. When Yan Xishan, Li Zongren and Feng Yuxiang united their forces to attack Chiang Kaishek, they were defeated. Yan Xishan escaped back to his home in Shanxi, Li Zongren back to Guangxi but Feng Yuxiang had nowhere to go. The Governor of Shandong, Han Fuqu, took him to Taishan. One day, some Christian students who were having a meeting there, sent for Feng Yuxiang to speak to them. Feng told them, "Some people say I'm not a Christian. This is not right. I am a Christian, but I believe there is no God."

After the Japanese surrender, I was in Chengdu to lead a service. Someone gave me copies of the *Tianfeng* magazines published in 1945. *Tianfeng* was first published during the Anti-Japanese War when its chief editor was Wu Yaozong. In his magazine, I read an article by him entitled, "Where is God?" The article started by saying, "In a modern man's mind, God does not exist. He is only there to symbolise all superstition. In terms of literary interpretation, God is a dictator and an evil king." This article revealed to me that Wu is an atheist, a "Christian" who does not believe in God's existence and even accuses God of being an evil king. What kind of Christian is he?

What beliefs does Wu Yaozong have? He is a Marxist and Leninist who gives the appearance of being a Christian but in reality does not believe in God at all. How can he lead the Church? Clearly, what he wants is not the Church. The purpose of the Three-Self movement is to destroy the Chinese Church. The 1920s saw the united front of the anti-Christian movement. That was outside the Church. The 1950s is seeing the "Three-Self" Church, an anti-Christian movement from inside the Church. It is much more effective to destroy the Church from within. His atheism is completely against the basic beliefs of Christianity, leading the Church to walk the road of Three-Self. This is deception. Therefore, from its first day, I wrote an article in *Spiritual Food Quarterly* opposing it.'

In fact, Wu made his position very clear in his book *Darkness and Brightness*:

'I studied theology and philosophy in the US for three years. My school was one of the most progressive seminaries in the US. Twenty years ago, there was a bitter fight between the fundamentalists and the liberals in the US. The fundamentalists emphasised faith but denied rational thinking. They think every word in the Bible was inspired by God. The liberals would apply scientific thinking and historical method to criticise and purify conservative beliefs. My seminary was liberal.'

After Mr Wu returned to China, he taught in Chengdu during the Anti-Japanese War, making frequent speeches in different universities. Once he made a speech at Yanjing University on 'Christianity and Communism', in which he tried to reconcile the two ideologies which are in fact completely different in nature.

At the end of the meeting organised by the Cultural and Educational Commission of the State Council, the delegates passed a united proclamation with specific measures to deal with American-supported churches. Both documents were compiled by the Religious Affairs Section of the Commission. After receiving official endorsement, they were published by the State Council in the *People's Daily* on 27 July 1951.

Notes

1.   *Tianfeng*, Vol. 19, 19 May 1951.
2.   *Tianfeng*, Vol. 21, 2 June 1951.

Chapter 6

Nationwide Accusation Meetings

After the meeting in Beijing, the Christian churches and organisations in Shanghai went into action. National flags were raised inside the church buildings. Public rallies were held to protest against Japanese armament and to support a peace agreement. Portraits of Chinese leaders were hung on the walls of the meeting rooms. Churches and groups had special meetings around the clock to prepare to participate in accusation meetings.

On 8 May 1951, churches in Shanghai held their own meeting to deal with American-sponsored churches. Liu Liangmo spoke about the national meeting, saying that it had woken many delegates up to the fact that they had been poisoned by the 'super political' teachings of American imperialism. According to him, the meeting demonstrated that Chinese Christians, like patriotic Chinese people from other walks of life, would unite under the leadership of the Communist Party and People's Government to work hard to eliminate the influence of imperialist cultural invasion and build a new China.

Chen Jianzheng, Archbishop of the Chinese Anglican Church, spoke of the accusation sessions as one of the most important elements of the meeting. According to him, in order to be able to accuse others, one had first to resolve one's own ideological problems. In a most inappropriate manner, he quoted from Luke 6:45–47 and Matthew 18:15–18 to explain that Christians made their accusations because they loved China and God, hated evil, and wanted to keep others from sinning. On 19 May, *Tianfeng* published an article by Liu Liangmo on the subject of how to conduct an accusation meeting:

'The central task for all Christian churches and groups is to have accusation meetings. What must we accuse? We must accuse imperialists, their servants and other decadent elements hiding inside the Church. How must we accuse? First of all, we must rid ourselves of our fear. Some think they should hide the sin and expose the good and do not want to accuse. Others don't think they can accuse. We must invite as many Christian leaders and church representatives as possible to participate in the city-wide accusation meetings and public rallies to sentence reactionaries. The vehement denunciation by the people of imperialists, bandits, spies, landlords and warlords will stimulate Christians to act righteously by condemning imperialists and their scum within the Church.

Second, thorough preparations must be carried out. Accusation committees must be established in all churches and leading organisations to consider carefully who will be accused and who will do the accusing. The second step is to have small group accusation meetings. We must encourage participants to speak as much as possible. People who are the most powerful at making accusations at these meetings can then be invited to big meetings.

Third, how can we make the accusation meetings a success? In condemning Chen Wenyuan, scum of the Church, Jiang Changchuan of the Wesleyan Church set a good example. "We are more than resolved to purify our church with righteous fire even if it destroy our own family. As regards bad elements like Chen Wenyuan, we must execute one if there is one and ten if there are ten. They must be completely eradicated." Accusations like this will touch many hearts.

Fourth, the accusation must take place in an atmosphere of seriousness. Chatting and laughing must be banned. The way the accusation is conducted is very important. To achieve the best result, the programme must alternate between being tense, relaxed and then tense again. When the accusation is really good, appreciation can be expressed with the clapping of hands.

To all the accusation meetings we must invite officials from the religious affairs department and the government, representatives from democratic parties and other experienced groups to act as our advisors. The best accusations should be sent to local newspapers for publication. They must also be submitted to the Preparatory Committee of the Anti-America Pro-Korea Three-Self Reform Movement of Chinese Christians.'

On 10 June Christian churches and groups in Shanghai held its first accusation meeting led by Wu Yaozong, who made this statement the basis of his attack:

'The purpose of American imperialists in sending missionaries to China was to use Christianity as the political instrument of its invasion of China to make China a colony of the US.'

He named some early missionaries who came to China before liberation as his examples before going on to accuse Chinese evangelists:

'Americans sent missionaries all over China in the name of spreading the gospel but their true aim was to gather information as special agents. American imperialists raised a group of "church leaders" to be their faithful lap dogs. These dogs included Chen Wenyuan of the Wesleyan Church, Zhu Youyu of the Anglican Church, Liang Xiaochu of the YMCA, Zhao Shiguan, Zhao Junying and Gu Renen of the Pentecostal Church, etc. These dogs served their American masters in different ways by engaging in activities that have undermined our motherland and our people. American imperialists used Christianity as their instrument to invade China's culture. Through this conspiracy China has come under a noxious influence. In particular, they used this so-called "spiritual" movement to cover their activities with a religious veneer. They misinterpreted the Bible and spread toxic "super political" teaching that was anti-Communist, anti-Soviet and anti-people. Their purpose was to instigate dissension between Chinese Christians and our people's government.'

Citing Gu Renen and Xiang Jun who, in order to be made examples, had been placed under arrest, he condemned the American plan as anti-China and anti-revolution. He also accused American imperialists of using Christian literature to launch a cultural invasion of China, and in particular, 'using the Bible to anaesthetise people in order to enslave them.' He finished by urging Christians to condemn American imperialism, actively support and participate in the Three-Self Movement to fight against it, support the Koreans, reform land ownership, and purge the reactionaries. To comply with the 1 June Directive of the National Anti-America Pro-Korea Committee, he asked Christians to make special donations to support Chinese and Korean soldiers.[1]

Jiang Changchuan of the Wesleyan Church and Cui Xianxiang of the Chinese Christian Church also made accusations at the meeting. The meeting passed a solemn resolution to promote love for China and for the Church. It also agreed to salute Chairman Mao and the Chinese People's Volunteer Army. At the end of the meeting, all the delegates shouted, 'Long live the Chinese Communist Party!' 'Long live Chairman Mao!'

On 21 June, *Tianfeng* published an editorial entitled 'We accuse':

'(1) We accuse American imperialists of using thousands of missionaries who under the guise of religion control the Church in order to undermine the Three-Self Movement. They work as spies to gather information for the invasion of China.

(2) We accuse American imperialists of using the All China Christian Progressive Council as their base for invading China and undermining the Three-Self Movement that loves China and the Church.

(3) We accuse American imperialists of using mainstream Christian denominations such as the Wesleyan Church to make contact with Chiang Kaishek's bandits and of placing Chinese and foreign spies such as Chen Wenyuan into the Church in order to invade China.

(4) We accuse American imperialists of using Christian publishers such as *Guangxuehui* to spread anti-Communist, anti-Soviet, pro-American, worship-American and fear-American sentiments and carry out the cultural invasion of China.

(5) We accuse American imperialists of using the YMCA and the YWCA under the guises of "democracy" and "freedom" to spread liberal ideas and invade China.

(6) We accuse American imperialists of using the spiritual movement of the Pentecostal Church to disseminate super political poison that is anti-Communist and anti-Soviet, to undermine the unity between the believers and the government and to destroy the Three-Self" Movement.'

In conclusion the editorial urged all Christians in China to take part in the process of accusation. This was a marching order for the Chinese Church to start their condemnation campaign and, within three months of its publication, churches all over China held similar meetings. The accusations in Nanjing, Shanghai and Qingdao were particularly successful.

Note

1.   *Tianfeng*, Vol. 23, 21 June 1951.

Chapter 7

Beijing Christian Tabernacle

Amidst the noise of accusation all over China, the Beijing Christian Tabernacle under Wang Mingdao's leadership remained silent and unaffected. As church after church fell under government control, believers would naturally go to the place where they could hear the Word of God preached. Following the accusation meetings the congregation at the Christian Tabernacle saw its biggest increase. Those who were afraid were encouraged and empowered by the Word of God; the weak became strong. During Sunday worship, the church building filled to overflowing, with people crowding the courtyard and adjacent rooms. There was a warm atmosphere of growth and prosperity. The Christian Tabernacle was indeed a beacon of light in the darkness of the night.

The Communists knew all about Wang Mingdao. They knew it would not be easy to get rid of him. They realised that if they tried to blacken his character, no one would listen. Even the street peddlers believed Wang Mingdao was a good man. Besides, his church had been established by the Chinese and had no foreign connections. It would not be easy to tar him with the brush of colluding with imperialism. Neither would it be easy to erase the memory of his fight against the Japanese invaders during their occupation of Beijing. The best scenario would be if they could persuade him to lead a Three-Self church. All they could do was wait patiently for Wang Mingdao to come round to their way of thinking.

When Gu Renen was arrested in Qingdao, the government together with the Three-Self Church, knowing that Wang Mingdao did not agree with Gu's actions, tried to make him speak out against him, but he refused. Later, when he was asked why he would not speak out, he said he was not willing to hit Gu when he was down. Earlier when people had praised Gu, he had criticised him for his dishonesty in word and conduct. But when Gu was suffering, he remained quiet.

After the April meeting to deal with churches with foreign funding, Wang Zizhong, Chairman of the United Christian Council in Beijing, sent for Wang Mingdao. 'You should join the United Christian Council,' he advised. 'No, I will not,' Wang Mingdao replied. 'Our faith is different from yours.' Wang later became the Chairman of the Three-Self Church in Beijing. He never really believed the Bible. Wang Mingdao once told this story to illustrate where Wang stood:

> 'Once a Mr Ning went to ask Wang about the Bible. Wang told him, "You must not believe all that is in the Bible. You can only believe selectively. Believe only those verses that can be believed, not those that cannot be believed." This confused Mr Ning who came to me with the same question. I asked him, "If you went to buy a dictionary and the shopkeeper told you you could only believe part of the dictionary, would you buy it? We buy dictionaries because we do not know all the words. If we can only believe part of it, should we buy it?" After that, Mr Ning never went to Wang again.'

In 1951, Yan Jiale, leader of Beijing Christian Congregation, was persuaded to join the Three-Self Church. He wrote a statement signed by ten people to support Three-Self. Wang Mingdao felt heavy when he read the statement, realising how isolated he was becoming. In late June, leaders of the Congregation began to lure and threaten those who refused to join Three-Self in an effort to make them change their position, ordering preachers not to mention the concepts of 'kingdom of darkness', 'Satan' and 'heaven'. Many brothers and sisters left the Congregation to join the Christian Tabernacle. Yan Jiale had thought that the Christian Tabernacle would not survive if it refused to join Three-Self. However, when he saw that the government did not interfere and that it grew in numbers at the cost of his own congregation, he

began to believe the government was not serious in its
intentions and reversed his decision to join Three-Self. In
those days, many churches lost their vision and could not see
the way ahead.

After Shanghai Christian Congregation joined the Three-
Self, its elder Zhang Yuzhi came to Beijing in October 1952.
On 20 October Zhang visited Wang Mingdao, accompanied
by Yan Jiale. The three men talked for two and a half hours.
He told Wang Mingdao that Brother Ni had joined Three-
Self. 'He can do whatever he wants. It's none of my business.
But I never will,' Wang Mingdao replied. 'From the very first
day of Three-Self, Chinese Christians lost their freedom of
belief. Do you want freedom of belief? Yes, but you say we
must join Three-Self. As soon as you join, you are compro-
mised and before long you become an atheist. They won't
even need to force you to say there is no God. You won't dare
to mention God yourself.'

Zhang Yuzhi asked Wang Mingdao where the Church
should be heading. Wang Mingdao said, 'It must walk the
road the disciples walked.' By this he meant that the Church
should follow the example of the disciples, imitating their
courage and perseverance. It should not give in to the threat
of intimidation but be faithful right to death. It should not
please man but spread the gospel in all circumstances. It
should teach only what is written in God's Word. He insisted
that the Church needed to repent of its mistakes. They
needed to be humble before God and ask for His mercy. He
warned them not to 'go to Egypt' for help.

After he returned to Shanghai, Zhang started meetings in
his home and stopped going to the Congregation. Wang
Mingdao sent him a few copies of the *Spiritual Food Quarterly*
for his church. During the Cultural Revolution, Zhang was
arrested and soon after executed for his faith. That was a time
of chaos, of random attacks and brutal killings. It was said
that he was very brave at his death. After the Cultural
Revolution, the government tried to give his family a few
thousand yuan as compensation. His wife refused to accept
the money, saying, 'My husband is worth more than a few
thousand yuan.'

Chapter 8

Growing Pressure

Shanghai was the base of the Three-Self Movement and often led the way for the national campaign, serving as an example for other churches and cities. After the accusation meeting held in Shanghai on 10 June 1951, similar meetings were held all across China. Beforehand preparatory meetings were held to study Liu Liangmo's guidelines on 'How to hold accusation meetings'. The accusations could only be made on the platforms of public rallies after they had been rehearsed in private. But many places lacked Shanghai's organisational standards and meetings often turned out to be absurd. Not only were the expected results not achieved, but they also exposed scandals inside the Church. In cities where the accusation meetings were successful, they were followed by the establishment of local Three-Self churches. The most progressive members and leaders of the local churches would be named as the new leaders. Behind the scenes these churches were directed by the Department of Religious Affairs. They often targeted pastors and preachers who had spoken 'inappropriately', forcing them to write 'self-confession' reports. Increasingly, the leadership of the Church was falling into the hands of the government. When Wang Mingdao realised the seriousness of the situation, he urged believers to be strong and courageous in their faith, wise and cautious in their speech, and loyal and diligent in their work.

After five days of preparatory meetings organised by the Beijing Christian Council, the Wesleyan Church planned to hold its own accusation meeting. But it did not achieve its desired aims. The influence of Wang Mingdao was too strong in Beijing. In December, pressure from the government began to mount. At a preparatory meeting on 14 December, a Mr Wang from the Department of the United Front spoke for three hours, urging all churches to hold their own accusation meeting. During the course of his address, he mentioned the name of Wang Mingdao. In February 1952, the Three-Self Church began to increase pressure on Wang Mingdao through their publication *Tianfeng*. On 21 February Wang Mingdao wrote in his diary:

> 'The police came with a request to use our hall. We told them that for reasons of faith we do not rent out our hall. Afterwards we were summoned to a meeting in two or three days' time. As we awaited their reply, Chang Linshi and Yu Yifang came with a copy of *Tianfeng* Vol. 301. In the report on church donations to support the Korean War, it said, "All churches launched donation campaigns except for a few such as the one led by Wang Mingdao." The purpose was to accuse me. But I don't think there is any reason for me to make a statement about it.'

The donation campaign was initiated by the Preparatory Committee of the Chinese Christian Anti-America Pro-Korea Three-Self Reform Council to support Chinese and Korean soldiers. Wang Mingdao did not try to stop other believers making donations, but he would not have anything to do with it himself.

On 10 August a key figure from the Beijing Three-Self Church, Zhao Fusan, visited Mr Wang Kecheng who was an elder of the Christian Tabernacle and taught at the Beiman Girls' High School. Wanting to divide the leaders of the Tabernacle and isolate Wang Mingdao, he asked Wang who the deacons were at the Christian Tabernacle. This was a new tactic by the Three-Self Church in Beijing. On 15 August Mr Qi Ruiting came from Tianjin to talk with Wang Mingdao about the situation in Tianjin. He had heard that someone had said that Wang Mingdao would have to be swept away with an iron broom. They were trying to scare him. In May 1953 the Christian Council banned all churches from inviting Wang Mingdao, Wang Cheng and Allen Yuan to preach.

In addition to growing pressure from the outside, Wang Mingdao also faced resistance from within his own church.

When some saw the good things the Communists were doing, they gave up Christ and became Marxists and Leninists, even proposing that not only the Bible, but also the writings of Marx and Lenin be studied at church. The most outspoken of those who believed this was Wang Enqing, and he influenced many young people. Some gave up their faith and joined the Communist Party. Under the influence of new ideologies after liberation, even Wang Mingdao's son, who was in his second year at university, began to doubt his faith. He did not completely give up his faith, but wavered between belief and unbelief. Because of his heavy workload, Wang Mingdao had no opportunity to talk with him until 6 July 1951. After talking together for two hours, they began to understand each other better. But from that time on, whenever the father thought of his son's unbelief, his heart was filled with sorrow. On New Year's Eve, 1951, Wang Mingdao spent time in God's presence. On the first day of 1952 he wrote:

'At 11.45 last night I was on my knees. I was reminded of my sin in pride and how often my thoughts, words and deeds deprive God of His glory. I saw how utterly corrupt I am. I could only confess my sins before God and ask for his forgiveness. Then I prayed for my son, asking God to restore his faith so that he does not wander astray. After prayer I felt the peace and power of God and went to bed at midnight. The topic for tomorrow's sermon is "The year ahead".'

Wang Mingdao loved his son deeply, and his son had great respect and love for him, too. The way Tianzhe lived out his life in his relationships and his work testified to the impact his father's teaching had made on his life. He understood his father's sorrow. In 1952, when he worked in Shanghai, he sent a telegraph to Brother Wang Enqing, asking him to comfort his father. But for the rest of his life, until he was called home, the deep pain in Wang Mingdao's heart because of his son did not subside. Information from his diary and his friends indicate that nothing hurt him more than his son's unbelief.

Chapter 9

Doctrinal Teaching Group

From March 1949 onwards a discipleship class had been held every Thursday in the small hall of the Christian Tabernacle with the purpose of teaching biblical doctrine. Twenty people had attended that first meeting. In the beginning of 1952 the group was relaunched and the name changed from 'Training Class' to 'Study Group'. Fifty people attended the first session on 17 January when Wang Mingdao taught on purity. A year later, the name was changed again, this time to 'Teaching Group', and personal testimonies and drinks were included in the evening as well as study. Thirty-two people attended. Towards the end of 1953, the name was changed again to 'Doctrinal Teaching Group'.

Under normal circumstances, discipleship groups were no more important than other forms of fellowship meetings but, when it came to the Christian Tabernacle, the government paid very special attention. Those who attended were considered the 'key members of Wang Mingdao's group' as distinct from the ordinary believers. This was because, after 1954, the group was not open to everyone but could only be attended by those who had been individually assessed. Only a few dozen church members were invited to the group, and they were considered the core of Wang Mingdao's church, the inner circle. If anyone from outside the church asked to be included, someone from the group would talk with them to assess their spiritual life. Then a report would be given to Wang Mingdao about them.

The main purpose of the group was to give instruction on the Bible so that group members would be equipped to teach the gospel. Wang Mingdao would speak first and then everybody else would have the opportunity to contribute.

Between 1954 and 1955, Wang Mingdao taught solely on the Bible, but after that he also spoke on topics such as the Three-Self leaders, why the Christian Tabernacle did not become part of the Three-Self Movement, and why it had not joined the North China Christian Union during Japanese occupation. He felt it was important to keep reminding people about these important lessons from the past in order to strengthen their faith.

After 1954, the situation became increasingly tense. The doctrinal teaching group had been swelled by the presence of some impostors who had won the trust of the church but who were spying for the government. Later, even policemen came to sit in the meetings. Wang Mingdao felt the weight of the pressure, because what he taught was in sharp disagreement with the official Three-Self guidelines. He said,

'The Three-Self Church is the most effective method used by those outside the Church to destroy the Church from the inside out. Throughout history no one has ever before thought of such a clever way to destroy the Church, but today it has been discovered.'

He regarded this as Satan's attack on the Church and thus a spiritual battle. To safeguard faith and keep the truth that had been passed down to the saints (cf. 1 Corinthians 15:3), the Church must remain alert, cautious and courageous. From the perspective of the government, the Christian Tabernacle was a watertight, impenetrable stronghold of the enemy. The doctrinal teaching group was its core, and must therefore be dealt with most seriously. Besides the 'wolves in sheep's clothing', the group had other problems. Cao Lianpu publicly announced, 'I don't believe any more.' These words deeply hurt Wang Mingdao. Then Cao Lianpu and Wang Enqing proposed a youth group to study the Bible alongside Marxism and Leninism, with the emphasis on political studies and also questioned why the church did not join the national Christian conference. In addition, they denounced those whom they did not regard as patriotic and loyal to the government, making life very hard for them.

These attacks from within and without deeply troubled Wang Mingdao.

In the late summer of 1954, as internal pressure continued to grow, Wang Mingdao held a meeting after a Sunday evening communion service in Brother Jin Guangding's room in Shijia Hutong to discuss the situation with his key leaders. It was attended by over ten people, including Liu Xiaojin, Shi Changling, Sun Zhenglu, and Wang Mingdao's wife. Wang Mingdao asked, 'Wang Enqing and Cao Lianpu think that we should have meetings to study political theories in the church. They propose a youth group which would meet in the small hall to study the Bible, Marxism and Leninism. What do you think?' Those present considered that people had sufficient opportunities to study Marxism and Leninism at their workplace and there was no need to do it in the church. The church was where the Bible is studied and it was not the appropriate place for meetings of another nature. If they insisted, they could go elsewhere. As long as they stayed, the answer was no. This may seem a matter of small significance but it throws important light on the pressure Wang Mingdao was feeling. In the past, for instance when faced with Japanese occupation, he had clearly discerned God's will and had not felt the need to go to others to ask for advice or sympathy. He had relied only on God, even if that meant risking losing his life. But under the present circumstances, he was hesitant and fearful. He needed help, sympathy and support.

Chapter 10

Infiltrators in the Church

In 1954, as the spiritual battle was waging, unbeknown to the church, false brothers and sisters had infiltrated both the inner circle and the fringe of the church and had won the believers' trust.

Beijing Christian Students' Union had very strong links with the Tabernacle, with most of the students attending Sunday services, and it was very influenced by Wang Mingdao. Both its Chairman and Deputy Chairman were students, but not all the leaders of the Union were. Some were teachers, others were government officials. They all participated in the Union prayer meeting, which was a very important meeting where all the decisions were made. The background of at least two of the group leaders was rather unclear.

One of them was Lou Guxiang. He was from Sichuan and was an Assistant Professor at one of the Beijing universities. Nobody knew exactly how he had ended up in the Student Union and the Tabernacle. He appeared enthusiastic and God loving and was very active in the church. After the former Chairman Shi Changlin joined full-time ministry, it was no longer convenient for him to live at home, so he stayed at Lou's place, and the prayer meeting was often held there. Being in charge of liaison at the Union, Lou knew everything there was to know. When the Chairman Huang Shaofu had anything that needed co-ordinating, Lou would be the one to do it. But Huang had no idea where Lou had come from. After Wang Mingdao was arrested in 1955, he suddenly disappeared. No one could find him, not even at his university. Years later, when people asked about him, Huang Shaofu would say, 'Oh, how naive we were!' In fact, he had been placed there undercover, and when his work was finished he was transferred.

The other suspicious person was Guo Qiyu, who at one time led the devotion group. When the Union wanted a guest speaker, it was her job to make the invitations and, as a result, she knew about everything that was going on in connection with the prayer meeting. For a long time she worked closely with Wen Yijun, the Deputy Chairman. After Wen was arrested, nothing happened to her. Not only that, but she was promoted. After graduating in pharmacy she got a job at a pharmaceutical research institute but, following Wang Mingdao's arrest, she was transferred to a medical college where she became the head of its personnel department. To have been given such a prestigious position meant she must have made a special contribution to the Revolution. Later, she told others that she had given up her faith. But the truth was she never had any faith. She had lied. Because the Union was closely connected with the Tabernacle, it was very easy for Lou and Guo to come to the meetings. They were thus able to gather information for the government.

Other infiltrators found their way inside the church and managed to become close to Wang Mingdao's wife; among them were Mr and Mrs Li Yingfu. Li had been the chief of staff for General Fu Zuoyi. When he had worked in Suiyuan, he had saved Communist underground workers. After liberation, he and his wife became public security officers. Because of his work with the resistance Li was held in great respect and worked with the Director of Beijing Public Security Bureau. His wife, who had been an opera singer, used the pretext of wanting to learn English to gain an introduction to Mrs Xiao, which put her in an ideal position to find out who the family's frequent visitors were. She reported everything that went on in the Xiao family. Through Mrs Xiao, Mrs Li also came into the Tabernacle and the Union. They even went to the Home of Grace in Fragrance Hills for 'spiritual devotion'. From there they gathered information about the Home of Grace for the government. Li Yingfu pretended to be very spiritual and earnest in his seeking of God. The morning after Wang Mingdao's arrest Mr Li was at the Union

Chapel at Nanheyan, where the Union had its office and held meetings, to 'pray' and 'study' the Bible. He was really there to find out what was going on.

Another suspicious person was Ong Lisheng. At one time Ong had been the personal secretary to General Zhang Xueliang, but little else was known about his past. Between 1954 and 1955 he often appeared among the pastors in Beijing who were refusing to participate in the Three-Self Movement and he often visited Wang Mingdao and told him things about other churches that no one knew. Before 1955 he wrote an article, saying that he was a Christian, but all those who knew him doubted his authenticity. After Wang Mingdao's first release, Ong was always in the Tabernacle, never wanting to miss a meeting. Whenever any of the elders wanted to take a walk with Wang Mingdao, he would always want to accompany them. It was obvious that he was working under cover.

It was not until after Wang Mingdao's arrest that the believers at the Christian Centre began to put two and two together about what really had been going on. These are just a few examples of those known to be working under cover for the government. There were probably others too, but the truth will never be fully known.

Chapter 11

Chinese Christian National Conference

By the beginning of 1954, after the national accusation meetings and the political studies, the Three-Self Movement had established and consolidated its leadership over the Chinese churches. The Three-Self Preparatory Committee had accomplished its mission. The next step was to hold a national meeting to set up the Three-Self Church formally. But even before that, a Three-Self Branch Committee was established in Beijing and pastors from different churches were summoned to a meeting to discuss the proposed Church's constitution. Mr Li, Director of Religious Affairs for Beijing People's Government, telephoned Wang Mingdao, inviting him to go to the city government offices that Saturday morning for a talk. At that time the official attitude towards Wang Mingdao was still the softly softly approach of patiently trying to persuade him to join Three-Self. It was ineffective, but none the less a clever strategy. As soon as Wang Mingdao joined Three-Self, they reasoned, he could work for the government.

Wang Mingdao arrived punctually for the meeting. After being received by a lady, Mr Li came out of his office carrying in his hand a copy of *Over Fifty Years*, Wang Mingdao's autobiography. As soon as they started talking Wang Mingdao realised that Li already knew a lot about him. He asked, 'Mr Li, what is it that you want to talk about?'

'Nothing in particular,' Mr Li replied. 'I thought it would be good to talk.'

Wang Mingdao began to tell him about the beginnings of the Christian Tabernacle. After a while, Mr Li stopped him, saying, 'Pastors in Beijing are meeting to discuss the constitution of the Three-Self Church. Would it be all right to ask you to come?'

'I won't attend,' Wang Mingdao answered. 'My thoughts and faith are very different from theirs. I don't associate with them. If they are meeting in a room, I won't go in.'

He continued telling his story for almost three hours, until the telephone rang. 'Mr Li, let me say goodbye. It's your lunch-time.'

'No rush. Let's finish our conversation.' Mr Li insisted. The talking went on for another ten minutes but then Mr Li warned, 'Let me give you some advice. Don't isolate yourselves from other people and harbour hostile attitudes towards them. It's right and proper that we should unite with one another.'

'It's not the Christians who are not willing to unite,' replied Wang Mingdao. 'But no matter what we do, we are despised and discriminated against. How can we unite?'

'We do understand the situation,' Mr Li said. 'We will educate our people to change their attitudes. They must not treat Christians like that.'

The meeting did not finish until 12.15 p.m.

That evening, the youth group, known as the Timothy Group, had a meeting in the small hall at the Tabernacle. More than ten young people were present. When Wang Mingdao told them about his talk with Mr Li, explaining that he had refused to attend the meetings to discuss the Three-Self Church, it became clearer than ever before that the Tabernacle would not join the Three-Self Church.

Soon afterwards the National Christian Conference was held in Beijing's old Lantern Market from 22 July and 6 August, attended by 232 delegates from all over China. They stayed at the guesthouses outside the city's Front Gate and were shuttled into the meeting by special buses every day.

At about this time, four delegates from Beijing Three-Self Church – its Chairman Wang Zizhong and Deputy Chairman Zhao Fusan, Jiang Yizheng and Ying Jizeng – came to see Wang Mingdao at the Tabernacle. Wang Mingdao was conducting a wedding when they arrived. When the cook came to announce their arrival, he asked her to tell them he was too busy to see them. An hour later, when the wedding was over, the uninvited guests came back. Wang Mingdao had always found these men difficult to talk to, particularly Wang Zizhong. He had never been impressed with Zhao Fusan who, before liberation, had been a great admirer of Dr Aidy, a promoter of liberal theology in the US. So he instructed his co-worker to tell them there was nothing to talk about. Thus he drove his guests away.

A few days later, when Wang Mingdao was talking with some people in the hall, the doorbell rang and he was informed that there were some visitors who would like to see him. Wang Mingdao took the card and read their names: Chen Jianzheng, Jiang Changchuan, Chen Zonggui, Zhu Guishen, Xie Yongqing. Most of them had come down from Shanghai for the national meeting. As their average age was over seventy, they were called 'The Five Old Men of Shanghai'. Wang Mingdao knew that they had come to try to persuade him again to attend the national meeting. So, once again he told Mrs Chi, his co-worker, 'Tell them I have nothing to talk about.' After a while, she came back to report that, if Wang Mingdao was unwilling to see them, they would like to see Mrs Wang. 'You can see them,' Wang Mingdao told his wife. Mrs Wang met them in the reception room. After some greetings, Jiang Changchuan said, 'When the Japanese organised the Christian federation, we said nothing bad about Mr Wang.' He was inferring that they were not his enemy.

'You know what his temper is like,' Mrs Wang replied. 'When he speaks, he never worries about saving face. If you see him, and things become heated, you will all be embarrassed. That would be terrible. So it is better not to see him.' Later a rumour surfaced: 'Even Wang Mingdao's wife knows his temper. You can tell how hard it is to deal with him.'

After their visit, a wave of accusations flared up. 'The Shanghai Five are highly respected men in their sixties and seventies. Wang Mingdao is only in his fifties. How could he refuse to see them? What a proud man he is!' The purpose of such accusations was to make Wang Mingdao confess his pride and accept that he should have met them. But Wang Mingdao maintained he had had good reason to refuse to see them.

At the national meeting, Wu Yaozong delivered an official report on the first four years' work of the Three-Self Reform Movement, listing four major achievements. First, the Chinese Church and Christian organisations had rid themselves of imperialist control and were now controlled by the Chinese believers themselves. Second, the elimination of all imperialist influence was now in progress. Third, with a better understanding of imperialism and a firmer commitment to patriotism, Chinese Christians had begun to participate in patriotic movements which would safeguard world peace. Fourth, new life was emerging in the Church in the new China based on patriotism and faith. After talking about the mistakes and problems, he proposed that the next steps in developing the Three-Self Movement were to:

'(1) Urge all believers to support the Constitution of the People's Republic of China and make their contribution to socialist construction.

(2) Urge all believers to resist the invasion of imperialism and work for world peace.

(3) Continue patriotic studies among the clergy to totally eradicate the influence of imperialism.

(4) Consolidate self-governing and improve the unity of the Church.

(5) Research the problems associated with being self-supporting and help churches to achieve this.

(6) Research the work of self-propagation governed by the principle of mutual respect in order to eliminate the vestiges of imperialist poison and spread the pure gospel.

(7) Implement the love of China and of Christ, encourage patriotism, obey the law and purify the Church.'

All these were political steps; there was nothing about spiritual development. He emphasised unity but it was political unity: it had nothing to do with biblical unity. He said,

> 'Our experience over the past four years indicates that imperialist powers never stop trying to accuse and destroy our unity. We must therefore apply our love for the Church and work for the unity of all Christians. If something promotes our unity, we will try our best to do it. If it harms that unity, we must identify it at once and correct it. For the sake of unity, we must accept the differences between churches, denominations and theologies and be governed by the principle of mutual respect.'

This speech was intended to make evangelicals respect the liberals and live in peace with them. Its overriding message was that no one should expose or criticise the erroneous teaching of the false prophets and false teachers because criticism and exposure would undermine unity. But Wang Mingdao knew that, if the Church became united with the liberals who did not believe, it would not be able to hold firm to the truth of the Bible. As Paul wrote,

> *'Do not be yoked together with unbelievers. For what do righteousness and wickedness have in common? Or what fellowship can light have with darkness?'*
>
> (2 Corinthians 6:14)

Such unity with false prophets goes against the teaching of the Lord who warned, *'Watch out for false prophets'* (Matthew 7:15; see also 2 John 7–11). If Christians gave up the Bible and their faith to unite with false teachers, there would be dire consequences.

The meeting also included accusation sessions. Because Wang Mingdao had refused to meet with the leaders from Beijing and Shanghai, it was arranged that Shan Letian of the Seventh Day Adventist Church should lead an attack against him. In the past the Adventists had always been isolated from other churches, but now its leader was not only invited to the meeting but was asked to take the pulpit! He made the following accusation about Wang Mingdao:

> 'I know Wang Mingdao well. Today, let me tell you one thing about him that you do not know. During the Japanese occupation of Beijing, he donated copper to the Japanese. He fraternised with them and supported them. When the Japanese needed copper to make bullets to kill Chinese, he led his church in donating copper to them. This is a very serious matter!'

Wang Mingdao realised that Pastor Shan was trying to make him come to the meeting to put an end to his 'revelations' – he was saying, 'We know what you have hidden in your closet. If you don't come to the meeting we will expose it.' But he paid no attention to the accusations. He simply explained:

> 'I did not "offer" copper. It was a copper levy. The mayor ordered every household to give copper. The police knocked on each door telling us how much we must give. Big, medium and small families were given quotas. When they received the copper, they would weigh it. Nothing less than the quota was acceptable. After we satisfied the quota, they would issue a slip with a stamp, "Copper", which we had to paste on our door. Otherwise we would have had to give more. That slip was on the door of the Tabernacle for many days. Maybe Pastor Shan saw it. He spoke about that to accuse me of supporting the Japanese, to find fault with me.'

Before the end of the conference, Brother Tang Shouling, the Chinese translator of *Streams in the Deserts*, came to see Wang Mingdao. When Mrs Wang saw him, she asked, 'I heard all the delegates went sightseeing today. Why didn't you go with them?' His word was the heart cry of a believing brother: ' "The harps were on the poplars" [cf. Psalm 137:1–2] how could I have the heart to sightsee!' With the Chinese Church becoming captive, how indeed!

The conference concluded with an edict which formally changed the name of the Three-Self Movement to the 'Chinese Christian Three-Self Patriotic Movement', and the establishment of a national steering organisation under the name 'Chinese Christian Three-Self Patriotic Movement Council'.

Chapter 12

After the National Conference

On 5 August Wang Mingdao and his wife took the train to Beidaihe, a summer seaside resort north-east of Beijing. The next morning Wang Hengxin from Xuzhou came to the Tabernacle to ask Wang Mingdao to sign a petition against nuclear war. Since Wang Mingdao was away, Mrs Chi received him, and Wang Hengxin asked her to sign it on his behalf. Mrs Chi refused, saying that Wang Mingdao would have to sign it for himself. In fact, the reason they wanted his signature was because Wang Mingdao's name was included on the list of Christian leaders at the conference even though he had not attended. Had they obtained his signature, they could have said that he had been part of it.

The Wangs stayed in Berdaihe for over ten days. When they returned to Beijing, they read in a national newspaper, *Da Gong Bao*, that rumours were circulating among the Americans that Wang Mingdao had been executed by the government. A British Labour Party delegation, led by the former Prime Minister Mr Ardley, was on a visit to China and was due to hold a meeting with Chinese Christian and Catholic leaders in Beijing on 17 August. Bishop Chen Jianzheng made a statement saying that there was no truth in the rumours that Wang Mingdao had been executed. 'I went to see him recently,' he said. 'He is still in Beijing and is fine.' Later on, however, this incident was used in the charges brought against Wang Mingdao, because he had not been willing to make his presence visible and dispel the myth.

On 23 September Wang Mingdao received an invitation from the Department of Religious Affairs to a meeting in Sun Yatsun Park for all Christian organisations and churches not willing to join the Three-Self Movement. This was yet another official attempt to persuade them. Over 100 people representing eleven organisations participated in the meeting, including the Christian Tabernacle, Christian Student Union, Christian Assembly, Xiangshan Devotional Bible School and Xiangshan Home of Grace, Allen Yuan's Gospel Assembly, Peng Hongliang's Gospel Assembly, and Pastor Yang's Meiyimei Church. The Tabernacle sent the most people, with over twenty participants. The atmosphere was very tense. A sister from the Tabernacle, who was not a deacon and not invited, was so concerned and fearful for Wang Mingdao's safety that she went to Sun Yatsun Park to see for herself what was going on. She did not go home until she was sure that everything was all right.

Two men sat on the platform at the meeting: Mr Li, who was in charge of religious affairs and his successor. Mr Li made a speech, urging everybody to join the Three-Self Church before inviting others to ask questions and make comments. Wang Mingdao was the first one to rise. He spoke for nearly an hour explaining why he was not willing to join, declaring 'There is no way that I will join because some of the leaders do not even believe in God.' Responding to a comment in Mr Li's address about the American rumour that Wang Mingdao had been shot, he said, 'When people make up lies about me even in Beijing, I can't stop them. How can I possibly do anything about American rumours thousands of miles away?' After Wang Mingdao, many others stood up to speak. In conclusion, Mr Li said he had been going to invite everyone for lunch, but since there was another meeting in the afternoon he would not press them to stay. The Indonesian President was arriving and the welcoming ceremony was to be held at Sun Yatsun Park. He asked everyone to take a book on American imperialism home as a gift from the government.

While Wang Mingdao was speaking on why he would not join Three-Self, an old lady poured some hot water into a cup and passed it to him. He was so thirsty from speaking so much that he took the cup and drank it all. The man chairing the meeting was paying such close attention to what Wang Mingdao was saying that he forgot all about the cigarette between his fingers. He lit a second one but it too burnt out without being smoked. Writing about the meeting later someone picked up on these details as symbolic of the mood in the hall: 'A cup of water is drunk, two cigarettes burnt out.' They illustrated how tense the situation was and how much Wang Mingdao was loved by his people. The meeting ended at noon. As those who came from Fragrant Hills would miss their lunch Wang Mingdao invited them to eat with him at the Tabernacle. They told Wang Mingdao, 'What you said at the meeting today was like a Bible study for us.'

As a result of the meeting, the government realised how firm Wang Mingdao's position was on the Three-Self Church. However, they were still not willing to give up their efforts to persuade those who would not conform, so, shortly afterwards, they came up with a new proposal, suggesting that the nonconforming organisations form an association in which they would study politics together under the supervision of the government. The new proposal would have to be answered, but it was difficult to know how. Peng Hongliang and Allen Yuan invited all those not with the Three-Self Church to a meeting at the Tabernacle. The invitation was sent by Allen Yuan, and this was later used to indict him of a serious criminal act. Over ten people came to the meeting, which was chaired by Allen Yuan. After he had spoken he asked everyone to share their ideas. Wang Zhen made the conclusive comment when he said, 'Anyone who is interesting in attending study meetings should do so as individual citizens not as pastors or under the name of any church.' And this was the basis on which they rejected the proposal.

When the government realised that Wang Mingdao was not to be persuaded, they decided to change their strategy. In early October in Beijing a process of accusation was initiated against him to try to force him into obedience. Any organisation which had members who were involved with the Christian Tabernacle was required to hold a meeting to bring the accusation against Wang Mingdao. The accusation was based on what Shan Letian had said at the national meeting. Government officials were sent to the meetings to report on Wang Mingdao's dealings with the Japanese. The accusation was always the same, 'The Japanese wanted to destroy China but they had no copper and couldn't produce bullets. Wang Mingdao gave them the copper. This shows that Wang Mingdao was a Japan worshipper.' Many members of the Christian Tabernacle stood up to oppose these denunciations.

At Jiaotong University, a professor stood up after hearing the report against Wang Mingdao. He told the secretary of the meeting, 'Sir, you don't have to say any more. I know Wang Mingdao. He could not have offered copper to the Japanese, because he opposed the Japanese organisation of the North China Christian Confederation. How can you say he was pro-Japanese? There is no reason to accuse him.' 'I don't know the details,' the secretary said, 'I have only repeated what I have been told.'

The Union Hospital also had an accusation meeting, which was attended by professors, doctors and nurses. After hearing the accusation Sun Zhenglu stood up and said, 'According to you, Wang Mingdao gave copper to the Japanese to show his love for the Japanese. Wang Mingdao is not that kind of person. During the Japanese occupation, he never joined the North China Christian Confederation organised by the Japanese. How can you say that he liked the Japanese?' Brother Sun was very gifted in speaking; he was powerfully persuasive and strongly influenced the accusation meeting at the Union Hospital. Soon afterwards he was transferred to the Second Military Medical College in Changchun.

At a meeting in Daoji Hospital and on a number of other occasions people voiced their support of Wang Mingdao. In Western City, Li Zaisheng and another believer went to the government to complain. They said, 'This accusation against Wang Mingdao for giving copper to the Japanese is groundless. They were taxing copper. Everybody in Beijing had to give copper, including us. How can you say Wang Mingdao offered copper to the Japanese? Wang Mingdao did not offer any copper to the Japanese. Not only that, he refused to join any Japanese organisation.' The main purpose of the accusation meetings was to exert pressure on Wang Mingdao to force him to join the Three-Self Church but, because so many people from the Christian Tabernacle stood up to speak for him, the meetings had to be called off without achieving their aim.

Since that strategy had failed, the government changed their policy again by trying to bring together all those in the Three-Self Church who would be willing to join forces against Wang Mingdao. Their new aim was to isolate Wang Mingdao. They hoped that once he realised his influence was dwindling, he would have to join. In January 1955, Mr Li, Director of Religious Affairs, invited church leaders to a meal at Xinqiao Hotel, but Wang Mingdao and his partner Shi Tianmin of the Christian Tabernacle were not invited. At first it was hard to understand why another of Wang Mingdao's partners, the leader of the Tabernacle's South City Preaching Centre, Yang Runmin, was invited, but the following story explains why.

In 1954, Beijing City Government's Civil Affairs' Bureau asked all civilian organisations to register their names, addresses, properties, persons in charge, and members. Because the Bible teaches that the church only has two ranks, elders and deacons, when Wang Mingdao made the declaration, he listed only the elders and the deacons. Under elders, he wrote Wang Mingdao and Shi Tianmin. Under deacons he named eleven people, including Yang Runmin. Mr Yang was upset when he saw this. He went to the Christian Congregation on Broad Street to say, 'This is Wang Mingdao trying to get rid of me. He doesn't want me to work at the Tabernacle.' When Mr Li of the City Government heard this, he thought there was some friction between Wang Mingdao and Yang Runmin, and that is why he invited Yang Runmin to the meal instead of Wang Mingdao. But what Mr Li did not realise was that, within the Christian Tabernacle, the two men most adamant in their position against Three-Self were Wang Mingdao and Yang Runmin. After receiving the invitation, Mr Yang not only refused to go but also refused to reply. This shows how strongly he opposed Three-Self. He said, 'Of course I will not go. The Religious Affairs Department is inviting us with one purpose: to destroy the Church.'

The only person not with Three-Self who participated in this get-together was Allen Yuan. Other leaders from the

Christian Congregation had said they would go but in the end they didn't. What was interesting was that Mr Li asked everybody to give thanks before the meal. Yet when the prayers were being said, only the Three-Self pastors were in the room. All the government officials left the room until grace was finished. This was so baffling that people did not know if they should laugh or cry.

On the same evening, there was an important meeting at the Christian Tabernacle, at which Wang Mingdao spoke on his experiences of spiritual warfare between 1950 and 1954. Even though there were only twenty-five people present, they represented a wide geographic area across the country. Some came from Jiuquan and Tianshui in Gansu in Northwest China, others came from Shanghai, Tianjin, Shenyang and Harbin, and still others from Baoding, Changli, Chifeng and Taiyuan. As a result of that evening Wang Mingdao's testimony was taken to many parts of the country, and did much to support and consolidate the witness of the local churches. This produced far-reaching effects and had a deep impact on churches right across China.

Chapter 13

Fight for Truth

After the Beijing meeting in the spring of 1951, a wave of vicious accusation campaigns swept across China. Initially the accusations were based on the supposed use of missionaries by the imperialists to infiltrate Christian denominations, organisations and publishing houses and in this way to bring about the invasion of China. As the campaign progressed, emphasis became focused on the Bible itself. Spiritual groups were accused of deliberately misinterpreting the Bible in order to spread the poison of imperialism. They were also blamed for instigating trouble between the Church and the government to destroy the Three-Self Patriotic Movement. With regards to the Bible, the authorities did not actually say that it was itself 'the poison of imperialism' but that it was being used to spread the poison in order to destroy government policy, undermine the unity of believers and hinder socialist construction. They maintained that the Bible must be subjected to testing against government political standards to see if it conformed to official guidelines. If it did not, it should not be believed or taught. This was an attempt to put a political straitjacket on preachers' minds and souls which, if it had succeeded, would have resulted in the teaching of the Bible no longer being guided by the Spirit and the Church existing in name only.

Towards the end of 1954, the pages of Christian magazines were filled with the rhetoric of accusation. One such article, which was published in *Tianfeng* under the title 'Accusing Wang Mingdao's Counter-Revolutionary Gang', tried to make the Bible the basis of its accusations. Taking the quotations, *'Do not love the world or anything in the world'* (1 John 2:15) and *'...don't you know that friendship with the world is hatred towards God? Anyone who chooses to be a friend of the world becomes an enemy of God'* (James 4:4), the article accused:

> 'These two verses made young people think that if they participated in socialist construction, they were becoming involved with the evil of the world. Wang Mingdao's Counter-Revolutionary Gang used deception to teach people the Bible. As a result, people were so confused that they no longer knew right from wrong, to the extent that they became insane.'

With reference to verses about the end of the world, *'... the elements will be destroyed by fire ... That day will bring the destruction of the heavens by fire, and the elements will melt in the heat'* (2 Peter 3:10, 12) it maintained:

> 'Wang Mingdao's Counter-Revolutionary Gang emphasised that everything made by man's hand would be destroyed, to make people feel pessimistic and hate the world. As a result, people thought, "No matter how good Communism is, when the end of the world comes, it will all end up in the fire." And so they lost their enthusiasm for socialist construction. How evil their motivation was!'

The Bible describes the present time as a *'wicked and adulterous generation'* (Matthew 12:39) and teaches that the world under Satan is 'dark' (Ephesians 6:12). The article said:

> 'According to the senseless logic of Wang Mingdao's Counter-Revolutionary Gang today's Chinese society is dark. Nothing could be further from truth. Today's Chinese society is marching along the bright road of socialist construction. Wang Mingdao's Counter-Revolutionary Gang rigidly maintained that the new China was dark. They went so far as to misinterpret the Bible by dividing history into gold, silver, copper, steel and clay. Their real purpose was to teach that from generation to generation the times are getting worse. This is not teaching the Bible but spreading poison.'

The Bible says, *'Do not be yoked together with unbelievers. For what do righteousness and wickedness have in common? Or what fellowship can light have with darkness?'* (2 Corinthians 6:14) and *'Watch out for false prophets. They come to you in sheep's clothing, but inwardly they are ferocious wolves'* (Matthew 7:15). These two verses were openly opposed by leaders of the Three-Self Church:

> 'Some people emphasised the difference between the existence and the non-existence of God. They taught that believers and unbelievers should not mix. This is imperialist poison.'

After the National Christian Conference in the summer of 1954, leaders of the Three-Self Church went even further in their speeches and articles in an attempt to warn people:

> 'The poison of imperialism overshadowed the true light of the gospel. Such poison and the truth can never tolerate one another, like water and fire. We firmly believe that God has a special call for the Chinese Church today. And that is to eliminate imperialist poison and purify the gospel. In the past, Christianity was used as an instrument to invade China. Nonsense and ideas far from the truth were taught as theology. Truth and faith became skewed. We must not only rid the truth of this poison but also spread the saving faith of Jesus Christ. For over a century, imperialists used every opportunity to misinterpret the Bible and spread imperialist poison among Chinese believers. They wanted to captivate all Chinese believers with their ideas. Consequently, there was much confusion within the Church. Relationships between believers and non-believers became problematic. The outlook was pessimistic. Even though the problems are complicated, their root lies in the imperialistic poison that harmed the Chinese Church, undermined the relationship between the Church and the people, and destroyed the head and heart of Chinese believers. As a

result, they fell into despair without even realising it. Imperialists have perverted the image of Jesus in order to use mission to achieve their scheme of invading our country. They tried to entomb the real Christ. They even spread the poison in the name of Jesus.'

After reading these allegations, believers who loved the truth became downhearted. They became confused about what was and was not biblical truth and what was imperialist poison. It was at this time that Wang Mingdao stepped out into the heat of the battle with an essay published on 12 December 1954 entitled 'Truth or Poison?', fiercely defending the truth that had been entrusted to the saints. In this essay, he clearly exposed the purpose and intention of the Three-Self leaders:

'What they refer to as "imperialist poison" is nothing other than the truth of the Bible. The reason they dare not spell out what they mean by "imperialist poison" is because they are afraid that believers would immediately see them for who they really are. These clever people tried their best to hide their real intention, but they did not realise that by going down this path of accusation they have in fact revealed what they were hiding in their hearts. They said, "Some people emphasised the difference between the existence and the non-existence of God. They taught that believers and unbelievers should not mix. This was imperialist poison. Their purpose is to stir up friction between believers and the people to destroy their unity. Others discriminate against those in the Church who hold different views to their own. This was imperialist poison too. The purpose was to divide the Church so that imperialists could easily take control." Don't these words clearly show us what they mean by "imperialist poison"?'

Wang Mingdao quoted from 2 Corinthians 6:14–18, Ephesians 5:6–10, Matthew 7:15–20, 2 Corinthians 11:12–15, 2 Peter 2:1–3, and 2 John 7–11 to show the difference between people who know God and those who do not. He reminded his fellow believers of what was clearly taught in the Bible, warned them to beware of false prophets and urged them to stay away from them:

'Maybe some will ask, "According to these teachings, should we always oppose those who do not believe, refuse to work with them, stand against them and despise them?" Our answer is, "No." We should not stand against anyone or refuse to co-operate with others. Neither should we despise anyone or oppose them. God wants us to glorify Him, witness to His grace and spread His gospel among non-believers. We must do our best to serve those around us. He taught us, *"Therefore, as we have opportunity, let us do good to all people, especially to those who belong to the family of believers"* (Galatians 6:10). *"All people"* means everybody around us, including those who worship false gods and those who are atheists. God also taught us, *"If it is possible, as far as it depends on you, live at peace with everyone"* (Romans 12:18). If God wants us to *"live at peace with everyone"*, how can we oppose them, refuse to work with them, stand against them and despise them? Someone may ask, "If God does not want us to oppose them, why did He teach us those things?" We must understand that it was because God wants us to know how different we are from those that belong to the world. In this way we can live a separated holy life. We can be prepared for the temptations that Satan uses non-believers to bring us and we will know how to fight off the temptations when they come. Sometimes, Satan uses people under his control to attack us. At other times he uses them to weaken us and tempt us, by putting human benefits and glories before us. Sometimes he will attract us to them and cause them to show us friendship so that we will be assimilated into the world. If we are not able to be discerning, if we do not keep ourselves separate, it will be very hard for us not to fall and be enslaved by the devil.'

Finally he exposed the intentions of those who twisted the truth of the Bible as 'imperialist poison':

'The real intention behind their work is to destroy the gospel from inside the Church on behalf of those who oppose God. Those who oppose God have learnt the lessons of over a thousand years of history. They realise that the gospel of Jesus and the Church cannot be defeated with arms. And not only that, but the more they are attacked, the stronger the gospel and the Church become, and the more they thrive. They have said that they would "engage in all kinds of anti-religious propaganda," and would "apply all the propaganda of popular science" to raise people's awareness until every vestige of religion is completely destroyed. Let me tell you clearly, these followers of Judas have distorted Bible truth as imperialist poison and have become part of the anti-Christian propaganda. But they do not stand outside to launch their attacks. They have sneaked into the Church. These attacks against Christianity are much more effective from the inside for they appear not as our enemies, but as our friends and family.

Those who oppose God are not afraid of a Church that has only the formal structures but no faith and life. Churches like this have no influence in the world. They cannot give life to people; neither can they touch anyone in their inner being. They can only decorate the world to make it look more cheerful and attractive. The enemy of God is not afraid of this kind of Church. And they do not hate it either. They hope that all churches will become like this. The structures and the buildings are still there, but the Church and gospel of Jesus have been destroyed.

The followers of Judas shout at the top of their voices, "Get rid of the imperialist poison" but they do not say what that poison is. Their purpose is to make believers doubt everything they read in the Bible so that they will not believe, scared of being poisoned. Their purpose is to make preachers doubt everything in the Bible so that they will not teach the Bible, fearful that they will spread the poison. Gradually, preachers will not preach and believers will not believe. If they succeed, the truth of the Bible would be eliminated and the Church would be destroyed.

"Do not be yoked together with unbelievers. For what do righteousness and wickedness have in common?" This is God's way of protecting His children. As long as we do not take off this protection, we are safe. The world wants to assimilate us. Unbelievers lure us to leave God and give up our faith. Their first step is to make us confused so that we cannot remember the difference between them and us. They want us to forget that we are a totally different kind of people, to forget that they are trying their best to lure us away from God. The enemy of God has no way of leading us away from the word of God, so the followers of Judas want to help him by lying to believers that it is "imperialist poison". God has warned us for our own safety to defend ourselves against false prophets and keep away from them. The false prophets' worst fear is that we will keep away from them. So they sing at the top of their voice, "Two become one", "Respect one another", "Accept one another", "Consider others better than yourselves". If we depend on the Bible which teaches believers to stay away from them and not interact with them, they call this "imperialist poison". This is the method they use to scare us in the Church so that we do not teach these lessons any more. Then they will be able to do whatever they want to in the Church. The enemy works his hardest outside the Church to make us abandon God. Those false prophets strive inside the Church to make us forsake God. If we obey God's teaching and keep His truth, if we keep our distance from unbelievers and stay away from false prophets, we will outwit them.'

Chapter 14

Debates and Battles

The publication of 'Truth or Poison?' caused a huge stir. One by one the Three-Self leaders stepped into the arena to fight back, some basing their arguments on misinterpretations of the Bible and others using political threats to try to scare Wang Mingdao. The first one into the fight was Mr Qing Mu who published an essay in *Tianfeng* entitled 'The Truth and Faith of 2 Corinthians 6:14'. He reinterpreted 2 Corinthians 6:14, *'Do not be yoked together with unbelievers'*, to justify the anti-imperialist patriotic movement, putting forward a meaning that had nothing to do with the original verse:

> 'This verse teaches us, first, not to participate in sin. But the cause of the anti-imperialist patriotic movement of the Chinese people is righteous. The imperialists interfered with our internal affairs, stirred up international tension and set about invading our country. Theirs were the sinful intentions. Our efforts to resist are righteous. Christians should participate in such actions. Second, the verse teaches us to keep the purity of our faith. The anti-imperialist patriotic movement is not a bad influence on our faith. In the movement, we realised that the imperialists were not only using military, political and economic means to penetrate China but also the Bible and its misinterpretation to spread their poison. By getting rid of the imperialist poison we will restore the purity of the faith. Thus, taking part in the movement will not weaken our faith but purify it. When Christians refuse to participate in the movement, it is not the Bible they are basing their reasoning on but imperialist poison.'

The essay was an attempt to make believers deny the truth of the verse so that they would participate in the anti-imperialist movement. After reading this essay, Wang Mingdao wrote in his diary, 'I read Qing Mu's essay in *Tianfeng* which misinterpreted the Bible.' Because the essay was full of misinformation, Wang Mingdao did not feel it was worth discussing and so he did not publicly refute it.

The second one to fight back was Ding Guangxun. In an interview in *Tianfeng* on 28 March 1955, he said,

> 'I would like to talk about two issues: one is opposition to the use of atomic weapons. The other is Chinese Christian unity against imperialism. As a pastor, what I like to talk about most is our Lord Jesus Christ. But world events have robbed me of the peace in my heart and prevented me from teaching the Bible and feeding the sheep. The problem is that some people do not like our new China. They do not like our attempts to build a better life for ourselves. They have waved the atom bomb in our faces to force us to our knees. No Chinese with any integrity would be able to bear this. In the face of increased efforts by the imperialists to invade us, as they intensify their use of Christianity to seek to divide us, and when the people of China hope that we will strengthen our unity in order to be able to resist, we find a minority of our own people working against us. Some people maintain that faith itself is the obstacle to unity. Many believers are confused and really think that this has something to do with faith. I doubt if this has anything to do with faith, but rather that those unwilling to unite for other reasons are exaggerating the differences between us. But what on earth are these differences? Of course, different denominations have different characteristics in their faith, their life and their organisations. But these only demonstrate the richness of Christianity. These should only make us thankful. How can they become the excuse for our divisions? I can personally testify to the fact that the Three-Self Patriotic Movement fully respects the differences in faith among different denominations. Mutual

respect sustains the faith. There is no need to make any adaptations to participate in this movement. What is more hurtful is that some people today are randomly accusing others of unbelief. What sort of behaviour is this? We will be held responsible for our words before God. Since men are saved by faith and Jesus died for them, how can we call them "unbelievers"! This is to accuse brothers before God, to curse them, to force God not to save them, condemn them and keep them out of heaven. Who are we that we dare to bear false witness before God in order to frame others? Can we bear the responsibility of doing such a thing?'

A few weeks later, Cui Xianxiang published an article in *Tianfeng* entitled 'We Must Consolidate and Expand Our Unity'. He wrote:

'The biggest characteristic of this unity is mutual respect for each other's faith. Although there are many theological schools within Christianity, the shared basis of our faith is the same. We must respect one another. Among Christians, there are differences within this common faith. But these are differences of emphasis and approach. In other words, within the wider unity of Christianity, there are small differences in the various denominations and groups.'

He went on to take up Wang Mingdao's point that 'If we hate the imperialist poison so much, if we must root it out, why don't we clearly define what it is?':

'Such people have never paid proper attention to the Three-Self Patriotic Movement. During the national accusation campaign, many people made it clear what they regarded as the imperialist poison. In study groups across the country, many co-workers confessed the imperialist poison that was mixed into their faith. Such poison was frequently exposed in Christian magazines. Anyone who was willing to pay attention would have realised what it was. If they know what it is but still make such comments, their hearts are clogged up with grease and their ears are too dull. *"They see but do not understand, hear but not know."* In order to remain physically healthy we need to discover and destroy bacteria. Likewise, in order to remain spiritually healthy we need to discover and destroy ideological poison. Denying the existence of bacteria and allowing it to multiply is bad for physical health. In the same way, denying the penetration of imperialist poison into our faith and allowing it to spread is detrimental to our spiritual health. Some people have gone so far as to use sarcasm and vitriol to attack those actively involved in the Three-Self Movement, accusing them of having impure faith and mixed motives. Are they attacking the Three-Self Movement, or are they attacking the people involved? If they are not against this movement, why can't they take part in it as someone with "pure" faith, "high" standards and "pure" motives to correct its shortcomings and strengthen the weaknesses of others? If they are not willing to participate, doesn't that prove that they are using personal attacks as a way of destroying the movement?'

A week later, Wang Weifan published an article in *Tianfeng* entitled 'Although We Are Many We Are One Body'. In it he talked about his experience when, soon after he was saved in 1947, he was told that some people in the Church claimed to be Christians but did not believe in the blood of Jesus, in the Word becoming flesh, in the resurrection, in miracles and in the Bible. He wrote:

'During my three years at Jinlin Union Seminary, I never met anyone who belonged to this imaginary group of unbelievers. Those three years were like a nightmare. Today, it is as if I have woken up from the nightmare: I feel the simplicity and purity of my faith again as I did when I had just been saved. Despite the fact that we do have some differences, they are only small differences within the wider unity. These small differences do not prevent faith but make our unity stronger and richer.'

Besides those already mentioned, Bao Zheqing, Zhang Guangxu, Chen Jianzheng and Sun Pengxi joined in the attack targeted at Wang Mingdao. The crux of all their arguments could be summarised in this one point: the Three-Self Patriotic Movement is a righteous movement and therefore it should be welcomed by believers and churches. Anyone who opposes this movement has a hidden agenda – to serve the interests of imperialism.

To respond to the points they raised, Wang Mingdao published an essay in the summer 1955 issue of *Spiritual Food Quarterly* called 'We Are for Faith'. To counter one of their central themes that there was little difference between the churches – just small differences within the wider unity of Christianity – Wang Mingdao reminded his readers that Wu Yaozong, who was the chairman of the Three-Self Movement, was a Modernist and therefore an unbeliever. He quoted from Wu's writings to prove that the differences between evangelical Christians and Modernists were not small ones but were like water and fire which could not mix at all. Then, one by one, he refuted each of the points made by Cui Xianxiang, Ding Guangxun and Wang Weifan in their articles. He began his counter-attack by quoting from Wu Yaozong's book *Darkness and Light* on the differences between fundamentalism and Modernism:

'The decade following World War I saw capitalism prosper in the world as never before, due to the innovations of science, the advancement of technology, progress in production techniques and the improvement of living standards. All such developments were the result of the development of human rationalism and intellectual thinking. Man could apply his rational thinking to understand the world, increase his happiness and solve his problems. However, when such thinking was applied to Christianity, it became Modernism. Modernism is against fundamentalism. The former represents progressive thinking, the latter conservative thought. Within Christian theology, there are five points which are disputed: the first one is about the Bible itself. Fundamentalism believes that every sentence and every word in the Bible was revealed by God. Therefore there are no mistakes whatsoever. Modernism maintains that although the Bible was revealed by God, we cannot interpret it literally. The Bible is not science or history. It is a guide to life and faith. The time covered in the Bible was about a thousand years. Over such a long period of time, it could hardly be conceived that no mistake was made in the legends and records of the Bible. Within this debate, the origin of man in the book of Genesis became the focus. Fundamentalists believe that man was supernaturally created by God. But Modernism accepts the theory of evolution that man came into being as a result of natural evolution, from apes and monkeys. The second issue concerns the birth of Jesus. Fundamentalism takes the view that Jesus was born supernaturally from a virgin. But Modernism argues that the birth of Jesus from a virgin is a fable. The third point is redemption. Fundamentalism believes that the death of Jesus on the cross made atonement for man's sin. This atonement changed God's anger towards man to forgiveness. This was one of the basic beliefs of the Reformation of the seventeenth century. But Modernism maintains that the cross was only an indication of God's love, which made it possible for us to become one with God. There is, therefore, no need to believe in an angry God demanding a sacrifice for the atonement of man's sin. The fourth point is the resurrection. The book of Acts says, *"I believe in the resurrection of the body."* This was written in the third century when Christians, like Egyptians, did not believe in the resurrection of the spirit unless there was resurrection of the body. Fundamentalism holds that the resurrection of the body of Christ was real. Otherwise Jesus could not have overcome death. Modernism does not deny resurrection, but maintains that it was not necessarily the resurrection of the body.

Additionally, there is no direct relationship between the resurrection of the body of Christ and Christian faith. The last point of conflict concerns the second coming of Christ. Like St Paul and early Christians, fundamentalism believes that Jesus will soon return in His physical body from the clouds to the earth. Modernism, however, argues that this is only a poetic symbol.'

Mr Wu had studied theology and philosophy for three years in a liberal seminary in the US that believed in Modernism.[1] In his essay, 'We Are for Faith', Wang Mingdao argued:

'In the recent two or three years, conflicts between fundamentalism and Modernism have emerged in the churches in the big cities. *The Life of Jesus* written by Zhao Zi, the former Director of Yanjing University's Religious Institute, is an example of Modernism in China. Most of the books on Christianity published by the YMCA Press in Shanghai were written by Modernists.'

After exposing the true face of Modernism, Wang Mingdao commented on Cui Xianxiang's essay 'We Must Consolidate and Broaden Our Unity':

'Mr Cui argues that "although there are many theological schools of thoughts within Christianity, the shared basis of our faith is the same. So we must respect one another." He also says that "within the overall unity of Christianity, there are small differences between various denominations and groups." Hence so-called mutual respect for faith was "mutual respect of the small differences within the overall unity." I have no idea if Mr Cui's "basis of faith" and his "small differences within the overall unity" include the difference between fundamentalism and Modernism. Mr Cui is the National Co-ordinator of the Chinese Christian Council. It is impossible for him not to know that fundamentalism and Modernism do not share basic beliefs. It is impossible for him not to know that the differences between the two are not small differences within the unity but water and fire that do not mix. If Mr Cui does know that fundamentalism is totally different from Modernism, what he said was not true. If he thinks that they are similar in their basic beliefs, we can conclude that Mr Cui is a Modernist.'

After this, Wang Mingdao rebuked Ding Guanxun's speech in *Tianfeng*:

'Mr Ding maintains, "As the imperialists increase their efforts to invade us, intensifying their use of Christianity and seeking to divide us, the people of China hope that we will strengthen our unity so that we will be able to resist imperialism, but we find a few people working hard to divide us. Why do we divide when this is falling into the hands of the imperialists?" What malicious talk! What a destructive accusation! Totally ignoring the differences in faith between us, such words are as sharp as knives piercing through the hearts of those who, for the sake of the purity of faith, refuse to co-operate with unbelievers. The accusation of aiding imperialist efforts to invade China and use Christianity were levelled as political labels to condemn those standing firm in their faith. "Those in the minority are causing division." How can "division" be caused? How can "division" only appear now? Twenty-five years ago, I called those with real faith to separate themselves from unbelievers.'

Wang Mingdao quoted from some earlier articles he had written, including 'To Unite or to Divide?' published on 23 January 1930, 'Warning against False Teachers' on 29 December 1935 and 'A Serious Warning to the Church Today' on 14 October 1936, to support the fact that he had always called for this separation. He did not want any division between those who truly believed but he whole-heartedly urged those with real faith to separate themselves from unbelievers. He went on:

'Mr Ding seems to have discovered evidence to prove that there was a connection between imperialism and our division. But he shied away from stating his evidence, leaving readers to wonder what it might be. The point is that whatever guesses readers might have made, Mr Ding did not have to be responsible for them. Wu Yaozong once told us that a heated debate took place between fundamentalists and Modernists in 1922. Among the fundamentalists was Bishop Manning from New York, and among the Modernists was Dr Harry Emerson Forsdick, Professor of Theology at New York Union Seminary.[2] I don't know if Mr Ding ever investigated whether their argument was "used by imperialism", if "imperialists ever sought to divide them"? As President of Jinlin Union Seminary, Mr Ding is certainly aware of the defining differences between fundamentalism and Modernism, yet he asks, "What on earth is the difference between our beliefs?" What is he trying to do? Mr Ding is obviously not exaggerating the differences but eliminating them altogether. This is to make people believe that those who are not willing to unite were not standing for their faith but are being used by imperialists.'

Commenting on Mr Ding's statement that 'We believe in the same Heavenly Father and the same Bible. We are redeemed by the same Christ and led by the same Holy Spirit,' Wang Mingdao argued:

'When these words are applied to those who truly believe, they are right. But when applied to Modernists, such words are totally wrong. Modernists do not believe the biblical record of how God created man. They do not believe the biblical account of how Jesus was born of the virgin. They do not believe the biblical truth of how Jesus died the substitutional death in our place. They do not believe the biblical fact that the body of Jesus was resurrected after His death. They do not believe the biblical promise that Jesus is coming again. Once they eliminate all these basic teachings of the Bible, I do not know how much truth is left. To say that they believe in the same Bible as we do is, therefore, not factual.'

Regarding the accusation that 'Somebody is randomly condemning others as unbelievers', Wang Mingdao said:

'"Unbeliever" is not a label. It applies to a type of people. These people say they are Christians but they do not believe the truth in the Bible that needs to be accepted with faith. They do not believe that man was directly created by God, that Jesus was born of the virgin, that Jesus died on the cross for our sin, that the body of Jesus was resurrected, that Jesus is coming again. They do not clearly say that they do not believe, but use ambiguous words to hide their unbelief. When necessary, they may say they completely believe the truth. But *"nothing hidden ... will not be exposed, and nothing concealed ... will not be made known"* [Luke 8:17]. Once they do not believe, they cannot conceal their unbelief for long. As such unbelievers do exist, how can this be "randomly condemning people"?'

Wang Mingdao also rebuked Mr Ding's use of the verse *'for God has accepted him. Who are you to judge someone else's servant? To his own master he stands or falls. And he will stand, for the Lord is able to make him stand'* (Romans 14:3–4):

'This is indeed a precious piece of teaching. However, Mr Ding did not quote the whole passage, but omitted what is before and after his quotation:

"Accept him whose faith is weak, without passing judgment on disputable matters. One man's faith allows him to eat everything, but another man, whose faith is weak, eats only vegetables. The man who eats everything must not look down on him who does not, and the man who does not eat everything must not condemn the man who does, for God has accepted him. Who are you to judge someone else's servant? To his own master he stands or falls. And he will stand, for the Lord is able to make him stand.

> *One man considers one day more sacred than another,*
> *another man considers every day alike. Each one should be*
> *fully convinced in his own mind. He who regards one day*
> *as special, does so to the Lord. He who eats meat, eats to*
> *the Lord, for he gives thanks to God; and he who abstains,*
> *does so to the Lord and gives thanks to God ... You then,*
> *why do you judge your brother? Or why do you look down*
> *on your brother? For we will all stand before God's*
> *judgment seat ... So then, each of us will give an account*
> *of himself to God.'* (Romans 14:1–6, 10, 12)

Paul wrote this because disputes about special days and food were stirring up problems for the church in Rome. *"One man's faith allows him to eat everything, but another man, whose faith is weak, eats only vegetables ... One man considers one day more sacred than another, another man considers every day alike."* These words were written for believers who all believed in Jesus, unlike unbelievers who do not believe that Jesus was born of the virgin, that Jesus died for our sin, that the body of Jesus was resurrected, that Jesus is coming again. These people in Rome had faith. They shared the same faith. They only differed in their opinions about special days and food. So Paul advised them not to despise and judge one another. To apply these words to those who obstruct the truth, false brothers and false prophets, is to misuse them completely. For such people, the scripture to quote is not Romans 14, but 2 John:

> *"Anyone who runs ahead and does not continue in the*
> *teaching of Christ does not have God; whoever continues*
> *in the teaching has both the Father and the Son. If anyone*
> *comes to you and does not bring this teaching, do not*
> *take him into your house or welcome him. Anyone who*
> *welcomes him shares in his wicked work."*
>
> (2 John 9–11)'

In 'We Are for Faith', Wang Mingdao commented on Wang Weifan's article 'Though We Are Many, We Are One Body':

'Anyone who knows anything about the Church is aware of the differences between fundamentalism and Modernism. How can such differences be fabricated all of a sudden? Mr Wang studied at Jinlin Union Seminary for three years. Did he ever read their journal? If not, can I introduce him to something from it? The founding issue of the journal carried an article by Peter Han, Deputy President of Jinlin Union Seminary. He said, "Jinlin Union Seminary consists of eleven organisations with different denominations, theological views and historical traditions. Fellow Christians in various parts of the country are deeply concerned about the problems of the unity of our faith. Although in theology we have both Modernist and fundamentalist views, we hold to what St Paul preached: one Lord, one faith, one baptism, one God. In order to promote the principle of mutual respect, Modernist and fundamentalist views are taught in separate courses. Thus mutual respect and teaching freedom are guaranteed." The same issue published another article by Zan Antang entitled "Ten Months at Union Seminary". He wrote: "Accordingly, Jinlin Union Seminary is made up of eleven theological schools including three Bible colleges independently set up by fifteen denominations. The church traditions we inherited and the religious life-styles we are used to are very different. Some are conservative in religious formality but progressive in theological thought. Some are simple and lively in their ceremonies but extremely traditional in their theology. Some are called fundamentalist, some spiritualist. Others are Modernist and progressivist." Both the Deputy President and the Professor of Jinlin Union Seminary admit without reservation that there are fundamentalists and Modernists within the school. The school even organises separate courses to accommodate both fundamental and Modernist streams. This separation proves that there is a distance between fundamentalism and Modernism. How could Mr Wang regard the differences as a fabrication?

Mr Wang said, "Despite the fact these differences exist between us, they are only small differences within our unity. These small differences do not prevent faith but make our unity stronger and richer." How is it possible for these words to be so similar to those of Mr Cui Xianxiang? Some people believe man was created by God. Others believe man evolved naturally from monkeys. Some believe Jesus was born of a virgin. Others think it is merely a fable. Some believe Jesus died to redeem sinners. Others deny the truth of redemption. Some believe in the resurrection of the body. Others maintain that resurrection has little to do with Christian faith. Some believe Jesus is coming back. Others think it is just a poetic symbol. In such unity, the Christian faith would be totally eliminated.'

Finally, Wang Mingdao declared his position:

'Let me solemnly declare: Not only must we keep away from unbelievers and their organisations, even when it comes to believers of Jesus, we can only unite in spirit not in organisation, because this is what the Bible teaches us. Regarding faith our attitude is that we accept and keep whatever is the truth. We totally refute anything that is not found in the Bible. To show our faith in God, we are willing to pay any price and make any sacrifice. Twisting facts and bringing false charges against us won't scare us off. A person's mouth grows on his or her own head. Whatever they want to say, they can say it. But facts are always facts. Not only can God see the truth clearly, those belonging to God can too, no matter how others twist it and make up false charges.

We are for faith.'

In the days of old, when Israel strayed away from Him, God sent prophets to convey His message, urging them to repent of their sin, abandon their rebellion and turn back to God. In the twentieth century, when God's truth was hidden and God's Church was without light, God raised up Wang

Mingdao as a prophet to protest loudly against the evil and urge believers to return from their sin to God and to live a holy life that is pleasing to Him. Wang Mingdao left no room for these false prophets in his rebuke. He warned believers to guard themselves against them and stay away from them for in this way they would avoid being influenced and trapped by their sin, which would cause permanent damage.

After the publication of 'We Are for Faith', Wang Mingdao's mission as the prophet of the time was over. He had spoken what God had wanted him to say, taught the truth God had wanted him to teach, and given the warning God had wanted him to give. Anything that would benefit the believers, he had said. There is no doubt that he was a prophet of his time who had faithfully accomplished all that God had intended. With his mission accomplished, he no longer needed to speak or write any more. He had done enough. God would now hide him, keep him and build him up to prepare him to face Him.

Notes

1.   See Wu Yaozong, *Darkness and Light*, p. 78.
2.   *ibid.*, pp. 189–191.

Chapter 15

The Grip Tightens

Wang Mingdao's two articles 'Truth or Poison?' and 'To Obey God or to Obey Man?', published in *Spiritual Food Quarterly* in the winter of 1954, answered all the accusations of the Three-Self leaders. With the publication of these articles, Wang Mingdao's became even more influential in the Chinese Church. Between the summer of 1954 and the spring of 1955, after reading his articles, many churches and believers across the country realised the true nature of the Three-Self Church and withdrew from it. In 1954 alone, following the national conference, many people (from as far afield as the North-east, North-west, Guangdong, Shanghai and Nanjing) visited Wang Mingdao to ask him about Three-Self. Many more wrote letters with similar questions. Wang Mingdao answered their questions one by one helping them to see the true face of Three-Self, with the result that many left after returning home. In 1955, the following organisations were among others to sever their relationship with the Three-Self Church: Qingdao Student Fellowship, the Third Street West Church, the Baptist Church and the Third Street Shazi Church in Changchun. After the Christian Assembly in Beijing had formally withdrawn from Three-Self, they took the unprecedented step of inviting Wang Mingdao to speak to their youth groups. In the beginning of April, churches in Nanjing started an anti-Wang Mingdao campaign but it soon collapsed in failure. Meanwhile, unofficial publications in Shanghai called for churches to leave Three-Self. In late May, the Christian Assembly in Xian withdrew and, in early June, the Christian Assembly in Hohhot followed suit. Across China, from the North to the South, from the East to the West, churches were leaving the Three-Self Movement.

Naturally its leaders were very angry about the withdrawals, and published articles and convened meetings to attack Wang Mingdao. In late February, the Three-Self Church in Shanghai held a meeting to accuse Wang Mingdao. In May, when the Shanghai Three-Self Church was formally established, all churches joined except the Christian Assembly, the biggest church in Shanghai. In the same month, the Three-Self Church in Xian held a meeting lasting seven days to bring accusations against Wang Mingdao, but he did not waver.

Despite all the official propaganda, as soon as believers heard Wang Mingdao speak, they were convinced by the Holy Spirit and understood the true nature of the Three-Self Church. Without the support of the government, the Three-Self Church would have been doomed. To prevent its complete failure, the government activated its hard-line policy on 18 May and arrested Xu Hongdao in Tianjin. Xu, who at one time was a co-worker of Wang Mingdao at the Christian Tabernacle, had gone on to pastor All Saints' Church in Tianjin. Like Wang Mingdao, he had refused to join the Three-Self Church. When China Inland Mission had left China they had vacated a three-storey building in Tianjin, which the government had indicated that Xu Hongdao could use. This was like the Foreigners' Chapel in Beijing, which the government had offered to Wang Mingdao, but he had refused. When Xu Hongdao had accepted the building, it had stirred up jealousy among the other pastors in Tianjin who had turned against him. In fear, Xu Hongdao left his church in Tianjin and returned to Beijing to become the pastor of Hemp Thread Lane Church. As soon as he took over, he invited Wang Mingdao to speak, and this made some people even angrier. They accused him of making connections with Wang Mingdao but, in fact, there had always been a lot of contact between his church and the Christian Tabernacle in Beijing, and these accusations had already surfaced earlier while he was still in Tianjin. This contact with Wang Mingdao laid him open to being accused of the crime of associating with bad elements to undermine the Communist Party and, when he was invited back to Tianjin to lead a meeting, he was arrested. Soon news began to arrive from other places that more believers who had refused to join the Three-Self Church had also been arrested. It began to look like a masterminded trap even though as yet there had been no arrests in Beijing. Mr Xu's arrest upset Wang Mingdao greatly but it did not alter his position. He still believed that it was government policy to respect religious freedom. In addition, he had never accepted any foreign gifts, and he attributed Mr Xu's arrest to his use of the China Inland Mission property. However, Wang Mingdao was wrong. The real purpose of the government action was to send him a warning shot: 'We have now arrested Xu Hongdao. We could easily have arrested you.' They were trying to make him reconsider before it was too late.

The publication of 'We Are for Faith' and, in particular, his clear attitude and firm position made the government realise that there was no room for any further negotiations. All the efforts by the government to change him had failed. The next step was to arrest him. In order for them to be able to achieve this without causing a backlash, there would have to be some ideological preparation. In July 1955, *Tianfeng* carried an editorial entitled 'Strengthening the Unity and Clarifying Right from Wrong', which defined the purpose of the Three-Self Patriotic Movement as:

- to unite all believers in China to eliminate imperialist poison in the Chinese Church;
- to mobilise Chinese Christians to participate actively in the anti-imperialist patriotic movement to safe-guard the peace of the world;
- to establish a Church in China that is self-governed, self-supported and self-propagating.

The editorial continued by clarifying the official attitude towards those who had not joined the Three-Self Church:

'To the minority who have not joined, we keep our door wide open and extend our hands and arms with love and patience. We hope one day we will meet in sincerity and live in peace.'

Immediately after this, the editorial turned sharply on Wang Mingdao:

'Of course, as we expected, there are a few who, like Wang Mingdao, persist in their error by refusing to adapt to current changes. They intend to destroy the Three-Self Movement. They will not budge an inch even if our mouths dry up in our efforts to persuade them. The more we succeed, the more they seek to destroy. So far as anti-imperialism and patriotism are concerned, they and we are indeed like fire and water that do not mix. Faced by the reality of the new China, they care nothing for the people. Their hearts grow harder by the day. Motivated by political hatred they do their utmost to undermine the anti-imperialist patriotic movement which is today the foundation of Christian unity. It is clearly the intention of Mr Wang Mingdao in the present circumstances to undermine this foundation by launching a so-called fundamentalist and Modernist debate. Doesn't his emphasis on division demonstrate his unwillingness to unite, why we do not know? Should we really abandon our anti-imperialist patriotic foundation to start a war between fundamentalists and Modernists? By doing so, wouldn't we be walking straight into the trap of the imperialists who want to divide us? Isn't this a crime that hurts our friends and delights our enemies? No matter who it is, if this is his intention and action, he is the enemy of the Chinese people, the enemy of the Church and the enemy of history. He must watch out for the fair judgement of God and the condemnation of both the believers and the people.'

The editorial finished with a solemn statement and an urgent call:

'We support anti-imperialist patriotism. This is the principle difference between us and Wang Mingdao's undermining work in the name of faith! We must draw a clear line between the political principle of anti-imperialist patriotism and Wang Mingdao. All Christians who love China and the Church should actively engage themselves in this battle.'

As a servant of God, Wang Mingdao declared: 'We Are for Faith.' As the servants of unbelievers, the Three-Self leaders declared: 'We support anti-imperialist patriotism.' Each had his own master. One belonged to the Spirit, one belonged to the world – like fire and water that could never mix. Having become the enemy of the people, the enemy of the Church and the enemy of history, Wang Mingdao was no longer under the protection of the law. What happened to him was, therefore, 'fair judgement'. The editorial was a signal of his imminent arrest. The same issue of *Tianfeng* carried many articles openly condemning him, including ones written by Qing Mu, Ding Lingsheng, Jiang Wenhan, Wang Weifan, Sun Pengxi, Yu Han, Ye Baoluo and Cui Xianxiang.

In late July, Beijing became a hive of activity. Mass campaigns were held on the campuses of colleges and universities, urging all those who met at the Christian Tabernacle to step forward and denounce Wang Mingdao's crimes. Anyone refusing to do so would be arrested immediately. Wu Dexiang from Tianjin was a research student at Beijing People's University. Because he often attended Wang Mingdao's church, the university demanded that he make an accusation against him. When he refused, they began to threaten him. Unable to face the increasing pressure, he jumped off a building and died on the way to hospital. On 2 August, a mass meeting was held at Beijing Medical College where Liu Yueqing and Shi Shanghao were being pressurised to make accusations against Wang Mingdao. Liu was from Fujian and had come to Beijing to study medicine. He had once asked Wang Mingdao to baptise him. Both men were arrested on the spot when they refused to co-operate. Wang Mingdao encountered increasing persecution. Outside the Church he was condemned in wave after wave of articles and speeches by the Three-Self leaders. Inside the Church, some people committed suicide when they could no longer handle the pressure. Some were arrested for standing firm to the truth. Others were weak and gave up their faith. Still others betrayed the Lord and their friends for political advancement. With mounting battles from the outside and fears from the inside increasing, Wang Mingdao faced more pressure than ever before. The battle had now been waging for four years since 1951. He was fighting a lonely battle and his physical and mental strength was exhausted.

One of the most painful experiences was the defection of his old friend, Dr Li Boheng from Tianjin. Before liberation, Li was a warm Christian who loved the Lord and the people, and he had enjoyed close fellowship with Wang Mingdao. After liberation he had worked at a coalmine, where, for a cup of red stew, he had traded the birthright of his sonship (Genesis 25:27–34). From that time on he told all those he met to give up their faith and trapped many believers. He had not met Wang Mingdao for many years, but on 3 August, when Wang Mingdao was in great danger, he suddenly appeared on his doorstep. His first words to Wang Mingdao were, 'Are you still so superstitious?' Wang Mingdao was shocked. 'Boheng, how can you speak like that? How can you say that I am superstitious?' But Li Boheng made it clear that he had given up his faith. He told Wang Mingdao, 'There is no need to pray for me.' He advised Wang Mingdao that in today's atheistic world there was no way of proving God's existence and that it was far better to speak about topics people were interested in and wanted to hear about. When Mrs Wang walked in, Li got angry. He stood up and told Wang Mingdao, 'You are too superstitious. We have nothing more to say to each other. I will leave. I will leave', and with that he left. This visit hurt Wang Mingdao deeply. Li's words and actions were a betrayal of God's grace. Wang Mingdao had no idea that, despite his rejection of God's grace, Li had nevertheless still been imprisoned during the Cultural Revolution and had met a tragic end. One day, having become thirsty and wanting some water, he was told to stretch his head out of the prison bars, which he did. Because he had a big head he was caught between the bars and beaten to death with a stick. No one can treat God as he did. It is a very serious matter for those who have tasted the grace of the Lord to betray Him. His was a desperate end.

That night, Wang Mingdao could not sleep. He finally dozed off after 1.30, but was shaken awake at 4.30 by terrible fear. In the morning of 4 August, news came that Huang Yuxian had been arrested during the night. At breakfast time, four people came in to check the cleanliness of the room, and they looked everywhere to study the layout of the house. On Sunday 7 August Beijing Medical College and the Union Hospital cancelled their day off in order to hold more meetings of accusation against him. At the meetings, the Chairman, Deputy Chairman and former Chairman of the Christian Union were all arrested. 'Before the rain comes down from the mountains, wind swallows up the pavilion.' Wang Mingdao's arrest was soon to follow, like thunder following the lightning.

Chapter 16

The Christian Tabernacle's Last Day

Sunday 7 August 1955 was a day that remained in people's memories for a very long time. It was the Christian Tabernacle's last day as a genuinely self-governed, self-supported and self-propagated church. Eighteen years had passed since its dedication on 1 August 1937 and the church had been through a lot. It had gloriously fulfilled its mission. Its pastor Wang Mingdao had completed his preaching work as the prophet of the time. Many events were indicating that changes would soon take place.

Tianfeng published an article in which the following warning was repeated four or five times: 'Wang Mingdao: your political position is wrong.' The fact that his name was published openly suggested that his accusers were no longer bothered about posturing. A few days later, a carpenter from East Hebei province came to give him a leaflet on uniting against the counter-revolutionaries and then, not long afterwards, Wang Mingdao received the visit from Dr Li Boheng. When he saw the look of fear on his old friend's face, Wang Mingdao realised his arrest was imminent.

Early in the morning of that last day, Brother Feng Qi, the doorman at the Christian Tabernacle, arrived with a vase of lotus flowers, describing them as Mary's perfumes prepared for anointing Wang Mingdao. He seemed to know something was about to happen. Recently, he had been moody, sometimes happy, at other times upset, worried and angry. No one knew why. At the Tabernacle he had always been difficult and seemed to harbour some kind of resentment against Wang Mingdao. His father had been a policeman, and with his family and political background he was easily bought. People speculated that he had been working for the government for a long time. Nevertheless, he had been with the Tabernacle for many years. When he realised that tragedy would soon strike Wang Mingdao, perhaps his conscience had driven him to bring some flowers.

Before the service started at 10.30 a.m., a student named Miss Li came to speak to Wang Mingdao: 'Grandpa, Grandpa, on my way here this morning, I was followed.' 'Don't fear,' Wang Mingdao comforted her. 'God is watching over us and keeping us safe.' But in his heart he had a feeling that something was going to happen soon. The chapel was very full that day, with perhaps 200–300 people spilling over into the courtyard. In total there were about 700 or 800 people present. Wang Mingdao preached on 'This Is How They Framed Jesus', powerfully condemning 'the disciples of Judas' who were fabricating crimes to persecute God's faithful servants. As soon as the service was over, someone told Wang Mingdao there seemed to be a lot of strangers there. After lunch, Wang Mingdao rested for a while. Then a girl from next door came to tell him she had seen some people peeking in from the outside as if they might try to climb in over the wall. Wang Mingdao became afraid. He thought they might try to come in at night.

About 200 people came to the Lord's Supper that afternoon. As the service drew to a close, Wang Mingdao realised this might be his last meeting, so he asked Zhang Jiyong and Zhang Shuaixun to fetch 200 copies of his autobiography as a gift for those who were present. In the evening, there was a prayer meeting. Among those attending were his fellow team members and the youth group, including Shi Changlin, Zhang Shuaixun, Wang Dueng. While they were praying, policemen were already waiting outside. Wang Mingdao was so tired that he dozed off, just as the disciples had done in the Garden of Gethsemane. *'The spirit is willing, but the body is weak.'* When he woke up, it was half past ten.

Wang Mingdao's attitude to the spiritual battle he was facing at this time was very different from the way he had fought back in 1942. His own account of that last battle is helpful for all those in Christ.

> 'On 8 December 1941 Japan declared war on Britain and America. That morning, all the places of worship established by British and American missionaries were closed and sealed. Church leaders were extremely anxious. After discussing ways of continuing their work, they set up a "Beijing Christian Preservation Committee". In the afternoon of 16 January 1942, a worker from the YMCA came to inform me that churches had set up a "North China Christian Federation Promotion Committee". He had been dispatched by the Chairman to urge us to join. He pointed out that if we failed to join, we could suffer dire consequences. At that moment, I had no clue how best to answer him so I told him I would reply by the evening. I discussed the matter with my wife and two team-mates, along with another brother. We all knelt to pray. Within a few minutes, a verse from the Bible came to my mind, *"Do not be yoked together with unbelievers"* (2 Corinthians 6:14). I stopped my pleas. I could only give thanks and praise because it had become clear how I should handle the situation.'

At that time, when the battle closed in, he did not rely on confidence in himself but went before the Lord to make his plea. He did not pray alone, but with his fellow Christians. This was one important reason why he won that battle. The history of the Church reveals that whenever God's people cry out to the Lord, He gives His commands, reveals His power and delivers victory to His people. In the battle of 1942, only a few minutes after he prayed, God's word came to him. He realised instantly how to deal with the situation. But in this battle, he did not have the same experience. He did not receive a specific word or power from God. He did what he thought was right, depending on his previous experience of victory in 1942. He lost hold of a simple heart that relied on God and God alone. This was a big mistake.

Back then Wang Mingdao had also had a similar experience to the Lord praying in the Garden of Gethsemane:

> 'In the evening of 30 April, when I got home for supper,
> my wife handed me a letter from the Federation Promo-
> tion Committee: "In view of recent developments and
> in order to advance the true spirit of self-governing,
> self-supporting and self-propagation of the churches, we
> who represent various denominations and groups of the
> Christian Church are in the process of setting up the
> North China Christian Federation Promotion Commit-
> tee. A central office was formally established on 18 April.
> In order to comply with regulations we are duty bound
> to set up a branch office in this city. Since your esteemed
> meeting hall is located within the designated area of this
> branch, it has become necessary for you to join the
> committee. In particular, we request you to send a
> representative to be present on 1 May at 10 a.m. to
> discuss plans for future progress. The meeting place is
> the Christian Church at the False Rice Market. Signed
> Beijing Branch Office, The North China Christian
> Federation Promotion Committee."
>
> For three or four months, the Promotion Committee
> had repeatedly approached me, but this time it was a
> written statement that clearly spelt out, "Participation is
> essential." In addition, we had to give a reply. This time
> it might not be possible to avoid crossing swords. That
> evening, at half past nine, after everyone else had gone
> to bed, I sat alone on the platform on the south side
> of the chapel thinking the matter over. To join this
> Babylon-like committee would be disobeying the will of
> God. Yet not to join would inevitably bring Japanese
> intervention. The church would probably be closed. I
> personally would find it hard to escape danger. I thought
> of my ageing mother. If she heard that I had been
> arrested, she would certainly be overwhelmed by anxiety
> and fear. After pondering in the moonlight, I went into
> the small meeting room and knelt down to pray. After
> praying I went back into the moonlight to ponder the

situation and once again to pray in the room. I went back and forth like this many times. Normally when I pray by myself, I hardly ever open my mouth. But that night I prayed in a loud voice, so much so that all my fellow-workers sleeping upstairs heard me clearly. I had a taste that night of the Lord's experience in Gethsemane. Not until 2 a.m. did I lie down on my bed. Thank God, He came to my aid. That night, He gave me strength, faith and courage to make the decision against joining the committee. I slept for only four hours. In the early morning I was able to write the reply and hand it to the church messenger.'

When our Lord was in the Garden of Gethsemane, *'in anguish, he prayed more earnestly, and his sweat was like drops of blood falling to the ground'* (Luke 22:43). After He prayed, He returned to His disciples. Then He went back to prayer. He went back and forth three times. Because of His enduring prayer, He was able to claim victory after His arrest before the council and court of Pilate. Wang Mingdao was like that. He pondered under the moonlight and then went to prayer in the room. He went back and forth like this many times. That was why he gained the victory before Mr Kawano, the Investigating Officer of the North China Cultural Bureau of the Japanese Asian Prosperity Department. But this time, when faced with the new battle, he acted very differently. He did not pray like the Lord Jesus. He even went to sleep at the most important moment. It was evident that Wang Mingdao preached the truth, that he was still enthusiastic and brave, but he lacked the spiritual power that only God could bestow. In this regard, failure was embedded in his victory. This is an important lesson for those of us who fear God and seek to serve Him faithfully.

Chapter 17

Arrest of Wang Mingdao

After the evening prayer meeting on 7 August, Wang Mingdao returned to his room. Noticing some letters on his desk he sat down in front of the south-facing window to read them. It was very hot so he took off his vest and carried on reading. Mrs Wang stood behind him reading the letters over his shoulder. It was nearly midnight when Mrs Wang heard a sound on the roof. She told Wang Mingdao that she was going to investigate. At the door, she walked right into policemen entering the house. They handcuffed her and forced her to sit on the couch, telling her not to move or speak. Wang Mingdao was still engrossed in his letters with no idea of what was happening outside. Suddenly he heard someone shouting at him from behind: 'Don't move!' He turned around to see a policeman pointing a handgun at him. In his shock his legs went from under him and he sat down on the bed. Another policeman came over with a warrant for him to sign. They handcuffed him and asked for the keys to the gate. Wang Mingdao realised that they had not come in through the gate but had jumped the wall. 'The keys are with the gatekeeper,' he replied. A policeman threw his vest to him, in so doing knocking his glasses to the floor. Then they pushed him into the yard. Over thirty people came in through the gate, some carrying guns, and surrounded him.

Wang Mingdao was so near-sighted that without his glasses he could hardly see a metre. When he had passed through the sitting room he had not seen his wife and he became worried. Outside, he asked a police officer where she was. When he was told that she had also been arrested, his heart was deeply troubled. He had never thought she would be arrested too. It was he who was against the Three-Self Church, not she. And even if they were against Three-Self, it was not a crime. He asked the police officers standing near him: 'I am a law-abiding citizen. Why are you arresting me?' Two officers quickly covered his mouth and pushed him back into the house. Stubborn as ever, Wang Mingdao kept yelling, 'Help, help, they are arresting me!' He was trying to raise the alarm and make others aware that he was being arrested unlawfully, as well as showing his protest. This was something the police would not tolerate. Covering his head with the vest, they pushed him onto a van and quickly drove away. At that moment, the sky in Beijing became dark. Soon thunder and lightening brought heavy rain that lasted right through until the next night. This was rare in Beijing in August. What was really unusual was that there was hardly any rain in the rural areas of Beijing, except some drizzle the next morning. Even heaven was showing its anger and sorrow at the persecution that the children of God were being forced to endure.

After they had taken Wang Mingdao away, Mrs Wang was also taken away. She did not even have time to change and was wearing a new pair of cotton shoes made by a sister especially for her. She did not want her new shoes to be damaged by the rain so she took them off and walked barefoot carrying the new shoes under her arms. The policemen gave her an umbrella but her feet were soaked by the pouring rain.

Besides Wang Mingdao, some of the Tabernacle's workers were also arrested on the same night, including Shi Tianming, Chizhang Hejin, Zhang Lifeng, the youth group leaders Shi Changling, Zhang Shixun and Ling Yunfeng. Other believers were also arrested, including Peng Hongliang from East Big Street Preaching Centre, Wang Changxin from Hemp Thread Lane Church, Chen Shanli from Fragrant Hills, Sun Zhenglu from Changchun and Lin Shanggao from Guangzhou. Including those arrested the day before from Beijing Medical College and Union Hospital, about twenty people were arrested during this first crackdown. The people of Beijing were horrified.

Chapter 18

Learning to Be a Prisoner

As soon as the police van stopped, the officers removed the vest that was covering Wang Mingdao's face and he realised he had been taken to a detention centre in Weed Haze Lane. Initially he was locked up in a room with a brick bed large enough for four or five people, but not long afterwards he was summoned for interrogation. As soon as he entered the room he asked, 'Where is my wife?', to which he received the reply, 'It is you that we want, why should we arrest her?' This was the first of his interrogators' many lies. That night they did not talk about anything other than his personal details, such as his work and family. Feeling these questions were personal, he said, 'There is no need for me to tell you my personal business.'

'You are no longer a citizen,' came the stern reply. 'You are a detained criminal. Whatever we ask you, you must answer.'

Back from the interrogation, he lay down on the bed but could not sleep: the same thoughts were going over and over in his mind: 'Why was I arrested? What crime did I commit? I never broke one law, never stole one item, and never did anything to be ashamed of. There is no reason for my arrest other than my opposition of the Three-Self Church. If I say Three-Self is correct and good they will let me go.' So the next morning as soon as he entered the interrogation room, he said, 'I am against the Three-Self. Three-Self is supported by the government. If I am against Three-Self, I am against the Communist Party.' After that, he lied, 'The Three-Self is correct and good.' He thought once he made such statement, his problems would be solved. But he was wrong. If he lied once, he would have to repeat his lie many times, he would have to lie again and again, more and more.

When the interrogator heard this, he knew now was the moment to put more pressure on. With a face like steel he barked, 'Confess your crime!'

'Confess what?' Wang Mingdao did not understand.

'You said you are against Three-Self.'

'But that's a problem of faith. It has nothing to do with any crime.' Wang Mingdao tried to reason, 'My opposition of Three-Self does not break any law.'

The interrogator gave him an even fiercer look, 'Opposing Three-Self is a crime.' This scared him so much that he began to feel very confused, and he confessed that he had committed the crime. Then the interrogator asked him who worked in his church. Wang Mingdao listed many names, but forgot Liang Lizhi, who had only been at the Tabernacle for three months after liberation. The interrogator asked him if there was any others. He said, 'No.' The interrogator realised he might have forgotten, so he reminded him, 'He came from East Hebei.'

As soon as he heard this, he remembered Liang Lizhi. The interrogator wanted to know if he knew about any problems concerning Liang and Wang Mingdao told him all he knew about him: 'At first he came to me to subscribe to *Spiritual Food Quarterly*. He told me he worked for the Meiyimei Church in Fengrun County. Many years later, just before Japanese surrender, he came again one night telling me he had come from Xian. When I asked him why he had been in Xian, he told me it was because Xian was free whereas Beijing was occupied by the Japanese. He had been unhappy idling away the hours in his hometown so he went to Xian to look up a friend. But in Xian he joined the Nationalist Party. I asked him how he could join such an unpopular Party, a Party that was nothing but tried to be in charge of everything and advised him to leave it immediately. When it was 11.00 p.m. I asked him to leave but he said all the hotels were full and he had no place to go. He pleaded to be allowed to stay the night, otherwise he said he would have to sleep in the street. I was afraid that the Japanese would shoot him, so I let him stay and sent him off early the next morning. After the Japanese surrender, he came again, saying that the Hebei branch of the Nationalist Party was sending him to Changli County to become the Party Secretary.'

The interrogator interrupted him, asking if he knew that Party Secretary was an important position in the Nationalist Party. Wang Mingdao answered, 'He never became one. The Party had already sent someone else. So later he left the Nationalist Party and asked if he could work for us. I was in need of a strong person so I offered him a job and helped him with police registration.'

'You were hiding a Nationalist spy!' the interrogator shouted.

'My police registration included his name. How could that be hiding? During the registration of the counter-revolutionary parties and groups after liberation, he went back to his home town to make a confession.' The interrogator looked at him and told him, 'He was a Party Secretary, and an important counter-revolutionary. You helped him. How can you guarantee that he did nothing for the Nationalist Party while he was with you?' Wang Mingdao replied, 'I cannot.' Later he thought he should have said, 'I can.' The Beijing Public Security Bureau would have been able to guarantee that he did not allow Liang Lizhi to engage in political activities during his stay. Otherwise, at the time they would have summoned him for interrogation or taken him to Changli County for cross-examination. From the day Liang was arrested to the day he was executed, the Beijing Public Security Bureau never asked Wang Mingdao about him. This proved that Liang never did anything political during his association with him. It was because he had not slept that night and was scared that he was feeling so confused. His mind was not working and he did not dare to say, 'I can.' Because he could not guarantee that, his crime of hiding a counter-revolutionary spy was established. Wang Mingdao began to confess crimes he had never committed.

Mrs Wang was also interrogated immediately after she was imprisoned. When she was brought in, she used her hands to dry her feet, as they were still wet from the rain. The interrogator asked her, 'Why are you not making your confession yet? Are you afraid?'

'No,' she replied.

'Are you going to try to deny it?'

'No.'

'Are you dishonest?'

'No.'

Since they had taken her hairslide away, her hair kept falling down and she kept trying to put it back with her hands. 'Don't play with your hair,' the interrogator ordered. 'Why do you think you are here?'

'Because I am counter-revolutionary.'

'Counter-revolutionary? For what reason?'

'Liang Lizhi was a member of the Nationalist Party,' she replied. 'We asked him to denounce his party. He did and he burnt his membership certificate in our stove. Then he lived with us. Three months after liberation, he went back to his hometown to make a confession. But for three months, he lived with us. Wasn't that protecting a counter-revolutionary?' She said these words to make herself a criminal.

For the first two interrogations, there were three men standing guard. They looked very foreboding. Mrs Wang did not understand why they looked so sinister. The interrogator asked her if she was afraid. She said she was not. The sessions often took place at night. As soon as she lay down, the door would open and a voice would scream, 'Time for questioning.' Every time Mrs Wang left her cell, she would ask God to give her the words to say. On entering the room she had to shout, 'Here I am.' Then she would quietly ask the Lord to help her speak. Once she was asked, 'Wang Mingdao preached, do you preach as well?' She replied, 'I can't preach. But sometimes in women's fellowships I do teach.' Then the interrogator asked her to preach. Remembering that before her arrest the women's Bible study had been on Romans 2, she shared a verse from that chapter with the interrogator: 'The Bible says, *"You, therefore, have no excuse, you who pass judgments on someone else, for at what point you judge the other, you are condemning yourself, because you who pass judgment do the same things"* [Romans 2:1]. We often criticise others. But just as often, if not more, we do the same thing. When we don't judge others, we do not commit the sin. But when we pass judgement on others, we are doing exactly the same.'

After sharing this, Mrs Wang thought she was asking for trouble using the opportunity to preach. But the interrogator did not say anything. Her interrogations were not as intensive as her husband's. The government focused the investigation on Wang Mingdao, thinking that once he gave in, his wife would follow. Little did they know how wrong they were.

Chapter 19

Interrogations

September arrived, and the weather was becoming much colder. Mrs Wang did not have a cover for the bed, and she was still wearing the same shirt and blouse as the night she was arrested. With no socks, she was often barefoot. She asked the authorities for permission to get more clothing. They agreed, telling her to write down a list of the things she wanted from home. After she had written her list, the person in charge told her to write a list for her husband as well. So she asked for his quilt, a blanket, some clothes and his glasses. Wang Mingdao's original glasses had been broken when he was arrested – this was his spare pair. Without his glasses he could hardly see people's faces, let alone their facial expressions, which was why he felt so disorientated during his first month in prison. After the items had been fetched, the prison guard took them directly to his cell and told him his wife had brought them. Wang Mingdao thought this meant she was at home so he believed that she was all right. The guard lied to him to keep up the story the interrogator had told him.

In late September, one interrogator told Wang Mingdao to write something down about his wife. He did not think there was anything to write about, but realised that he had to write something. So he wrote, 'She is anti-Communist as well.' Since this was what he had said when they arrested him, he thought she must have been arrested for the same reason. As time went on, he began to realise that his wife had in fact been arrested with him. In October, the guard brought a pair of old winter shoes and some winter trousers. He left the garments on his bed without saying anything. Wang Mingdao had worn the winter shoes before but the trousers were new. He thought they must have been made by his wife at home, or maybe they had been brought in by Sister Chi. In fact, both his wife and Sister Chi had been arrested on the same night as he had been.

In the prison, the interrogators worked closely with the guards. Often, too, the inmates were acting on their instructions. Once they realised Wang Mingdao was easily intimidated, the interrogators and the guards used the same methods to scare him. The interrogators would make the inmates feed Wang Mingdao terrible stories. Because what the interrogators said and the inmates said was so similar, he could hardly tell what was government policy and what was just gossip. The interrogators told him that it was government policy to treat those who confessed leniently and those who resisted harshly. The inmates told him, 'The more you confess, the quicker you'll be released. The worse you claim to be, the more honest they will think you are.' They also warned him, 'If you refuse to confess, the interrogators can become extremely angry and take you out to be shot. You'll die a terrible death.' Night and day they tried to scare him. Wang Mingdao was plagued by crippling fears.

The Communists maintained a strong party line and it was very dangerous not to accept it. As part of the process of interrogation highly pressurised political studies were conducted to make them accept the official dogma and apply it in thought and action. It was extremely dangerous not to tow the line. There was no alternative. The interrogation was repeated over and over again. In general, the interrogators would not tell the prisoners what to say but guided them in such a way that they eventually confessed with their own mouth whatever the government wanted them to. In the end they had to give in. There was no way out except by saying what they wanted. At the beginning of September, the interrogators insisted that Wang Mingdao confess what he had done to 'instigate resentment between believers and non-believers, between the Church and the government.' Wang Mingdao said, 'When Director Li spoke to me, he asked us Christians not to isolate ourselves from those who did not believe. I told him he could not blame Christians for that.

We were the ones who were being discriminated against. Mr Li accepted that this was the case and promised to instruct non-believers not to look down upon Christians.' After a few days, the interrogator told Wang Mingdao they had seen Mr Li who refused to accept that he had ever said such a thing. Wang Mingdao testified that Mr Li did make such a statement and he clearly remembered the time and date he had done so. But the interrogator maintained that Mr Li had never said this. Wang Mingdao became very angry about this and, in the presence of the interrogators, he called out, 'Heaven!' A few days before that, the interrogator had told him never to mention the word 'God'. But when he called out to heaven, he was calling out to God. After this the pressure became so intense that he was forced to say that he had made up the story.

During interrogation, the accused could only say what the government wanted them to say. They could not tell the truth against the government's will. On one occasion the interrogator asked about the fact that Christians were making accusations against one another. Wang Mingdao explained that the Bible did not permit such behaviour. There was no way that the interrogator would allow him to make such a statement so he tried to scare him by saying, 'Are you still maintaining your position?' This statement was spoken with so much force that Wang Mingdao became terrified that he would be shot. He gave in and told the interrogator, 'I do not know now what the situation was. Maybe I said something that was not suitable.' The more the interrogators wanted him to confess, the more they tried to scare him. The more Wang Mingdao wanted to be released, the more he gave in. By doing this he put himself in a vulnerable and passive position. Wang Mingdao's failure started on the night of 7 August. During the daytime, he had been bold and brave, but that night he totally gave in and gave up. What was it that made him act like such a different person? In 1990, when asked about this, Wang Mingdao admitted,

'Soon after liberation I went to Tianjin where I saw the slogan written on the wall in white paint declaring

"Freedom of religion". I thought this meant the Communists were promising to all Christians that they need not be afraid because they would guarantee them freedom of religion. I firmly believed this. I believed the Communists would not interfere with personal beliefs. That was why I published so many articles to fight for faith. My failure had to do with my spiritual victory in 1942 against the Japanese. I thought that, although the Japanese were harsh and powerful, I had not given in, so what was there to fear? Conventional wisdom says that victory can come from fear and failure from haste. Fear is the source of blessings and haste the source of tragedies. My failure was in my haste and lack of fear. Why was this? I fought the Japanese for eight years and did not give in. I thought I was great, forgetting I was a man with a weak body. I was asked once who were more scary, the Japanese or the Communists? I said the Japanese because they could not speak Chinese. I thought that since the Communists were Chinese I could therefore reason with them. Now I know the Communists did not want to reason. Their guns scared me to death.'

Chapter 20

Living with the Other Inmates

Wang Mingdao spent the first two days in prison in a cell on his own but on the third day he was moved to another prison where he had to share a cell with two other inmates. One was called Meng Guanghua, and the other Huang Kedao. Meng had helped the Japanese to fight the Chinese. Huang never revealed anything about himself, and no one knew what he had done. From his accent, he was from the North-east. He knew some people in the church in Shenyang. As to why he had been arrested, nobody dared to ask him, because he was very rough. When he opened his eyes wide, even Meng Guanghua was afraid of him. There was a strange irony about Huang Kedao's name and Wang Mingdao's. *Mingdao* means 'to understand the truth', while *kedao* means 'to contain and destroy the truth'. Perhaps he was there to destroy Wang Mingdao. Wang Mingdao suspected that he was a policeman disguised as a prisoner to spy on him. Over a period of four months, Wang Mingdao suffered terribly at the hands of these two inmates.

As soon as Wang Mingdao was moved into the new cell, he asked Meng Guanghua where they were. Meng told him they were outside the city but Wang Mingdao could hear a bell and he knew there was no Catholic church outside the city. Later he learned he was being detained right beside a Catholic church inside the city. The two inmates soon realised their new cellmate was easy to scare and they did their best to intimidate him. Meng Guanghua told Wang Mingdao: 'You've got to confess your mistakes. If you resist, your interrogators will become extremely angry. Two people will come in, force your arms behind your back and take you out to be executed', adding, 'There is a bullet called a four-seven bullet. When it enters your brain, you don't die immediately but suffer a slow and miserable death suffering from pain and blood loss for hours.' Wang Mingdao thought he was telling the truth and became very fearful. To him it sounded worse than being pulled apart by five horses. They were doing their best to scare him. The three men slept on the same bed, with Wang Mingdao in the middle. Many times at night they would slap him on the face to wake him up. When Wang Mingdao asked them why they beat him, they pretended they were only dreaming. Even if this sort of behaviour was not actually organised by the government, it was tolerated. No matter what was going on, as long as it helped to break a person and make him confess, any behaviour was welcomed. Wang Mingdao had to put up with their abuse day and night. Meng Guanghua's language was vile. He would speak and Huang would listen. Sometimes they would sing silly songs just to annoy Wang Mingdao.

One morning, they asked Wang Mingdao, 'Besides your wife, have you ever had any relationships with any other women?'

'No,' Wang Mingdao replied.

'That's impossible,' they said. 'You have preached for over thirty years and have been to over twenty provinces. Thousands of people have heard you speak. There must have been some young women running after you. You must have had a few relationships. You must confess it. It will help you.' Trying to tempt Wang Mingdao into making a confession they gave an example of a priest who confessed having sex with his own mother and was released a few days later: 'We are not doing this for ourselves. When you leave, you can't take us with you. We can see how much you're suffering. Once you confess, you will be able to leave in a few days.'

'How can I confess something I have never done?' Wang Mingdao replied. 'If I confess, I will have to name someone. If I accuse somebody falsely, how will they ever forgive me? They would have to kill me. Chinese women take their purity very seriously. If I falsely accuse them, they will find me and beat me, I'm sure.' The two inmates kept on asking him the same question over and over again. Why? It was not until after his release that Wang Mingdao realised after reading an article in *Tianfeng* that a famous church leader had confessed to sexual sin after his arrest. He was two years younger than Wang Mingdao. The inmates thought if he had had problems of this kind, how could Wang Mingdao not have done? So they asked him the same question every day trying to get something out him. But Wang Mingdao had never had a problem in that area, and eventually they had to give up.

In his youth Wang Mingdao had been tempted in this regard, but, thanks to God, he had stood up to the test. Over the years he had shared some of his experiences to warn young people serving the Lord in ministry to guard themselves against the temptation of the enemy:

'My first test came when I was leading a service in Guangzhou. A woman preacher once came to see me with a few other sisters. She introduced one of them to me, saying she had been widowed recently. The next day when I was having a meal, this sister came with some food for me to enjoy. She sat with me and chatted for a long time. Two days later, she came with more food, telling me I must try a Guangdong speciality. "Thank you, please take them back," I told her. "I have enough food here. Next time you come, please do not come alone. Bring some sisters. If you want to talk about anything, write it down beforehand. Don't just talk about whatever comes into your head. That is not good." I lived in a large compound with the gatekeeper, who lived in the room next to the gate. I was in a big house at the back. There was no one else. Had I wanted to do something sinful, it would have been very easy. Thanks be to God. He was watching over me. The thought never entered my head.

The second time I was tempted was in Bongbu. I was there one summer to preach. I went into an inn and asked for a single room. When he took me to my room, there was a young woman waiting at the door. I told her to leave. "Why close the door when it is so hot?" she asked and refused to leave. "I don't want anybody to stand here. Please leave me alone," I told her and forced her to leave.

The third time I was tempted in this way was in Hong Kong. When I got there, a brother came to meet me. He took me to the biggest hotel run by Christians. The hotel would not allow prostitutes in. However, they had arranged it so that prostitutes could come to visit without an invitation. After the brother took me to my room on the third floor, I went to have a shower. Even after I had locked the door, a well-dressed woman came to the door playing the harmonica. She followed me from my room to the shower door. After my shower she was still playing. I saw her but paid no attention to her. She just kept on playing at my door. There was nothing I could do about it. Finally I had to turn off the lights. When she realised there was no chance she left. Thanks be to God. I stood up to the test because He was watching over me and kept me. The temptations did not lead me into impurity.'

On New Year's Day 1956, after Wang Mingdao had been imprisoned for five months, Huang Kedao told everyone to share their thoughts. Wang Mingdao said, 'Ever since I came in four or five months ago, I have prayed every day for God to deliver me. So far He has not done so.' Hearing this, Mr Huang and Mr Meng concluded, 'Well, your faith is very shaky. Why don't you write down that you have given up your faith? If you do, you will have a meeting with them within days.' Indeed, not long after Wang Mingdao had submitted his report, he was summoned to a meeting. During every interrogation up till now he had had to stand up but this time it was different. As soon as he walked in, the interrogator pulled up a chair and asked him to sit down with him by the fire. It was in the middle of winter and was very cold. The interrogator told him, 'I have read your report. I am happy that you have given up your faith. I have two things to tell you now. The first is that I want to kill you. The second is that I think you have some talents which can be put to work for the government.'

'I have given up my faith, what can I do for the government?' Wang Mingdao asked.

'Preaching, of course,' the interrogator said.

'Without my faith, how can I preach?' Wang Mingdao asked.

'That hardly matters,' the interrogator said. 'You can perform. Just like an actor. When Mei Lanfang was acting Princess Yang his name changed to "Princess Yang". He was a man but on the stage he became a woman.'

'That I cannot do,' Wang Mingdao explained. 'In order to perform I will have to lie. Whenever I lie, I become overwhelmed with pain.'

'That's because you're not used to it. After a while, you'll get used to it.' But the interrogator realised that he was not going to agree and sent him back to his cell.

As soon as he returned, Mr Huang and Mr Meng wanted to know what had happened. He was not ready to tell them until a day later. Huang Kedao replied, 'If the government wants you to act as if you are preaching, you should act.'

'I can't act,' Wang Mingdao said. 'In order to act, I would have to lie. Whenever I lie, I get a terrible pain in my heart.'

'That's because you're not used to it,' Huang Kedao advised him. 'The pain will go if you keep on lying.' Wang Mingdao could not accept this but he could not stand up to them either. By now he was totally controlled by them.

Because he refused to act out his preaching, many days went by without any further meetings. He missed his wife. Coming from the south she was used to eating rice, not steamed cornflour bread. At home meat dumplings did not satisfy her, she always had to have rice. Now that she was imprisoned, how would she be able to survive with just cornflour bread? Fearing that she would soon starve to death he wrote another report to say that he had accepted the interrogator's advice to act out his preaching. Sure enough, he was summoned to another meeting. 'Very well,' the interrogator said, 'you can perform now.' How could he act? He had never even been to a theatrical performance. To act, he would have to shut himself off from reality. How could he do that? During the interrogation, he was nicely treated. The interrogator thought he was finally going to co-operate with the government. However, in his heart, Wang Mingdao realised that he had written the report to say he had given up his faith because he thought God was not being fair and loving to him. He had not heard his prayer. But in his mind he had not changed at all. He still believed in the existence of God. Even when he confessed with his mouth that God was an illusion, his heart firmly believed that God was right there with him. His experience over many decades had proved that God is real.

In late January, Huang Kedao was suddenly transferred. When he failed to return at meal time, Meng Guanghua told Wang Mingdao he must have been executed. 'You should watch out,' he said. 'It's your turn next. You'll be shot soon.' Hearing this, Wang Mingdao became increasingly nervous. Mr Meng then asked which room was used for his interrogation. 'You must have killed before, haven't you? Why don't you just confess it?'

'How could I kill anyone?' Wang Mingdao was horrified. 'I can't even kill a chicken. How could I kill another human being?'

Over five months, these two men had made him suffer so much that, by the end, he was too terrified to speak. After Huang Kedao left, it remained just the two of them in the cell. Because there was no one else, the abuse became even worse. One day, Guanghua beat him so hard that Wang Mingdao fell to the floor. 'If you beat me, I will tell the guard,' Wang Mingdao shouted in vain. Then Meng Guanghua threw himself on the floor and yelled even louder, 'You beat me, you beat me. You beat me to the floor.' What could be done against such a monster! Wang Mingdao lived with these two inmates for a long time. They beat him numerous times and abused him physically and mentally day and night. He lived in such terror that he almost had a nervous breakdown. It was not until July in the second year that Meng Guanghua was transferred, too. The period of terror and hardship was finally over. Soon after, Wang Mingdao was transferred to another prison where the conditions were much better.

Chapter 21

The Closure of the Christian Tabernacle

After 7 August, when all the believers living in the compound were arrested, police officers occupied the premises, and the gates and doors were firmly shut; no believer was allowed in. Access was only available to the church building through the main entrance facing the street which was opened during worship times. The Tabernacle existed in name only.

The police masked all the windows of the building with paper so that no one could see in while they carried out a very thorough search, even digging up the concrete floor of the toilets. They were hoping to find some weapons or equipment for spying but they found nothing. However, they did find something which was used to besmirch Wang Mingdao's reputation. In the office upstairs there was an unlocked box containing a large amount of money. It had been sent to the account of Wang Mingdao's magazine, *Spiritual Food Quarterly*, by the uncle of one of the sisters in the church, Sister Sheng, to pay for his children's education. After Wang Mingdao had received the money, he had passed it onto Sister Sheng, who put it in the box and left it upstairs. There had also been another large transaction through the account of *Spiritual Food Quarterly*. A Mr Reng Zhengfang from the North-east, who had made a lot of money doing business in Lanzhou, had paid money into the account so that he could buy a house in Beijing. After these two discoveries, the rumour began to spread that Wang Mingdao had big savings. Later, Yang Chaotang wrote in *Tianfeng*:

'In the past I had a lot of respect for Wang Mingdao. But from what was discovered, it appears he was anti-new China and resisted the laws and regulations of the people's government. Even in his personal life, he was far from honest and pure. Once he told his audience he lived by faith and had no savings in the bank. It is shocking to discover that he had such big savings.'

When he read these words later, Wang Mingdao was deeply hurt. Even his old friends no longer trusted him, choosing rather to believe the lies put out about him by his enemies.

The police occupied the compound for over a year and, during this time, they used Wang Mingdao's private telephone and read all the newspapers and magazines to which he subscribed. Yet they paid the premises' bills with cheques sent to Wang Mingdao from different parts of China. Despite using up all his money they accused him of having big savings. Wang Mingdao felt he was badly wronged.

On the morning of 8 August news of Wang Mingdao's arrest spread quickly. Brother You Yipo was due to meet Huang Shaofu and Shi Changlin at Union Chapel to plan a student summer camp. When they arrived, however, there was no one there. They waited and waited until Sister Kou Shuzheng came with news of the arrest. 'How can this be?' Brother You asked. Then he realised that one of the Ministry of Public Security's plants, Mr Li Yingfu, was sitting in the corner behind them pretending to be praying and reading the Bible. You left immediately and went to the Tabernacle, where he saw that the front and back gates were closed. He then went to see Sister Gao who warned him not to go back because, another brother, Li Dianan, who had been seen there, had been detained by the police for a long time before being released.

Brother You went to see Sister Dong who suggested that since the shepherd had been attacked and the sheep scattered, they should pray. When he came out, he noticed someone was following him. The man was about thirty years old and carried a basket as if he was a sweet-seller. He remembered seeing the same person every time he went to visit Brother Chen Yihe. He quickly jumped onto his bike and rode straight home. He told his wife, 'I may not come back again. If I don't, go to Brother Li's home.' Then he put a Bible, a toothbrush, some soap and toothpaste into his bag and left. First he went to Brother Li Zaisheng's home and then to the homes of other brothers and sisters to tell them to meet at Brother Li's. From there they were to proceed to the Tabernacle for the Monday evening prayer meeting. They would pray specifically for Wang Mingdao.

It was pouring with rain and everyone was carrying an umbrella. When they arrived, they saw water had flooded the steps leading to the front gate. The gate was wide open and all the lights were on. No one knew who had turned them on. They all went in. Several dozen people attended the prayer meeting that night including some who were not from the Tabernacle. Mr Li Zaisheng led the meeting: 'Tonight we have come here to pray, because we believe in God. Nothing not permitted by God would come to us. If it has been permitted by God, we can only pray. There is nothing else to say. We must trust God. Nothing else. God's servant has been arrested. All we can do today is pray.'

After prayer, Mr Li said they should send someone to ask why Wang Mingdao had been arrested. Brother You Yipo was elected to be their representative, and Brother Chen Yihe volunteered to go with him. They left via the front gate and went to the side gate at the back. A policeman opened the door and asked them what they wanted. 'Why was Mr Wang Mingdao arrested?' Brother You asked. 'What crime did he commit? You must tell us.'

'Don't you even know that?' the policeman answered. 'You must know we arrested him because of his counter-revolutionary activities.'

'What counter-revolutionary activities?'

The policeman did not reply but asked, 'What is your relationship with him?'

'We are believers from this church. He is our pastor,' Brother You answered.

'Then, how can you come to ask that question? You must know why!' the policeman said.

'We came because we did not know,' Brother You said. 'We were sent by our brothers and sisters.' At this point, someone inside the room ordered the policeman, 'Don't speak to them.' With that he slammed the gate shut.

When they returned, it was still raining heavily. Gradually those who had come to the prayer meeting dispersed, until the two men were left with only Brother Zhang Jiyong and Brother Shi Yajun. They were planning to stay there for the night but after a while, at about ten, a plain-clothed man came, saw them there, and then went again. Shortly afterwards, a jeep carrying two policemen arrived at the front gate. 'What are you doing here?' they asked.

'We are having a meeting.'

'What meeting?'

'To pray for Wang Mingdao.'

'This building belongs to the police now. You must all come with us.'

They were taken to the police station where they were placed in separate rooms for interrogation. They were asked about their previous occupations. Brother You said, 'I haven't done much. I came to Beijing to study.'

'What else? Why don't you confess?'

'There isn't anything else.'

'You are lying.'

'I have answered all your questions about my past.'

'If you resist, you will face harsh punishment.'

After a while, the jeep returned, this time with warrants for their arrest, and they were taken into a room where Brother You and Brother Chen were officially arrested. Once they signed the warrants, they were handcuffed and taken to the detention centre.

On 9 August, Mr An Menghua from Tianjin came down to Beijing to see Wang Mingdao. Having no idea what had happened, from the train he went straight to the Tabernacle. As he was knocking at the door, the police asked him whom he was looking for. 'Wang Mingdao,' he said. They opened the door to let him in and arrested him immediately. After a few days, he was taken to Tianjin and sentenced to ten years' imprisonment.

Many children were deeply distressed by Wang Mingdao's arrest, among them Little Huiren, a boy who lived in the neighbouring house and often came to the Tabernacle with his parents. He especially liked listening to Wang Mingdao's stories. When he heard Grandpa Wang had been arrested and that he might never see him again, he stood outside the door facing the Tabernacle and cried. He could not be comforted.

An old doctor, Brother Wang, once promised before Wang Mingdao's arrest that he would go with him if he was arrested. After Wang Mingdao's arrest, he was not able to keep that promise. So he started to grow a beard, vowing, 'The day Wang Mingdao is released is the day I shave my face.'

Wang Mingdao was particularly partial to the sweet dumplings which were the speciality of Tianjin. Whenever he went to Tianjin, Brother Zhen Pingdao would invite him to come and eat sweet dumplings with him. Sometimes when he came to Beijing, he would bring some for the pastor. After Wang Mingdao's arrest, Brother Zhen stopped eating sweet dumplings. If he was invited to eat them, he would say, 'Thank you. I can't eat any: my pain is too great.' The first time he came to Beijing after Wang Mingdao's arrest, when he heard the announcer on the train say, 'Ladies and gentlemen, we will soon arrive in Beijing, the capital of our great motherland. In no time you will be able to meet with your family and friends', he was overwhelmed with pain: 'I no longer have a home here. Where can I go? In the past I could go to the Tabernacle. That was my home. Where can I go now?' He could not hold back his tears. From the heart-cry of a little boy to the determination of an old friend, such was the deep love of the sheep for the shepherd. The servant of God will never labour in vain.

In the evening of Wednesday 10 August, Yang Runmin, the only preacher at the Tabernacle that had escaped arrest, came to see Brother Li Zaisheng. Privately he asked him, 'I came to tell you something important. Can you go with me to the Religious Affairs Office at 8.00 tomorrow morning?'

'Why should they want to see me?' Brother Li was puzzled. 'I am not a preacher. Neither am I a deacon. I am only a believer. I won't go.'

'The Director wants you to come with me,' Mr Yang said.

'Didn't I just tell you? I am not a preacher. Neither am I a deacon. I am only a believer. I won't go. If the Director wants to see me that much, tell him to send a car.'

The Director must have learned that Mr Li had led the prayer meeting on Monday. Mr Yang was the person the Religious Affairs Office had designated to be Wang Mingdao's successor. That was why he had come to see Mr Li. When Mr Li refused to listen to him, he had to leave.

On 14 August, the first Sunday after Wang Mingdao's arrest, many people attended the service. The main hall was crowded, and people even filled the back yard where bikes were usually parked. As there were so many people, bikes had to be left outside. Yang Runmin stepped onto the platform and announced, 'Last Sunday, both Mr and Mrs Wang Mingdao were arrested.' As soon as he said that, most people in the congregation started to cry. Some were crying so much that they had to leave the meeting. Through the windows masked by paper, people could just see the policemen, who were staring in between the gaps, hoping to find out who had come to the service. The sermon was on the topic 'I Won't Abandon You as Orphans' taken from John 14. People reacted differently to Yang Runmin's message. Some were comforted; others thought his quoting of *'Trust in God. Trust also in me'* meant they should trust Wang Mingdao and Yang Runmin himself. After the service, many left in tears never to return. When the shepherd was attacked, the flock was scattered: each went their own way.

Chapter 22

The Man Who Asked to Be Arrested

After Li Zaisheng had returned home after the prayer meeting on 8 August, his wife had asked him, 'Everyone is in prison now, why aren't you?' Mr Li had replied, 'I don't know what to do. I don't want to be the only one left on the outside, but I don't know how to get myself arrested.' After that, she kept asking him the same question, 'Everyone has been arrested except you. You are still on the outside pretending everything is fine. What are you afraid of? The time has come. Why are you still playing around at home?' Mr Li said, 'Fine, I'll go and get arrested.' Then he told his youngest son, 'Tonight I won't cook for you. Let's go for out for a hotpot meal. Then you can come home, and Dad will go to the police and not come back.'

Mr Feng, the chief policeman, dealt with Mr Li and asked him what he could do for him. 'You know what's happening in Beijing,' Mr Li replied. 'Wang Mingdao has been arrested. Wang Mingdao and I are the same kind of people. I won't wait any more. Here I am. Do whatever you want with me.'

'Fine, Li Zaisheng,' Mr Feng said. 'We think you are a patriotic Christian but if you want us to do something with you, we can. But first of all, you will have to admit that you are acting in defiance of the constitution, because the constitution guarantees freedom of religious belief. If you admit that you are defying the constitution, we can make the appropriate arrangements for you today.'

'That I will not admit,' Mr Li said.

'In that case, you can go home.'

The following Saturday, 13 August, people were sent from Beijing University's Medical School, where his wife worked, to speak to him. 'What is your relationship with Wang Mingdao?' they demanded. 'A faith relationship,' he said. 'That is all.' The next day was a Sunday. In the morning he went to a service of worship. In the evening he was arrested. At that moment he felt such a tremendous sense of joy that no one could understand it. He was joyful all the way – when he was pushed onto the jeep and when he was detained at the police station. The police told him to be serious, but he could not control himself. He was so joyful that he could not stop laughing. In the end, they had to tell him to squat facing the wall. He thought even this was funny. 'No wonder they call prison a squat!' This made him laugh even more. At night he could not sleep, but that too he thought was funny. 'I'll be home soon,' he told himself. They thought he was a fool but, in fact, his personality was like that: he was a real joker. For example, no one was allowed to climb up to the small window in the cell to look out, but every now and then he would do it. Whenever he was caught, he would have to stand facing the wall, but it didn't stop him.

One day the head of the prison asked him about Liang Lizhi. 'Do you know that Liang Lizhi was executed?'

'Yes.'

'Why was he executed?'

'Because he believed in Jesus.'

'He was a spy.'

'Yes he used to be. But he stopped. When he gave the key back to the Nationalist Party's office, it was I who delivered it.' When the head of the prison heard this, he had nothing more to say. Li Zaisheng thought, 'I came in because of my faith in Jesus. I did not commit any crime.' When asked during interrogation if he was against the Three-Self Patriotic Movement, he said, 'Yes.'

'Do you know what crime you are committing by opposing the Three-Self Patriotic Movement?'

'No, what?'

'Counter-revolution!' The head of the prison quoted the

Bible to support this, *'Everyone must submit himself to the governing authorities'* (Romans 13:1).

'You're right,' Mr Li replied. 'But there is one thing I won't do: disobey my faith.' They were unhappy about this but they was nothing they could say.

Mr Li had little education and spoke in a casual way, but there was wisdom behind it. During the Anti-Japanese War, he had been a businessman in East Hebei. He had owned many shops and made a lot of money. He had used his shops to shelter people working with the Communist underground resistance and had supported the movement financially. No could deny he was a patriotic man with a good track record. Later he had accepted Jesus, sold his business and moved to Beijing where he had got to know Wang Mingdao and begun to learn from him. Mr Li was an excellent cook and often cooked for Wang Mingdao. After liberation, he had been given the opportunity by the government to become an official. But he had not felt it was the Lord's will and had not taken the post up. He remained content humbly serving the Lord and His Church. He was one of the people closest to Wang Mingdao.

Whenever someone was interrogated, there was always a People's Liberation Army soldier walking around or standing in the background. Everyone treated Mr Li kindly as he had a medical history of tuberculosis and could in fact have died at any time while he was in prison. They made quite a few concessions because of his ill health, such as allowing him to walk slowly. After he returned to his cell, he would say, 'What a wonderful Father you are! You are feeding me so well that I am spoiled. Look, now I even have an escort to accompany me.' They were not happy about this and asked him why he was denouncing the government in that way. But there was nothing they could do about it, as Mr Li had committed no crime at all. At meal times, he closed his eyes to give thanks. When they would not allow this, he began a hunger strike. Two days later, the guard came to tell him that he must not disobey the rules. 'A meal is a meal, and a problem is a problem. As for saying grace, do you have to close your eyes? Why don't you thank God with your eyes open? Why don't you just change your way of doing things a bit?' After that he gave thanks with his eyes open.

During interrogation, interrogators often slammed the table, yelling, 'I'll have you executed!' Li Zaisheng was never afraid: he just said to God: 'Lord, it's up to you. You're all I have. It's all in your hands now. If I am to be executed, let your will be done.'

One day, when some inmates tried to force him to condemn the Communist Party, saying that he had not truly confessed unless he had condemned the Party, he became very angry with them: 'I may do so outside. But I will never do so in prison. I am not like you. Do you know who I am?' Then he told them about his background in the Communist underground movement. Naturally they reported him to the guard. Later, an underground activist whose life he once saved came to the prison to identify him. When he testified that Mr Li was indeed who he said he was, the government was ready to release him. On 31 August, having been imprisoned for just half a month, he was to be released as a demonstration of the government's leniency with those who co-operated. He knew exactly what they were trying to do, and he refused to leave. He thought it was better to die inside. After this, they put him with other prisoners who were also suffering from TB. The prisoners never had to make their beds because they sat in them all day long. It was a comfortable life with special meals for the sick, not just cornflour bread. Sometimes they were even given meat dishes and hotpot. Mr Li was there for almost a whole year.

In early July of the second year, he was summoned to the office and told, 'Pack your things. We are sending you home this afternoon.' He knew if God did not want him to leave, it would not happen. He did not know this revelation was from the Holy Spirit. After he returned to his cell, he said nothing about it. In fact, he was not released that afternoon. In the middle of July, the guard summoned him again, 'We did not release you last time. What did you think of that?' Mr Li replied, 'I gave it no thought. Every day I remain here, there must be a good reason.'

'Last time we had not finished our paper work and your release was delayed. But this afternoon we will release you.'

'Fine.' He returned to his cell with the same thought, 'If God does not want me out I will not be released.' Once again, it did not happen.

Towards the end of July, he suddenly thought, 'How nice it would be if I could be out on 25 July.' This was a special day because it was Wang Mingdao's birthday. With this thought in mind, he began to hope he would be released on that day. On 25 July, from early in the morning to 3.30 in the afternoon, he waited and waited. When nothing happened, he gave up, thinking there was no hope any more. At about 4 o'clock, the door was kicked open. 'Li Zaisheng, pack up your things,' the guarded ordered. He thought he was going to be transferred. But then the guard added, 'Pack everything, do not forget anything.' He packed everything into a big bag which he carried on his back. He left the cell and walked to the office. Once he was there, they gave him a haircut and a shave. 'Li Zaisheng, you have gained weight, do you know that?' they asked.

'Oh yes,' he replied. 'How could I not? If I hadn't gained weight, I would not have done my best for the government. From morning till evening I have had the best possible meals. After eating there is nothing to do except wait for the next meal. How could I not gain weight?'

'That is enough. You can go home now.'

'Thank you very much!' He picked up his bag and left the prison. Immediately he began to sing, 'All the songs I sang yesterday I am singing again today. Glory to God! Hallelujah.' He kept on singing until he got to the gate of Beijing University Hospital, where he hired a rickshaw to take him home.

As soon as he arrived home, he began to collect the trash and sweep the street. A neighbour was amazed to see him so active, 'I was in prison for three months and, when I came out, I had to rest for half a year. You were there for a year and have come back as if nothing had happened.'

'How can you say that?' Mr Li replied. 'There is nothing to beat it: free food, free hotel, free medical care. To tell you the truth, I didn't say long enough!' He found life outside prison a lot more complicated. There was always something to do and people making demands. One day he was so fed up that he packed a bag and went back to prison. When he reached the gate, he asked to be allowed back in. The police asked him what he wanted. 'I want to come back to stay,' he said. 'Living outside is not as easy as living inside. A phone call today and a visit tomorrow. A trip here and a trip there. Do this, do that. I am fed up.' An old guard came out and told him there was no reason for him to be prison. 'No, I didn't stay long enough. I want to come back.'

After that, no one dared to bother him any further.

Chapter 23

Dire Straits

After dozens of interrogations, by the spring of 1956, Wang Mingdao had confessed to having committed at least twelve crimes against the government. Among these, his only true 'crime', to which he had confessed immediately after his arrest, was opposing the Three-Self Movement. The rest was lies. Under pressure from his interrogators at a time when he could not think clearly he had confessed to the crime of sheltering reactionaries. The refusal of Director Li to corroborate the truth of his statement had led to him being accused of two further crimes: damaging the relationship between believers and non-believers and encouraging believers to oppose the government.

He also confessed to having undermined the 'Three-Purge' Movement. At the beginning he had supported the movement but later he had realised many lies were being fabricated in a deliberate attempt to deceive the people. When he confronted these lies he was labelled as a criminal who was acting in defiance of the movement. For instance, a believer who attended the Tabernacle had been imprisoned on a completely trumped-up charge of embezzlement and had been locked up in a room so small that he could not lie down but had to sit up all the time. After a long period of confinement he had developed such bad piles that he could bear it no longer and falsified a confession that he had embezzled a large sum of money, promising that on his release he would return the money. After his release, having no idea what he should do, he went to Wang Mingdao for advice. He was told to be honest about what he had done and ask the government to reconsider his case. This was what he did. Nothing happened to him. He really had not stolen any money at all. Wang Mingdao had discussed his plight with other believers and they had all agreed that no one should be forced to suffer so much without cause. However, this was used as evidence to accuse him of being against the Three-Purge Movement.

He was also forced to admit to undermining the Anti-America Pro-Korea Movement as well as obstructing the military service law. During the Korean War, a young man in the Tabernacle had asked him if Christians should join the army. Wang Mingdao explained that there were two points of view among Christians on this subject. Some thought it was acceptable to join the army to protect one's country. Others interpreted Christ's teaching that those who lived by the sword would die by the sword to mean that Christians should not use weapons against anybody and should rather go to prison than join the army. Wang Mingdao believed personally that a Christian should not join the army. He had expressed this view openly before liberation, but afterwards it would have been seen as undermining government efforts to fight the Americans on behalf of the Koreans.

Wang Mingdao was also forced to confess that he had made personal attacks on Mr Wu Yiaozong and opposed the Three-Self Patriotic Movement, an organisation founded and promoted by Chinese Christians themselves. In his articles to defend faith, he had called Mr Wu a Modernist, an unbeliever and a false prophet. As far as the Three-Self Movement was concerned, he had said that history would not show that it had been initiated by Chinese Christians. After Wu Yiaozong's death, a memorial was held for him in Shanghai, at which the Deputy Director of the Revolutionary Committee in Shanghai, Zhang Chengzong, had clearly stated that the movement was developed by Wu under the care and instruction of Chairman Mao and Premier Zhou. So the movement was not started by Chinese Christians but by Wu himself. But no one was allowed to say such things. If you did, you were committing the crime of opposing a movement initiated by Chinese Christians. In 1951, Wang Mingdao had written a book on Christians and Marriage in which he taught that Christians must not divorce. This was used as evidence for his crime of damaging the new marriage law. Such crimes were not really crimes or his crimes but, by confessing to them, he piled them up onto his own head. He went deeper and deeper into the mire, until it threatened to swamp him completely.

At around this time a special interrogation was organised so that he could reconfess all the crimes to which he had already admitted, with the intention of making him more aware of his crimes. It was a day of dark terror for Wang Mingdao. His trembling voice as he read his crimes revealed how scared he was for his life. With these twelve crimes, there was hardly any political movement since liberation he had not opposed. It made him the most hardened criminal and most out and out counter-revolutionary that it was possible to encounter. Wang Mingdao clearly understood what fate awaited a criminal who stood so accused. It is easy to imagine the fear in his heart.

This interrogation was secretly recorded and tapes were circulated among the active members of the Christian Taber-nacle in different districts of Beijing. After listening to the tapes, everyone was required to reflect on Wang Mingdao's confessions. In a discussion in the Western City District, Sister Huang Xiaotong stood up and said, 'In the past, Wang Mingdao has always been a faithful servant of God who taught completely according to the Bible. If he really confessed these twelve crimes, he is no longer a faithful servant of God.' When others heard what she had to say, they were amazed at her courage. That power came from the Lord. She was no longer afraid. She packed a small bag and got ready for her arrest waiting patiently at home each day. For many nights when she went to sleep she did not undress because she wanted to be ready when the police arrived. But what the Lord did not permit never came upon her.

In fact, the organiser of the meeting welcomed what she said. Afterwards, the Communist Party Committee for West-ern City District sent three officers to the school where she worked to talk with her. One of them said, 'Wang Mingdao is a counter-revolutionary. You must distance yourself from him.'

'No,' she replied. 'Wang Mingdao is a faithful servant of God.'

'The government has classified him as a counter-revolutionary. You must denounce him,' another of the officers said.

'To know whether a person is good or bad, you need to ask those who have frequent contact with him. I live across the street from the Tabernacle. I used to go to all the meetings there. I talked with Wang Mingdao often. He always listened to me very patiently. He answered all my questions very carefully. His attitude was gentle and kind, humble and patient. When I worked on propaganda for the street committee, twice I wanted to give up my faith. Both times after I heard Wang Mingdao's preaching, my faith was restored. He is a faithful servant of God!'

The three officers took turns to try to change her mind but it was no use. She was an active opponent of the Three-Self Movement. After the arrest of Wang Mingdao and his wife, the Christian Tabernacle had joined the Three-Self Church. She had written to resign her membership, stating that by joining, the Tabernacle was yoking itself with impurity and prostitution. From this it is clear that even when Wang Mingdao fell, his brothers and sisters were able to stand because of his faithful teaching. They did not follow the person of Wang Mingdao but the truth that he taught.

After that special interrogation, the government ordered Wang Mingdao to write a new report on his plan to redeem himself with good work. After he submitted that plan, the government thought that they had achieved what they had set out to achieve, and they were ready to release him. The day when Wang Mingdao would be able to walk out of prison was drawing near.

Chapter 24

Wang Mingdao Released

After Wang Mingdao agreed to act as if he was preaching, the government began to think about when to release him. But for Wang Mingdao himself, there were so many questions. What would he do after his release? Should he join Three-Self? If he didn't, he would be back in prison again. If he did, what did the future hold? What was more important was how his wife would react. Would she agree with him? Would they be able to go forward together? These questions filled his mind.

In May, the interrogator instructed him to write a letter to his wife, which they would pass on to her. So he wrote, 'I have confessed that I undermined the Three-Self Patriotic Movement and defied the government's religious policy of freedom in faith. I hope you have also changed your position.' Wang Mingdao was in a weak and confused state at the time. He hoped he would receive some help and encouragement from her but, to his disappointment, he did not get a reply. By 27 August, although there had been no official announcement, the government had decided to release them. The prison doctor told him that, starting from that day, he would have the same meals as the sick inmates. 'I am not sick, why I am being the same meals as the sick?' He was puzzled. 'You just take what you are given. You do not ask why,' the doctor told him. The sick received meals of rice and wheat bread – they didn't have to eat cornflour bread. Sometimes there were even meat dumplings. This was like heaven.

At about the same time, Mrs Wang was given a new room. She was also allowed special meals and even to read the newspaper. The doctor told her she could write a shopping list of anything she needed for her health, so she wrote down soil beans and sunflower seeds. The doctor was bemused and told her she could order things like biscuits, milk, apples and pears. She had never imagined she would be allowed to ask for such luxuries, but she followed the doctor's advice and wrote them down. At home, Mrs Wang had never read the newspaper, but now that she was given her own copy, she read it to pass the time, even memorising the twenty-four lunar seasons of the year. Also, when the government published simplified characters for the written language in a move to promote literacy, she copied them down twice. Her handwriting improved while she was in prison. She had no idea that the government was about to release her. She would frequently check her thoughts to see if she was harbouring any wrong ideas. She had not been asked to do it, but she did it anyway to keep a track of her thoughts.

On 14 September, Wang Mingdao was summoned to the office once again. The interrogator told him, 'You and your wife have both made good confessions. Tomorrow you will see each other.' Wang Mingdao was joyful and fearful both at the same time. He was happy because he would see her soon. But anxious because this meant that their release was imminent. What awaited him outside? He had promised to join the Three-Self Church. If he did not, there was no doubt that he would be back in prison again. The very thought of prison filled him with terror.

The next day, he was summoned to the meeting room. When the guard brought his wife into the room, he told them, 'You two have confessed your crimes. The government will treat you leniently. In a few days' time, you will be released. You can have some time to talk about the future.' When they saw each other, they did not know whether to smile or weep. Wang Mingdao sat on a chair and held his wife's hand for a long time, speechless. Mrs Wang was shocked by his distressed state. There can hardly be anyone in the world who has ever looked more miserable. She thought his mind was like the twisting branches of a tree that were impossible to unravel. After a long while, Wang Mingdao said, 'Something has happened to my faith in God. I have promised to join Three-Self.'

'How can we live without God? With your personality you would never fit in. You won't be able to do it.' Mrs Wang knew that her husband would never be able to join that organisation. 'What can we do?' he replied. 'We will have to do what we are told.' They could not say any more, knowing they were being listened to.

After the meeting, the guard summoned Mrs Wang to ask about their talk. She told him, 'He told me his faith was wavering. He even wanted to join the Three-Self. We have always trusted the Lord. How can we live any other way?'

'So he wanted to join?' the guard asked.

'He can't. There is no way. Other people can act out a pretence, but his character would never allow him to do that. He just won't be able to do it.'

'It will be all right,' the guard said.

But she insisted, 'How can he ever preach again? If he no longer believes in God, how can he teach others that God is real?'

'Isn't there a verse in the Psalms about the fool saying in his heart there is no God? He can still teach that,' the guard said.

'How can he teach that? The Communist Party does not believe in God. How can he teach that?'

'Why not? It is your belief. You can teach it.' The Party understood that once a person had lost his faith, he could teach whatever he liked: without the work of the Holy Spirit it wouldn't make any impact, so the Party didn't have any problem with it. Whatever a person taught, it didn't really matter any more.

A few days later, Wang Mingdao and his wife met again. She realised that the government had not allowed Wang Mingdao to ask for food to be brought in, so she wrapped up some milk powder for him. Mr Li, the head of the prison, was afraid there might be something hidden inside so he poured it out to have a closer look. When he found nothing, he allowed it to be taken to Wang Mingdao. While they were talking, the guard came in to tell them someone had arrived to see them. It was Mrs Chi. Wang Mingdao took her hand and wept. Wang Mingdao held Mrs Wang's hand with one hand and Mrs Chi's with the other. After a long while, he asked about her daughter. They had a long talk. Before leaving, Mrs Chi asked them if there was anything they would like. For over a year Wang Mingdao had had nothing but cornflour bread so he asked for some cake and fruit.

Some time later Wang Mingdao was summoned again and told, 'You and your wife have made good confessions. The government has decided to release you.' News began to spread outside the prison about Wang Mingdao's imminent release. The Director of the Religious Affairs Department invited all the pastors in Beijing to a meeting to ask them if they had anything to say about the plan. They all expressed their support for it. On 28 September, the day before his release, the guard told Wang Mingdao that his door would no longer be locked. 'You can go out into the yard to exercise and see the flowers.' They also returned his watch which had been confiscated when he was arrested. Then they sent him to a barber to get him ready for his release. That afternoon, he was seen by Mr Zhang, Director of the Public Security Bureau, in the reception room. Wang Mingdao was behaving so nervously that Mr Zhang asked him, 'Are you insane?' 'I did not use to be,' he replied, 'but now I have a weak mind.' Mr Zhang got Wang Mingdao some tea. Government officials had always been nice to him, hoping he would eventually become a leader of the Three-Self Movement.

That night, Wang Mingdao had to go with two officers to write a simple confession. He later learned that one of them was Li Guang; the other one had curly hair but he did not discover his name. They told him how to write the confession. He wrote the draft; they changed it; he revised it; they changed it again. This was repeated over and over again: 'I am a counter-revolutionary. I was arrested by the Beijing Public Security Bureau.' They told him, 'There is no need to write too much.' So he wrote, 'I am a counter-revolutionary.' After that, they wanted him to write, 'With the help of the government and my colleagues, I have made great improvements in my thinking.' Wang Mingdao refused, saying that since his arrest he had never seen any colleagues. They told him writing this would be good for him. Wang Mingdao had only ever been interested in his yes being yes and his no being no, but now he had to write whatever they wanted him to. Then he wrote down the confessions he had made. Finally they told him to write, 'There are many crimes I have committed but I cannot spell them all out today.' Wang Mingdao refused, saying that all his crimes were written down in the confession. Again they told him that it would be good for him to write that down: 'If anyone in the future exposes any other crimes of yours, the government can tell them that you had confessed them already.' The confession took the whole evening from 9.00 till 12.00 to write – they had to revise it so many times – and it was a pack of lies. When it was finally completed, the two officers sent for some meat pancakes and gave one to Wang Mingdao. Wang Mingdao refused it. They told him there was no need to stand on ceremony. 'It's late. Just eat it,' they said. With that Wang Mingdao took it and returned to his cell.

As soon as it was daybreak, Wang Mingdao got up. At 8.00, as he was just finishing washing, the two officers came to ask him if he was ready. 'I just got up. I am packing,' he told them. 'Don't worry. You don't need to pack. We will pack for you. Your wife can bring your things home with her when she leaves. You come with us.' They escorted him out of the prison where a car was waiting. As they helped him into the car, he asked, 'Wasn't I told by the interrogator that my wife would leave with me? Why am I on my own?' One of them explained, 'She has not finished her paper work yet. We will make sure that you are both home for Nation Day.' In the car, one sat on his right and one on his left. As the car wound its way across the city, one of them pointed out a building that had once been the imperial court but was now the meeting hall for the National People's Political Consultancy meetings. Wang Mingdao realised that they had pointed it out to him because he would have to attend meetings there. Eventually the car stopped outside an unmarked office of the Public Security Bureau. Mr Zhang, the Director, met Wang Mingdao and in the course of their conversation told him, 'Canadian newspapers printed reports that your wife died in prison and you were sentenced to fifteen years. Now that you are being released, the rumours will stop.' Then he pointed to one of the officers with him and said, 'His name is Li Guang. If you have any problems, contact him. I will ask them to go with you to the city government offices to meet the Director of the Religious Affairs Bureau. Then they will leave and you can get a car to take you to your home.' When they arrived at the Religious Affairs Bureau, the Director told him to be at Wang Zizhong's home at 2 p.m. that afternoon for a meeting. Wang Zizhong was the Chairman of the Three-Self Committee in Beijing. Wang Mingdao thought, 'Wang Zizhong is an unbeliever. If I as a criminal go to his place to meet him, that will be the end of any reputation I might have left. But the Director has told me to go, so how can I not go?' He pondered this all the way home in the rickshaw.

He had been in prison for 419 days, between 7 August 1955 and 29 September 1956. He arrived home to discover that the police had vacated the building a few days before his return and that the Tabernacle had been restored to its original condition. Feng Qi was back in his job as the gatekeeper, and Sister Wang was cooking again. As soon as he saw Wang Mingdao, Feng Qi came to greet him, saying that they had been expecting his release for a while. Wang Mingdao walked into his room where he met Sister Wang. She said, 'We heard you were coming back. Director Li spoke to the pastors, asking them if they had any comment to make about you being released. Everyone supported the decision.' They immediately sent for Sister Chi who came to join them for lunch. Wang Mingdao was hurting deeply in his heart. The lunch in his mouth was tasteless. He did not know what he was eating.

In the afternoon, he went to meet Wang Zizhong, who was waiting for him when he arrived. He held his hand, 'You have come out. This is good. Tomorrow afternoon at 2.00, go to the YMCA to read out your confession.' Wang Mingdao thought, 'My God! I resent the YMCA the most. He wants to send me there to read my confession.' It was extremely hard for him because he had once published an essay denouncing 'The Evils of the Modern YMCA'. He had vowed never to step inside its doors, whether in Beijing or Shanghai. Now he was being ordered to go there. He was deeply troubled. But he knew he dare not refuse, as Wang's order held as much weight as a government order. If he refused to go, he would without any shadow of a doubt be sent straight back to prison. He would just have to forget about his reputation and go.

That evening, many believers visited him. Among them was Sister Liu who loved Mr and Mrs Wang dearly. She told Wang Mingdao, 'You must watch out. People have changed.' Wang Mingdao realised what a difficult situation he had returned to. Although she mentioned no names, Wang Mingdao knew whom she was talking about.

Before their arrest, Wang Mingdao and his wife had lived downstairs next to the reception room. When he returned, all his belongings were piled up so a bedroom was made for him upstairs. They moved in a big iron bed from Sister Chi's room and made it very cosy for him. There were double happiness paper cuttings on the doorway and flowers in the yard to welcome his return. That night, however, as he lay in his bed alone, his heart was very troubled. He was back in the real world but he had no idea what his next step should be. Never before had he felt so terrible.

Chapter 25

A Miserable Day

September 30 was a Sunday. Before the service started, Mrs Chi went upstairs to tell Wang Mingdao people were arriving and would like to see him. 'I won't come down,' Wang Mingdao said, feeling that he could not face anyone. Even when the choir started singing, he was still not willing to go down. Before the service was over Mrs Chi came up again to ask him to go and say hello to everyone. 'They are all waiting to see you,' she said. Wang Mingdao finally came down. As soon as he saw an old brother Xu Xingyi, he called out to him and shook his hand before quickly returning to his room without saying anything to anyone else.

At 2.00 p.m., Mrs Chi came to tell him Mrs Gao had arrived to escort him to the YMCA. When they arrived at the YMCA, they did not use the front door but a side door. As soon as they entered the meeting room, he saw Wang Zizhong waiting inside with a heavily bearded old man who looked familiar but he could not recall who he was. Mrs Gao introduced him as Chen Zonggui. Wang Mingdao knew him from a long time ago and had in fact lived in his house for eighteen days. But because of his beard, he had not recognised him. After being introduced, Wang Mingdao shook his hand, but did not say anything.

Over one hundred people were present at the meeting, which was chaired by Wang Zizhong. He started by saying, 'Wang Mingdao has returned a changed man. Now he supports the Three-Self Movement and is willing to join us. Let's give him a hand.' Everyone clapped their hands. But had he really changed? He might have changed on the outside, but deep inside he had not changed at all. He hated the Three-Self as much as he hated snakes. He still believed its purpose was to destroy the Chinese Church from the inside out. His confession was false, not true. After the applause, Wang Mingdao stood up to read his confession. His confession had no title but when it was published in *Tianfeng*, the title 'My Confession' was added by the editor. As he read, he felt as if he was being punished. His head was lowered, his hands were shaking, his voice was trembling. In the past, when he had preached or spoken, he would never write it down beforehand. He would never lower his head either. But that day he could not look up. He could not bear to look at anybody. After he finished, Wang Zizhong led the audience in applause for him, and everyone clapped. All Wang Mingdao wanted to do was to find a place to hide. San Letian who had once accused him of donating copper to the Japanese cheerfully came up to him. He was happy because he thought Wang Mingdao had admitted his crimes. A Dr Tian who once belonged to the Tabernacle also shook hands with him. He put his arm on Wang Mingdao's shoulder and told him, 'Mr Wang, you have made a lot of progress. Now you are here at the YMCA reading out your confession.' His words were worse than a slap across the face. Wang Mingdao regarded that day as the most miserable day of his whole life: it was worse than facing a firing squad.

After the meeting, he left the YMCA as soon as he could. Miss Bei caught up with him and tried to sign him up for a Three-Self study group. Wang Mingdao told her, 'I am barely alive. How can I go to a study group? I won't.' Miss Bei refused to give up but just kept on following him. He decided he would go to visit the sister church of the Tabernacle in Sweet Rain Lane but nothing would deter her. When they were nearly home they met a young man who took Wang Mingdao by the hand and said, 'Mr Wang, it's good to see you. But we hope you have not changed. If you have changed, we would rather you had died in prison.' In his heart Wang Mingdao agreed, 'Amen! It would have been better if I had died in prison.' Miss Bei tried to hurry him away, asking, 'Who was that young man? How could he say such a counter-revolutionary thing?' When he arrived home,

many people were waiting for him. September was a very
pleasant month, neither too cold nor too hot, and they sat
outside in the yard, enjoying the summer sun and talking. At
4 o'clock, a young man who had been at the YMCA meeting
earlier came to see him. He told Wang Mingdao he would
like a word with him in private. When they were upstairs, he
asked, 'Did you write the confession letter yourself?' How
could Wang Mingdao say no? If he did, he would be locked
up again. So he said, 'Yes, the words were written by me.' As
soon as he heard this, the young man realised that even
though Wang Mingdao had written the words down, he had
not meant them but had been instructed to do so by the
police.

After Wang Mingdao read his confession, his wife was
released. She left prison just before dark, hiring a rickshaw
to bring her and all their belongings back. It was drizzling on
the way so everything got wet. As soon as she got home, she
went to the meeting room to play the piano and sing her
favourite song:

> 'To praise the Lord I want to raise my voice,
> My voice comes from my heart and reaches the heaven,
> I meditate on the character of the Lord and watch His
>   deeds,
> I begin by praising and finish with joy!'

In prison she had longed to sing this song, and she had made
up her mind that the first thing she would do as soon as she
got home was to sing it as loud as she could. She had always
been an optimistic person. After this she and Wang Mingdao
went upstairs where they were able to talk freely. Regret and
fear filled Wang Mingdao's heart: regret because he could not
believe he had fallen so far that he could no longer face
meeting anybody; fear because if he did not watch what he
said and did, he would be sent back to prison.

That evening many of the sisters came to see him. They all
told him, 'Mr Wang, in the future you must watch what you
say. Don't speak too casually. People's hearts have changed.'
This reminded him of what Sister Liu had told him the

night before. Their words made him even more scared, and afterwards he no longer found it easy talking to anybody. Living in such an environment of fear and mistrust was like living in hell.

Chapter 26

Torment

Three days after their release, the Wangs were told to report at the police station, and from then on they were required to do this every other week. The police were very polite to them, sitting them on a couch and offering them tea, sunflower seeds and sweets prepared especially for them. Two officers would sit one on either side of them. One of them was obviously responsible for seeing them because he was always there and, even if he was not, he would come as soon as a phone call announced their arrival. Whenever he spoke to them he was always polite, pleasant and considerate of their needs. The authorities were still pressing hard for Wang Mingdao to join the Three-Self Church.

While the Wangs were in prison, they knew nothing of what was going on in the outside world. After their release, they saw that many believers were still simply and purely in love with the Lord, and holding firmly to the truth that Wang Mingdao had taught them. These people hoped that Wang Mingdao had not changed, that he too was still walking in the ways of the Lord. How could they betray them by joining Three-Self? They could not be honest with anyone about what they were feeling – that was why it hurt so much.

Some of those who had joined the Three-Self Church were pleased that the Wangs had been released and could hardly wait to find a way to use the situation to their advantage and ingratiate themselves with the government. Since her efforts on 30 September, Miss Bei had returned to Fragrant Hills. However, from there she wrote a letter to Wang Mingdao which was also signed by her colleagues, praising Wang Mingdao's confession at the YMCA: 'Your confession pleased all those who belong to God,' she wrote. Wang Mingdao was so upset when he read her letter that he threw it on the ground. A few days later, two relatives who still attended the Christian Tabernacle, Sister Sheng and Brother Liu, visited Wang Mingdao. They told him, 'Wu Yaozong is a faithful Christian who wholeheartedly serves the Lord. You should not oppose him.' Wang Mingdao was deeply upset when he heard this. Wu was a false prophet, yet they praised him as a faithful believer who wholeheartedly served the Lord. How could Wang Mingdao tolerate that? But there was nothing he could say. The moment he criticised anything, he would be back in prison. So he threw himself onto the concrete floor and begged them to stop, 'My good nephew and good niece, please forgive me. Please stop immediately. Please do not go on. I am on my knees before you.' With that he bowed low before them three times. The visitors were so embarrassed they had to stop. After that, a Brother Dong from Shanghai, who was at one time an enthusiastic supporter of Wang Mingdao, came to visit. He had a meeting place in Yuyuan Street in Shanghai which was modelled on the Tabernacle. They used the same hymn-books and even shared the same name. There had always been good relationships between the two men. Later he had joined Three-Self and had become Wu Yaozong's assistant. He told Wang Mingdao that Wu was a humble man. When he heard this Wang Mingdao became extremely angry, and Brother Dong left never to return.

On the other hand, some believers in the Tabernacle had been kept by God as His faithful remnant. They refused to relate to the Three-Self Movement in any way. When the Tabernacle had joined Three-Self after Wang Mingdao's arrest, Sister Huang Xiaotong had written a letter severing her ties with the church. She never went back. By the time Wang Mingdao was released, she had moved away and was suffering from ill health. When she heard they were still living at the Tabernacle, she sent her good friend Sister Zhu to say she would like to meet them. Of course, they were very keen to see her as well. When they arrived on their visit, they saw someone familiar standing outside but could not remember who he was. Then they realised they were being watched.

Sister Huang told them that by joining the Three-Self Church the church had prostituted itself. After she showed them her letter of resignation from the Tabernacle, they realised that, no matter what, they must not join the Three-Self Church.

Wang Duen was a brother who deeply loved Wang Mingdao. He had not been arrested and when he heard that Wang Mingdao had been released, he phoned to ask if he could visit. When he came Wang Mingdao took him upstairs and began to pour out his heart to him, weeping as he told him how he hated himself for falling so far. As Wang Duen listened, his heart was very troubled, but somehow he could not shed any tears himself.

Mr You Yipo was released from prison one month after Wang Mingdao. The first Sunday after his release, his wife suggested, 'Uncle Wang is also out. Let's go and see him.' They realised that Wang Mingdao was deeply troubled but they did not say anything. Wang Mingdao did not want to go to the service but remained in his room while they went. He was sitting around so much that his legs had become very swollen. After the service, they went upstairs again to see him again. All Wang Mingdao could say was, 'I have failed you.' He knew that these young people had been arrested because of him. He felt he owed them a lot.

Not long after Wang Mingdao's release, Brother Sun Zhenglu, who was arrested in Changchun, was released too. As soon as he returned to Beijing, he phoned from the railway station and, after learning that Wang Mingdao really had been released, hired a rickshaw to take him to see Wang Mingdao before going home to Mountain Old Lane. When Li Zaisheng heard that Wang Mingdao had returned, he went back to cook for him. Most people were afraid of associating with Wang Mingdao but he was not. One day, Xu Hongdao came to visit. As he went upstairs, Mr Li followed him. He told them, 'I thank God for going to prison after you. Once I was released, you came out too. If it had not happened like this, I would not have been qualified to cook here.'

Mr and Mrs Zhen Pingdao also came to Beijing to see Wang Mingdao. Mrs Zhen came first, returning home on the same day, to be followed by her husband the next day. After making arrangements to stay in the house of an old friend, he came to the Tabernacle. But Wang Mingdao was so troubled that for a long while he could not say very much. A few days later, he came to visit again. This time Mr and Mrs Chen Hesheng were also there. Wang Mingdao told them, 'We are all on the same stage. We perform to the world and to the angels. Look, we are performing right now.' After having said this, he steered the conversation onto a new topic and, from that time on, he never talked about whether or not he would join the Three-Self Church.

On 16 October 1956, Li Zaisheng and Zhen Pingdao invited the Wangs to go on an outing with them to Taoranting, the Comfort Pavillion Park. Mrs Wang trusted them so she agreed. Mr Ong Lisheng was present when this was discussed and he asked if he could go as well. It was hard to exclude him so they all went together. Li and Zhen wanted to talk to Wang Mingdao, but with Mr Ong there it was difficult because they did not trust him. He had once served as the private secretary of the Nationalist Army General, Zhang Xueliang. Before Wang Mingdao's arrest he had often attended the Tabernacle and, after his release, he came back. The strange thing was that, although many people kept their distance from Wang Mingdao, Ong was not afraid to relate to him closely and he never got into trouble for doing this. He was never watched by the government either. They concluded that he must be a government spy. In the park, they were all trying to persuade Wang Mingdao to preach again. Wang Mingdao could not do this, but neither could he admit it either. His heart was full of contradictions and pain. Li Zaisheng felt Wang Mingdao was no longer being open and asked him, 'Brother Mingdao, do you have any doubts about me?' Wang Mingdao put his right arm on his chest and said, 'My heart is full of doubts.' When Ong Lisheng, who was right beside them, heard this, he began to laugh: 'There are very few people like you in this world.' For lunch, they had brought with them some bread, bacon, fruit and sweets, and they sat talking as they ate. They talked about the Comfort Pavilion and the tomb of the Fragrant Princess who had been hung by order of the empress during the Qing Dynasty.[1] Wang Mingdao was very moved by the story of the princess's sorrowful death and wrote down the inscription from the princess's tomb on a sweet wrapper. Then he recited it from his heart:

> 'The expanses of space spell sorrow. The vastness of the world witnesses injustice. The mourning song is stopped short. The bright moon is cut in two. The Forbidden City is spoiled by red blood. The redness is disappearing. The blood is fading away. A trace of fragrant smoke marks the end of a soul. To be not, not to be, only a butterfly remains.'

Wang Mingdao used this poetry to express the sorrow and restlessness in his own heart which could not be spoken of in any other way. Someone must have reported this to the government, because it was later used as evidence of his crime of speaking out about the unjust treatment he had received.

Many people welcomed opportunities to meet Wang Mingdao after his release. Others, especially those who had also been released recently, were afraid of being arrested for associating with him and they stayed away. But with his good friends the connections remained. Nothing is able to sever the links between true friends whose hearts are joined together.

Wang Mingdao continued to be torn apart by fear. He felt he was walking a knife-edge. But Mrs Wang was not fearful at all. She managed to remain as optimistic as she had always been. One day he asked her, 'What should I do? I just can't see myself acting out my preaching.' She tried to encourage him and told him not to be afraid. Once every two weeks, they still had to go to the police station and this was becoming more and more of a burden to them. Every time they were asked, 'Have you thought it through yet?' They always replied, 'No, we haven't. We're still not ready.' But why had they not thought it through? There had to be a reason. They were invited to meeting after meeting, with programmes and agendas being constantly sent to them. They also received prayer letters with information on meetings, sermons, Bible studies and prayer requests. Mrs Wang showed the police the programmes. 'How can we go to meetings such as these?' she asked. 'These people do not believe in God. They use human methods to decide what to preach on and what to pray for. Of course, we cannot say that we always hear from God, but at least we have a will to obey Him and to preach on what He has told us. There are meetings arranged for every day of the week. How can we go to their meetings? For example, if they pray, shall we close our eyes? We just can't. We won't go.' Thus, step by step, they backed out. They were both suffering from ill health and could not go to the meetings anyway.

Mrs Wang had started to feel ill before she was released. One morning in May, after her walk in the yard, she had felt very hot so she drank some cold boiled water. In the afternoon she had developed a high fever. At night, she could not stop coughing. Even the guard outside told her to be quiet. Once she was released, she was constantly sick and could not go to any meetings. This really was the protection of the Lord. She stayed close by the side of her husband. Wherever he was, she was there with him. This was because she was afraid that he might take his own life. On one occasion, at the police station, an official wanted to take Wang Mingdao out for a walk. Mrs Wang told him, 'I am suffering with bad health. My heart can't rest if he leaves me.'

'Don't worry,' the official said. 'I will walk him to the park and then bring him back to you. Is that okay?'

'No,' she replied politely. 'I just can't let him go.'

They often suggested that they take him out for a walk but she always told them she was afraid he might kill himself. 'Because his father committed suicide, I am afraid he has the same tendency. It's hard to say what he might do if he felt he was in an impossible situation. I just can't let him go.' Sometimes she would say, 'If he committed suicide it would be a great loss for the government.' As a result, government officials were never able to get him on his own. Had he been out with them, they might have put pressure on him, and then he would have been finished. So Mrs Wang's sickness was a hidden blessing that God used to protect them both.

Wang Mingdao's heart was so heavy because he could not share with anyone else what was hidden there. His fellow believers had been very happy when he was released, thinking that they would soon hear him preach again. But why didn't he preach? What had happened? They could not understand. He could not tell them that the government was putting him under pressure to join the Three-Self Church but that he did not want to. Some of his feelings he could not even share with his wife. And what she knew, she could not tell others either. So many important feelings were suppressed in their hearts that they could hardly breathe. Whenever he thought about them, he nearly went insane. One morning, he picked up the boiling water on the stove and, with his trembling hands, was about to pour it over himself. Even though he did not do it, he seemed capable of doing something terrible to hurt himself. In his family home in Sweet Rain Lane, some renovations were taking place and there was some wet lime to whitewash the wall in the yard. On one occasion he took some, put it into his mouth and was about to swallow it. Fortunately, Li Zaisheng witnessed it and forced him to spit it out. His mouth was so badly burnt that the skin peeled off. In many ways he was acting very strangely. Sometimes he crawled down the stairs to the reception room and then screamed at the top of his voice. Mrs Wang was sick in bed and could not follow him downstairs. She heard him screaming but did not say anything. She understood what a hard time he was going through.

Some time later Wang Mingdao became sick as well. After the period in prison when he had eaten a very restricted diet his stomach could not take too much meat. This, together with the worry and fear in his mind, broke his health. He contracted measles. A doctor in Chinese medicine thought this was due to his bad mental state and upset stomach. Most patients with measles have the rash in small patches, but in his case it was all over his body. His face, ears and legs became swollen. Even his digestive system was infected. For three days, he could not even take water. The smell in his mouth was vile. He stayed in bed for a month, playing with stamps to pass the time. He often sat in one spot for hours, with no sound, no word, no movement. The Three-Self Church still kept sending them invitations to the meetings but, since his legs were too swollen to walk, they could not go. This too was a blessing from the Lord. Zhao Zicheng, the former Dean of the College of Religious Studies in Yanjing University, came to see him and realised how sick he was. He tried to comfort him, saying that he should rest in bed. The police telephoned them many times, asking them to go to their regular appointment, but eventually they realised they were too sick and gave up. Occasionally after this they would just ring to say hello and to express their good wishes to Wang Mingdao.

When she heard that her daughter and son-in-law were released, Mrs Wang's mother in Shanghai wanted to see them as soon as possible. Of course, they wanted to see her very much too, so they wrote a number of letters asking her to look for a house for them in Shanghai. They had no idea that the government would not allow them to leave Beijing. When she found a house for them, she waited and waited but they did not come. In the end she had to send Wang Mingdao's son, Tianzhe, to Beijing to find out what was going on. Mrs Wang thought Tianzhe's visit might have a double purpose and might be connected in some way with the government's ongoing efforts to make them join the Three-Self Movement. There was a sense of increasing frustration on the government's part as to why there had been no progress.

Wang Mingdao and his son conversed together but he could not share with him what was really in his heart. One day, as Wang Mingdao sat on the couch, his heart was hurting so much that he began to slap himself on the face. Tianzhe went to him immediately. He sat by his side and held his hands, asking him to tell him the reason for his pain. 'I can't tell you,' Wang Mingdao said. 'I will have to take it to the grave.' He knew Tianzhe was a good son, but he was naive. If he told him, he was afraid he would report it back to the government. Then they would definitely send him back to prison. Wang Mingdao loved his son very much. He often praised him but he never talked with him much about his time in prison. He buried all his pain in his heart. One day, to help him forget, Wang Mingdao asked Tianzhe to go to the cinema with him. At the time, the classic film *Yang Naiwu and the Little Cabbage* was showing. Halfway through the film, when Tianzhe had to go to the toilet, Wang Mingdao started to cry secretly. The hero of the film Yang Naiwu had a sister who worked in the imperial court in Beijing. When she visited her brother and heard of the miscarriage of justice he had suffered she decided to defend her brother's case. Because of her help, the case was reversed. Wang Mingdao thought, 'Yang Naiwu had a sister who could help him. My sister has died. Who can come to help me?' Suddenly he was reminded of the misery of his life and he began to cry.

Tianzhe had come to visit during the Chinese New Year when he had three days off and he had also asked for a few days' holiday in order to be able to stay a bit longer. After seeing how sick his mother was and how much his father was suffering, he could not leave. So he kept on writing letters to ask for more days' holiday. After twenty days, he had to go back to his work. Back in Shanghai, he wrote a letter to his mother asking his father to write a few words to him but Wang Mingdao did not reply. During those days, he was in such great torment. Every day he thought of committing suicide. One reason was that he believed he had lied so much that he could no longer face living and another was that he was so afraid of being sent back to prison again that he thought it would be better to be dead.

After Tianzhe returned to Shanghai, the government there told Mrs Wang's mother that her daughter and son-in-law could not leave Beijing so she decided to go to Beijing to visit them.

When Wang Mingdao was released, the Tabernacle had a new board. Among the new board members were those who had been arrested and then released such as Yan Jinguang, Liu Xiaojin and Wang Enqing. Tian Jiafeng who lived in Sweet Rain Lane had also become a board member. Wang Mingdao requested many times to be allowed to resign, but they dared not say yes. This did not change until March

1957, when Wang Mingdao realised that he would have to try something else. He decided to go to Mr Li, the Director of the Religious Affairs Bureau, to ask to be permitted to hand in his resignation. Mrs Wang told Mr Li, 'He is no longer qualified to preach. He does not believe himself. How can he preach?' Mr Li replied, 'That's no problem. Even if your church has only one person, the government won't blame you. If it has two thousand people meeting, the government won't interfere. You just run the church.' What he meant was that as long as Wang Mingdao joined the Three-Self Church, they did not care what happened to the church. Mrs Wang thought that the government might have something else Wang Mingdao could do. Once when a believer at the Tabernacle, Mrs Liu, came to visit, she comforted him by saying, 'Get better quickly. There is hope for the future. You might be able to go abroad.' Mrs Liu had joined the Three-Self Church in the very early days. She thought that once Wang Mingdao had recovered, the government might send him to work abroad.

That day, Mrs Wang asked again and again for them to release Wang Mingdao from his duties. 'He must resign. There is no other way,' she said. 'Let me warn you,' Mr Li said, suddenly becoming very serious. 'You are treading a very dangerous slippery slope. If you persist in going down that road you alone will be responsible for what happens.' Mrs Wang insisted, 'There is no way that he can continue to be a preacher. He cannot preach any more.'

When they returned to the Tabernacle, they made the decision to move back to their family home in Sweet Rain Lane. On 7 April, the day before they moved, Miss Bei came to the Tabernacle to visit Wang Mingdao again. She said, 'Brother Mingdao, Brother Mingdao, all the churches in Beijing are fighting to invite me to preach. I am so busy.' Wang Mingdao understood that what she was really saying was, 'If you join Three-Self, you would get lots of invitations to preach and you would become very popular.' In his heart Wang Mingdao said, 'Do you think they respect you? They are just using you to lure me to preach again.' Wang Mingdao paid no attention to what she said.

Their move, the next day, marked the end of Wang Mingdao's long association with the Tabernacle and he never entered its gates again. Sadly, too, it was the end of many years of friendship with their close colleague Mrs Chi. The brother who helped them move, Big Brother Qin, took all the coal to Sweet Rain Lane, not realising that some of it belonged to Mrs Chi. When Mrs Wang went back to return the coal that did not belong to them, Mrs Chi was unwilling to take it back. Her words signified her desire to sever her relationship with Wang Mingdao.

Note

1. The Fragrant Princess was born into a Muslim tribe and later became the wife of the tribe elder. She was said to have been born with a special fragrance on her body. When the Qing Emperor regained the territories to the north-west of China, he stole her from her tribe and brought her back to the palace as his princess. The princess never gave up her desire for revenge. On one occasion, when the emperor was out, the empress summoned her to her court to ask her what she wanted. She replied by saying if she could not take revenge she would rather die. The empress then lured her into another room where she was hung. When the emperor returned, he could not restore her back to life. He buried her near the Comfort Pavilion and wrote a heartfelt inscription for her. Her tomb remained for nearly 200 years. In 1952, when the Communist government was enlarging the park, the tomb was destroyed.

Chapter 27

Rearrested

Six months and nine days after his release Wang Mingdao and his wife moved out of the Christian Tabernacle, completely severing their ties with it. Wang Mingdao planned to change his name and live quietly for the rest of his life, but things were not that simple. The government would not let him off that easily. In fact, by resolving to resign from the board of the Tabernacle, he had planted the seed for his rearrest.

The Wangs' determination not to heed Director Li's warning left the government with no other option. They had also stopped their regular meetings with the police, who had lost interest in them and had not followed it up. Although they began to relax, their problem did not go away. Wang Mingdao knew that the government had released him because he had agreed to join the Three-Self Church and act his preaching. As he was no longer willing to go through with this, rearrest was inevitable. With this thought gnawing constantly away at the back of his mind, he was very troubled.

To keep his mind off his fear, he began to look for things to do. The floor of his house was paved with bricks but he wanted to change it to cement. He divided each of the rooms into two or three squares and tackled them one by one, breaking and removing all the bricks, mixing the sand for the cement and then laying the cement one section at a time. All the furniture kept having to be moved, and then, once the floor was paved, everything had to be cleaned and dusted. He worked on and on, methodically and diligently, and without saying anything, even when people came to visit him. Sometimes he would go to the cinema without telling his wife, who would worry not knowing where he was. She could not rest until he came home, which was sometimes late in the evening. Life was hard.

Originally Mrs Wang's mother had come to Beijing to visit them for a short while. While she lived with them at the Tabernacle, she was registered at the police station as a temporary resident. Later she moved with them to Sweet Rain Lane. When her departure date came, her ticket was bought, but a sudden headache prevented her from leaving. Mrs Wang went to the police station to try to transfer her police registration from Shanghai to Beijing. She managed to do this and, in fact, all three of them made it onto the electoral roll. At election time, when they each received their ballot papers, Wang Mingdao thought his troubles were over. He was wrong.

In late April, Tianzhe came to Beijing on business. He was undertaking experiments at the Agricultural University for a month. In the morning he rode his father's bike to work and at night he returned home to sleep. His arrival gave Wang Mingdao some comfort. He planned to go out with Tianzhe to watch the May Day parade, but it was not to be. On 29 April he was arrested again. Mrs Wang thought that her son's presence in Beijing at that time must have had something to do with the government: was it just a coincidence that he was there to look after her mother after their arrest? If he had not been there, what would have happened to her if she had completely gone to pieces? At least in this way the government showed them some consideration. The government had waited for more than a year after the move to Sweet Rain Lane before they took action. They only issued the warrant for their rearrest when they finally realised that Wang Mingdao would never agree to join the Three-Self Church.

April 29 was a strange day, to say the least. Mrs Wang had spent the day working on the sewing machine making some winter shoes, but it had been frustrating because the needles had kept breaking, one after another five or six times. They had eaten meat dumplings for supper. Not long after Mrs Wang's mother had retired to bed, there was suddenly a knock on the gate. The front gate was locked so Wang Mingdao went to see who they wanted. 'The one whose surname is Wang,' came the reply.

'Where are you from?' Wang Mingdao asked.

'The police.'

'The gate is locked. Let me go and get the key.'

Wang Mingdao went straight to tell Mrs Wang's mother, 'Get up, they have come for me', and she got up immediately. Mrs Wang opened the gate and two policemen entered. Seeing Tianzhe they asked for his identification, and Wang Mingdao thought for a moment that he had made a mistake. Maybe the police had come to check Tianzhe's registration. But, as soon as he sat down, a third person walked in whom Wang Mingdao immediately recognised: it was the man who had interrogated him in prison. He stood up and invited him to sit down. The man had a good look at him and asked him what his name was. Then he ordered him to sign the warrant for his arrest before he was handcuffed. Wang Mingdao asked, 'For the whole year since I was released I have done nothing. Why are you arresting me?'

'We will deal with that tomorrow in court,' the man replied sternly.

Before they took him away, he went to kiss Mrs Wang. He wanted to kiss her mother as well but decided against it, as it was not the custom, and in the end went without shaking her hand. When they got to the gate, there was a car waiting. They pushed him in and sat one on each side of him. The car drove off.

After they had taken Wang Mingdao away, they took Mrs Wang's mother to a different room where she could not see what was going on. Tianzhe stood on the threshold of the room and watched as his mother was handcuffed. When Mrs Wang realised they were taking her away she said she would like to say goodbye to her mother but, afraid that the neighbours would hear the commotion, they refused.

Early the next morning when Wang Mingdao was summoned for interrogation, the interrogator handed a document to Wang Mingdao. 'You asked me why we arrested you, take a look at this. This is why,' he said. It was the

Redeeming Plan he had written before he was released. In the plan he saw his promise, 'After my release I will lead my church to join Three-Self.' After reading it through, he said, 'I am wrong. I have not kept my words and have broken your trust. I shouldn't do this to a friend, let alone the government.'

'The government is very different from your friends. It is a very serious offence to lie to the government.'

Then Wang Mingdao realised that the government regarded his failure to join the Three-Self Church as a grave offence.

After that first session, Wang Mingdao had a new interrogator. On the top left-hand corner of the record, there was a place where the interrogator was supposed to write down his name. The old interrogator had never bothered and Wang Mingdao had always referred to him to other inmates as 'the one with the moustache'. The new one always wrote down his name: he was Gao Guangzhi. He was polite to Wang Mingdao and was never angry. As far as he could tell, he never lied to him either.

At Mrs Wang's interrogation, the officer who regularly met them at the police station was present. When she walked in, he said angrily, 'You do not understand trust, do you? Why did you say his father committed suicide?' As he spoke, he pointed his finger at her. She answered, 'His father did commit suicide. I was afraid he would do the same.' He was especially angry with Mrs Wang for saying that the death of her husband would be a great loss to the government.

Both of them were in the new prison in Beijing which had been built behind the old one. It was much cleaner and much more pleasant. Mrs Wang was assigned to a cell with two sisters who were arrested for the first time in 1957, Song Tianying and Xiao Yuzhong. Sister Li Renzeng, Sister Guosun Huiqing and Dr Chen Shanli, who were also rearrested at the same time, were in the same prison too. From 1958 onwards, inmates were allowed to read the newspaper. Wang Mingdao read in *People's Daily* that Bishop Gong Pingmei had been sentenced to life imprisonment. This was what he feared the most. In order to reduce his sentence, he carried on lying.

Not only did he repeat all his false confessions but he promised once again that he would join the Three-Self Church when he was released.

Most of the interrogations revolved around the false crimes to which he had already confessed. There was only one new accusation. The interrogator asked him if he had ever been to a foreign embassy to ask for political asylum. 'I am Chinese. I live in Beijing. To which embassy could I have gone to ask for protection?' Wang Mingdao replied. 'This is not London or Washington. The foreign embassies are all in Beijing, right under the nose of the Chinese government. How can they protect me?' Wang Mingdao had only ever been to one embassy in his life and that was many years ago when he had gone to the Dutch Embassy to meet an old couple. He could not imagine where they had got hold of this piece of information.

Mrs Wang was hardly interrogated at all. On one occasion they asked her about a handgun owned by Sister Po Xiangting who had served in the Korean War and had said that she had left her gun at Mrs Wang's home, but it was a lie. On another occasion it was because of a letter Wang Mingdao had written on his interrogator's instruction. In it he said he had failed to join the Three-Self Church because of Mrs Wang's opposition. That was why they wanted to work on her. On that day, the interrogator told her, 'Wang Mingdao wrote you a letter', but he would not show it to her. She begged over and over again to be allowed to see it and eventually she was given it to read. In it Wang Mingdao had written, 'I would like to be given the opportunity to work again. I have gained some new understanding of the problems with the Bible. For example, the opinion I held about military service in the past was wrong. Now my view has changed, and I have a new interpretation.' Wang Mingdao was still in great mental anguish at that time, and needed some encouragement from his wife. But she did not reply: she did not know what to say.

In the spring of 1959, they were moved to a new wing built in the traditional style of a quadrangle, where they were put to work making toys. The women would make the bodies and heads of toy cats, and the men would put the eyes on. After that, the women would paint the whiskers. Wang Mingdao's job was to paint the eyeball; Mrs Wang knitted sweaters. She had no idea Wang Mingdao was there until one day her roommate Zeng Yuhua told her secretly that she had seen him. She was shocked, 'Why was he here?' Later she saw him through a gap in the window. She could not look for long because she did not want the other inmates to know what she was doing. Male inmates were often let out into the yard for exercise, and sometimes she caught sight of him there. Once, when all the women went out to the toilets, she saw him working on the other side of the window. Another time she knew he was ill because she heard the kitchen staff yelling, 'Wang Mingdao has a bad stomach and he needs a light meal.' She knew his health was not good.

Inmates were allowed to write home for fish liver oil and other basic medicines. Although neither of them were in good health, they did not want their family to know. She could not admit in her letter that she knew anything about what was happening to her husband, so she thought long and hard before writing, 'Anshi has ill health and needs some medicine too.' Anshi was her dead brother, who had been born in the same year as Wang Mingdao. At home they sometimes referred to Wang Mingdao as Anshi and she knew her mother would understand immediately. Later her mother wrote back, 'There is some for you, and some for Anshi. You can rest assured.'

Wang Mingdao saw his wife a few times too. Once they even walked by one another, but they could not speak to each other. In September 1959, they were transferred to another part of the prison. Zeng Yuhua was transferred ahead of her and, when Mrs Wang arrived, she told her that she had seen Wang Mingdao walking in the little alley behind the block. She kept a look out for him and saw him right there. He looked miserable.

A few months after their transfer, a terrible famine hit Beijing. As their prison was needed for another purpose, all the inmates were relocated to a prison outside the city wall to the north near Virtue Victory Gate. The building had once been a Daoist Temple and in structure it was like a cobweb. The office was right in the middle, and all the rooms and cells radiated out from this central hub. During the Korean War many American prisoners of war had been sent there. It had good showers and English books. The best part, however, was that while they were there they were not interrogated at all. It was a cold winter. Food was scarce and of a very poor quality. In February 1960, before Chinese New Year, they were transferred again, this time to a detention centre south of Beijing which was divided by a thin wall from the Beijing Prison. The detention centre housed prisoners whose cases had been concluded and who were waiting to be sentenced. Once they were sentenced, they would be sent to Beijing Prison or a labour camp. Both Wang Mingdao and his wife stayed in the detention centre for five or six years. It was never the government's intention to lock them up for life: they still hoped that they would join the Three-Self Church and work for the government.

Chapter 28

Life Imprisonment

The prison regime was very strict. Inmates were not permitted to talk to one another, even if they were in the same cell. Neither were they allowed to greet each other using gestures or make signs to one another. Even if they were husbands and wives, parents and children, the same rules applied when they met. If they saw one another, they must behave as if they did not know each other.

Every time they were transferred to a new location, all the inmates would have to line up to have their photograph taken. One day, Mrs Wang suddenly saw her husband in the line. As he was not wearing his glasses she did not think he would recognise her. She wanted to make a noise to attract his attention, but she was too afraid. All she could do was to put her nametag on, have her photo taken and walk away. In fact, Wang Mingdao had seen her in her yellow dress. Every Friday night, there was a film show for the inmates. They saw each other there a few times but they were not permitted to say anything, which was very upsetting for them both.

Soon after Mrs Wang arrived, Song Tianying and Xiao Yuzhong, who had been arrested in 1957, were sentenced to physical labour and transferred to Beijing Prison. There they were permitted to receive visitors and their families would come to see them. Since the detention centre had no showers, all the prisoners had to go to over to the prison when it was their turn to take a shower, and sometimes it happened to be visiting day. On one occasion she saw Xiao Yuzhong's aunt and Sister Yuping with their children. They recognised her in the distance and nodded. Another time she met Xiao Yuzhong's mother who waved to her. Prison regulations prevented her from doing anything in return.

During the second half of 1962, Wang Mingdao began to vomit blood. One morning as he was washing, he felt sick and threw up blood. This continued for many days and he lost so much blood he thought he was going to die. Yet he didn't want to die without his wife and son at his side. The doctor tried to stop the bleeding and told Wang Mingdao not to move when he ate, drank, or used the toilet, warning that there might be a serious emergency if he did not heed this advice. Wang Mingdao thought, 'How can I eat and use the toilet without moving? If there is any emergency, I will die. If I die, how can I be held responsible?'

It was at this time, when he was severely weakened by the illness, that he was summoned to appear in court. That day, when he walked out of the building, he saw his wife standing with a bowl of water. He was overwhelmed with sorrow. They were so near to one another, and yet so far away.

Although she had seen him a few times, she had no idea where his cell was and absolutely no idea that he had been vomiting blood. One day, one of the inmates picked up some shorts that had been blown onto the floor and put them on her bed. When Mrs Wang saw them, she recognised the white pattern with blue stripes immediately. She had made them for her husband! She washed them, mended them and gave them to a guard. 'These are Wang Mingdao's shorts. They were blown onto the ground. Please hand them back to him so that he knows lost things can be found.' Wang Mingdao had no idea how he got them back, but at least she knew he was in the same building.

The indictment, issued by Beijing People's Prosecution Court at the beginning of 1963, was filed against both Wang Mingdao and his wife (Liu Jingwen). It was based on the false confession made before his release and was being presented to Beijing Intermediate People's Court for sentencing:

Beijing People's Prosecution Court

Prosecution

(1961) Beijing Prosecution of Counter-Revolutionary No. 47

Wang Mingdao, male, sixty years old.
Birthplace: Beijing.
Residence: East City District, No. 29 Sweet Rain Lane.
Status before arrest: Christian preacher.
Present status: Detained.

Liu Jingwen, female, fifty-one years old.
Birthplace: Dinghai, Zhejiang.
Residence: East City District, No. 29, Sweet Rain Lane.
Status before arrest: Christian preacher.
Present status: Detained.

The case was concluded after investigation by the Beijing
Bureau of Public Security. After further investigation and
evaluation by this court, all the evidence confirms that the
prosecuted listed above have committed the following crimes:

1. Since liberation, the accused Wang Mingdao and Liu
Jingwen have continually sought to undermine the policies
and decrees of the People's Government and to jeopardise
various socio-political movements. During the Anti-America
Pro-Korea War, the accused Wang Mingdao actively engaged
in counter-revolutionary propaganda by saying 'Christians
cannot join the army' and 'Christians cannot make donations
towards fighter planes and rocket missiles.' This was a plot to
destroy the Anti-America Pro-Korea efforts. During the Three-
Antis Campaign, the accused condemned the movement as
'full of lies and brutalities'. This was to encourage believers to
resist the movement. After the passing of the military service
law, the accused used many preaching opportunities to speak
against the law, saying, 'Those who live by the sword will die
by it'. This was to keep Christians from joining up for military
service. Following the Campaign to Suppress Counter-revolutionaries, the accused Wang Mingdao gathered a dozen key
members of his counter-revolutionary group hiding within
government organisations and schools, including Wang
Shaowu, You Yuebo, Chen Yihe, Gu Chenghua, etc., to spy
on the movement and secretly plot to destroy it.

2. The accused Wang Mingdao frequently spread counter-
revolutionary propaganda which condemned modern society
as 'corrupt' and 'evil'. He described the Communist Party as

'demonic' and 'belonging to Satan'. He fabricated lies that 'the government will destroy the Church' and 'persecute Christians' in an attempt to use religion to stir up hostility among believers against the socialist society and against the government, contaminate relationships between believers and unbelievers, and condemn the exposure of criminals as 'mutual persecution' and 'mutual hatred'.

3. The accused Wang Mingdao and Liu Jingwen went out of their way to oppose the Three-Self Patriotic Movement initiated by Christians from all over the country. They accused the Three-Self Movement as 'the idolatry between the Church and the world'. They condemned the government for 'using the Three-Self Movement to destroy the Church'. They labelled those in the Church who joined the Three-Self Movement as 'the lap dogs of the government' and 'wolves in sheep's clothing'. The accused Liu Jingwen read Wang Mingdao's anti-revolutionary speeches in the church to encourage believers to stay out of the Three-Self Church and urge those who had joined to leave. Because of the secret efforts of the accused Wang Mingdao and Liu Jingwen, some churches in Beijing, Changchun and Qingdao left the Three-Self Movement.

4. The accused Wang Mingdao and Liu Jingwen provided shelter and protection to the counter-revolutionary element Liang Lizhi, Secretary of the Nationalist Party in Changli County. During Japanese occupation, Liang frequented the residence of the accused. After liberation, Liang stayed in their church under a false identity for a period of over three months.

5. The accused Wang Mingdao and Liu Jingwen were arrested by the government for their counter-revolutionary crimes on 7 August 1955. Under the government's policy of leniency, they were both released in September 1956 for re-education. However, after their release, the accused maintained their counter-revolutionary position and continued their destructive activities. On a number of occasions they told their believers that the crimes to which they had admitted in prison were 'exaggeration' and that their repentance was 'failure and weakness'. The accused Wang Mingdao even claimed that he was mistreated, trying to

encourage counter-revolutionary believers, released because of our leniency, to hold firm to their reactionary positions and resist the government. The accused carried on with their plot to oppose the Three-Self Patriotic Movement, condemning those who joined the movement as 'Judas' and 'prostitutes'. He claimed, 'As I was against them in the past, so now I am still against them. We have no common ground.' During the Consolidation Campaign, the accused Wang Mingdao and Liu Jingwen held secret meetings with Huang Xiaotong, a key member of a counter-revolutionary group. They used the opportunity to claim their 'unfair case' as a miscarriage of law, intending to fight the government to the end.

In summary, the accused Wang Mingdao and Liu Jingwen have extensively spread their reactionary lies and consistently undermined government decrees and political campaigns. They formed counter-revolutionary organisations, encouraging believers to oppose the government and providing shelter and help for counter-revolutionaries. After being released in 1956 by the government, the accused continued with their destructive activities. Their crime is serious and they have become reactionaries who refuse to repent. Based on Items 2 and 6 of Section 7 and Items 1, 2, 3 and 13 of Section 10 of the Counter-Revolutionary Decree of the People's Republic of China, this court presents the above charges. Please pass judgement and pronounce the sentence as determined by law.

To: Beijing Intermediate People's Court

Prosecutor: Zhang Xiaowei

29 April 1961

Attached Document 1: The accused Wang Mingdao and Liu Jingwen were arrested on 29 April 1958 and are at present being held at Beijing Detention Centre.
Attached Document 2: Preliminary prosecution of the case.

Both Wang Mingdao and Mrs Wang were required to appear in court, on separate occasions, to answer the charges. Once again he pleaded guilty. It took the court six months to pass sentence. By the time he was summoned back to court to hear his sentence he was so weak that he could hardly walk and had to be transported in an open-top bus. The notice of the sentence read as follows:

Beijing Intermediate People's Court

Sentence

(1961) Intermediate Sentencing of Counter-Revolutionary No. 548

Prosecutor: Zhang Xiaowei, Beijing People's Prosecution Court.
Accused: Wang Mingdao, male, sixty-three years old.
Birthplace: Beijing.
Nationality: Chinese.
Education: University.
Status before arrest: Unemployed and formerly Christian preacher.

1919 Taught in elementary school.
1921–1925 Studied the Bible.
1925 Itinerant evangelist, later established evangelical centre in Fried Noodles Lane.
1937 Established Christian Tabernacle in Family Shi Lane and became its pastor.
1955 Arrested for counter-revolutionary activities.
1956 Released after re-education under the government's policy of leniency.
1958 Re-arrested for counter-revolutionary activities.

Residence: East City District, No. 29 Sweet Rain Lane.
Present status: Detained.

Accused: Liu Jingwen, female, fifty-four years old.
Birthplace: Dinghai County, Zhejiang Province.
Nationality: Chinese.
Education: High School.

Status before arrest: Unemployed and deacon at the Christian Tabernacle in Family Shi Lane.

1918–1926 School years.
After high school: Taught at Hangzhou Bible School.
After marriage with Wang Mingdao: Worked in church.
1953 Church deacon.
1955 Arrested for counter-revolutionary activities.
1956 Released after re-education under the government's policy of leniency.
1958 Re-arrested for counter-revolutionary activities.

Residence: East City District, No. 29 Sweet Rain Lane.
Present status: Detained.

The accused were judged by this court and found guilty of the following crimes:

Since liberation, the accused Wang Mingdao and Liu Jingwen have consistently maintained their counter-revolutionary positions and their hostility towards the socialist system. They have used religious opportunities to launch their campaign against political movements and government decrees. During the Anti-America Pro-Korea War, the accused Wang Mingdao actively engaged in counter-revolutionary propaganda among Christian believers to prevent them from joining the army and donating money for fighter planes and rocket missiles. During the Three-Antis Campaign, the accused used destructive lies to undermine the movement. During the implementation of the military service law, the accused took every opportunity to threaten believers and encourage them to boycott the law. Following the Campaign to Suppress Counter-revolutionaries, the accused organised a series of meetings for believers working in government organisations and schools to persuade them not to expose criminals. After Christian believers initiated the Three-Self Patriotic Movement, the accused Wang Mingdao and Liu Jingwen did their utmost to oppose and destroy the movement. They used opportunities to speak to believers and write in condemnation of the Three-Self Movement and its leaders. The accused Liu Jingwen read Wang Mingdao's anti-revolutionary articles in the church to stir up believers against the Three-Self Church. In 1954, the accused

Wang Mingdao encouraged counter-revolutionaries Lin Chuifeng and Sun Zhenglu to undermine the work of the Three-Self Movement in Qingdao and Changchun. Under their influence, some churches in Changchun and Qingdao left the Three-Self Movement, as did the Broad Street Church in Beijing.

The accused Liu Jingwen not only gave all her support to the counter-revolutionary activities of the accused Wang Mingdao, but often planned and plotted for him and acted behind the scenes on his behalf. In May 1955, after reactionary Xu Hongdao was arrested, Wang and Liu encouraged his wife Zhang Deeng to go to Tianjin to make trouble for our government. In addition, the accused Wang Mingdao frequently made reactionary speeches and spread lies to condemn the new society and accuse the Communist Party. He rebuked people who exposed criminals as 'persecuting one another' and instructed them to oppose the government. After liberation, the accused Wang Mingdao and Liu Jingwen provided shelter and protection for the counter-revolutionary element Liang Lizhi, Secretary of the Nationalist Party in Changli County, Hebei.

The accused Wang Mingdao and Liu Jingwen were arrested by the government on 7 August 1955 for counter-revolutionary activities. Under the government's policy of leniency, they were released in September 1956 for re-education. However, after their release, the accused maintained their counter-revolutionary position and continued with their destructive activities. On a number of occasions they claimed to believers that they were mistreated. They tried to unite with other reactionaries and believers who were released due to the government's leniency in order to continue with their efforts against the Three-Self Patriotic Movement, to condemn those who joined the movement and to claim 'there is no common ground with the government'. After the Christian Tabernacle in Family Shi Lane joined the Three-Self Church, the accused Liu Jingwen secretly plotted to leave the Tabernacle with Wang Mingdao to show their opposition. In 1958, the accused Wang Mingdao and Liu Jingwen made connections with many reactionaries and believers to hold secret meetings seeking to reverse their case and plan their actions against the government.

The above-listed criminal acts of the accused have been thoroughly investigated and ample evidence of their guilt has been gathered. The accused Wang Mingdao and Liu Jingwen have admitted their principal crimes and the guilty verdict for their case is beyond doubt.

It is proven that, after liberation, the accused Wang Mingdao and Liu Jingwen used religious opportunities to fabricate and spread reactionary lies to undermine government decrees and political campaigns. They actively encouraged believers to oppose the government and secretly provided shelter and help to counter-revolutionaries. After being released in 1956 by the government, the accused refused to repent and continued with their reactionary stand and activities. Because of the serious nature of their crimes and their entrenched reactionary positions, despite the best efforts of re-education, they deserve the most severe punishment. To keep social order and consolidate the people's democratic dictatorship, this court passes the following respective sentences in accordance with the nature of their crime, based on Items 1, 2, 3 and 13 of Section 10, Section 13 and Section 17 of the Counter-Reactionary Decree of the People's Republic of China:

1. The accused Wang Mingdao is found guilty of counter-revolutionary crime and is sentenced to life-long imprisonment with all political rights permanently revoked. The accused Liu Jingwen is found guilty of counter-revolutionary crime and is sentenced to fifteen years' imprisonment (from 29 April 1958 to 28 April 1973), with her political rights revoked for a further five years after release.

2. The accused Wang Mingdao's properties, consisting of twelve rooms in No. 29 Sweet Rain Lane in the East District, are all confiscated according to law.

Should the accused find this sentence unacceptable, two copies of the Letter of Appeal must be received within ten days from the second day of this sentence. These copies can either be passed onto Beijing Higher People's Court by this court or sent directly by the accused.

Director: Xue Guanghua
Judge: Zhang Shirong
Juror: Wang Yunhui
Juror: Zhang Hongguang

18 July 1963

Secretary: Zhu Xintian

Wang Mingdao could not accept his sentence and decided to appeal. He knew that since the final sentence had been reached as a result of discussions between the Religious Affairs Department, the Three-Self Church and many others, an appeal was unlikely to make any difference, but he decided to go ahead anyway. Mrs Wang, on the other hand, believing that everything that had happened had been permitted by God, humbly received from Him what He deemed fit.

Two months after Wang Mingdao made his appeal, he was summoned to the court once again. He pleaded guilty once again to most of the crimes of which he stood accused, only denying having committed any counter-revolutionary activities following his release. The higher court paid no attention to his appeal and passed the following final sentence:

Beijing Higher People's Court

Final Sentence

(1963 Final Sentence No. 497)

Accused: Wang Mingdao, male, sixty-three years old.
Birthplace: Beijing.
Status before arrest: Unemployed and formerly Christian preacher.

1955 Arrested for counter-revolutionary activities.
1956 Released after re-education due to the government's policy of leniency.
1958 Re-arrested for counter-revolutionary activities.

Residence: East City District, No. 29 Sweet Rain Lane.
Present status: Detained.

The appellant has applied to this court concerning the case of counter-revolution, and in particular, the sentence of life imprisonment with all political rights permanently revoked as stated by Beijing Intermediate People's Court Sentence (1961) Intermediate Sentencing of Counter-Revolutionary No. 548 of 18 July 1963. The appellant maintained that, although after his release he believed he had been treated unfairly, and resigned from the church in passive resistance of the government, he did not form links with other released reactionaries and believers with a view to continue his opposition of the Three-Self Patriotic Movement. The appellant also maintained that he did not take any opportunities to seek to reverse his case. The appellant wishes to have his case re-examined and to be given a more lenient sentence. After re-examination of the case by the joint court, a decision regarding the final sentence has been reached as below:

Since liberation, the appellant Wang Mingdao has consistently maintained a reactionary position and hostility towards the socialist system, using religious opportunities to launch campaigns against political movements and government decrees. During the Anti-America Pro-Korea War, he actively engaged in counter-revolutionary propaganda among Christian believers to prevent them from joining the army and donating money for fighter planes and rocket missiles. During the Three-Antis Campaign, he furiously condemned the movement with destructive lies. Following the Campaign to Suppress Counter-revolutionaries, he organised a series of meetings to persuade believers working in government organisations and schools not to expose criminals. Following the establishment of the Three-Self Patriotic Movement by believers, he did his utmost to oppose and destroy the movement, using published articles and speaking engagements to condemn the Three-Self Patriotic Movement and bring accusations against its leaders. He encouraged the reactionaries Lin Chuifeng and Sun Zhenglu to undermine the work of the Three-Self Movement in Qingdao and

Changchun. Under his influence, some churches in Beijing, Changchun and Qingdao left the Three-Self Movement. In addition, after reactionary Xu Hongdao was arrested, the appellant Wang Mingdao encouraged his wife Zhang Deeng to go to the People's Government of Tianjin to make trouble. After liberation, he provided shelter and protection to the counter-revolutionary element Liang Lizhi, Secretary of the Nationalist Party in Changli, Hebei.

The appellant Wang Mingdao was arrested by the government for his counter-revolutionary crimes on 7 August 1955. Under the government's policy of leniency, he was released in September 1956 for re-education. However, after release, he maintained his counter-revolutionary position and continued his reactionary activities. He claimed to believers that he was mistreated, and tried to make links with other reactionaries and believers who were released due to the government's leniency in order to continue their efforts against the Three-Self Movement. He condemned those who joined the movement and claimed that 'there is no common ground with them'. To show his opposition, he left his own church after it joined the Three-Self Church. In 1958, he made connections with many reactionaries and believers to hold secret meetings seeking to reverse his case.

The above-listed criminal acts of the appellant have been re-examined. The appellant did not deny all his counter-revolutionary crimes before his first arrest. But he raised arguments against his reactionary crimes after his release, denying his ongoing destructive activities against the Three-Self Patriotic Movement and his attempts to reverse his case. The matter has been thoroughly investigated and the crimes have been proven beyond doubt by documentary evidence and the testimony of witnesses. Therefore this court does not deem the grounds raised by the appellant as sufficient evidence. This court holds that after liberation the appellant used religious opportunities to fabricate and spread reactionary lies to undermine government decrees and political campaigns. He actively encouraged believers to oppose the government and secretly provided shelter and help for counter-revolutionaries. After being released by the government, he refused to repent and continued with reactionary activities. Thus he has become an obdurate reactionary despite the best efforts of re-education. The original sentence of life imprisonment with political rights permanently revoked was consistent with the nature of the crime and based on law. This court found nothing in the sentence that was improper. Therefore, this court has reached the following verdict:

The appeal is rejected and the original sentence upheld.

Director: Liu Yong
Judge: Jiang Shufeng
Judge: Feng Jiajun
Acting Judge: Ma Ying

21 September 1963

Secretary: Jiao Yuping

Decree for Punishing Counter-Revolutionaries:

Section 7 Death or life imprisonment, five years or longer imprisonment in less severe cases for those participating in counter-revolutionary groups engaged in one of the following activities.

Section 7.2 Organising or participating in counter-revolutionary groups after liberation.

Section 7.6 Continuing with counter-revolutionary activities after being re-educated and released by the people's government.

Section 10 Death or life imprisonment in particularly serious cases, three years or longer imprisonment in less serious cases for those fabricating and spreading lies for the purpose of counter-revolution.

Section 10.1 Inciting people to resist the implementation of government decrees on collecting grain, tax and on military service.

Section 10.2 Creating barriers to destroy the unity among various nationalities, social classes, democratic parties and the relationship between the government and the people.

Section 10.3 Engaging in counter-revolutionary propaganda by fabricating and spreading lies.

Section 13 Death, life imprisonment, ten years or longer imprisonment for those providing shelter for counter-revolutionaries.

Section 17 Those found guilty of these crimes will have their political rights revoked and part or all of their properties confiscated.

From preliminary prosecution to final sentence, Wang Mingdao never dared to admit that his crimes were fabricated. Had he done this, he would have been regarded as resisting the people's democratic dictatorship and the punishment would have been even tougher. His only hope had been that he might receive a lighter sentence rather than life imprisonment. But now he had received the sentence he had feared, which meant he would never leave the prison again. What Wang Mingdao did not realise was that man's end is God's beginning. He had reached the depths of despair, but God had not abandoned him.

Chapter 29

He Stood Up

After Wang Mingdao's appeal was rejected and he knew he would spend the rest of his life in prison there seemed no hope any more. He had reached rock bottom. But it was this place of deepest despair that God used to save him and to turn his life completely around.

After receiving his life sentence Wang Mingdao felt there was nothing left to live for. He was angry because he was trapped. He was overwhelmed with pain and regret, and ashamed because he felt like a complete failure. All he could do was wait for death. In his anger he cried out to God, 'How can you be so brutal as to allow me to be attacked like this?' But in the depths of despair, he suddenly remembered a passage in the Bible that he had memorised at the age of twenty-one:

> 'But as for me, I watch in hope for the LORD,
>   I wait for God my Saviour;
>   my God will hear me.
> Do not gloat over me, my enemy!
>   Though I have fallen, I will rise.
> Though I sit in darkness,
>   the LORD will be my light.
> Because I have sinned against him,
>   I will bear the LORD's wrath,
> until he pleads my case
>   and establishes my right.
> He will bring me out into the light;
>   I will see his righteousness.'   (Micah 7:7–9)

God's word worked wonders in his heart and brought him out of utter despair and pain. It was not until the sentence of life imprisonment was passed that he realised his judgement had come from God. His many lies were detested by God and they greatly angered Him. When he realised this, all his complaints to God vanished. He said, 'I deserve this sentence. I even deserve to be put to death. I must suffer the consequences of God's judgement, because I have made Him angry.'

Once he saw his grave failures, he decided to retract all his lies. He asked God for an opportunity to confess his lies and, as soon as he had prayed this prayer, fear left him. Peace returned to his heart. After this, whenever he remembered that moment, a sense of peace and joy from the redeeming love of the Lord overwhelmed his heart. Thanks be to God! Within days he was transferred to the prison hospital for rehabilitation where he was given a private room. Though his pneumonia was healed and he no longer needed to be hospitalised, the prison doctor told him that the infected parts of his lungs were already seriously damaged: God had a better plan. He wanted to give His servant a quiet place to concentrate on writing his confessions.

The rehabilitation centre was in a pleasant situation and had a garden full of flowers. The window of Wang Mingdao's room faced south and, as it was autumn with many sunny days, it was bright and warm. At night there was light and there was even a fireplace in the room. One could hardly ask for a better place for writing. Even the food improved, and there was often meat on the plate. Wang Mingdao would never have dreamt of such luxury. Even though he was on a life sentence, he was being treated like a special guest.

The second day after he was moved to the rehabilitation centre, he was called to the office where a man with a gold tooth spoke with him. Two other men were present. From their clothes Wang Mingdao could tell they were high-level officers. Wang Mingdao asked the man who he was, and he introduced himself as the prison director, Mr Zhang. The other men were Mr Liu, the manager of the prison hospital, and Mr Xing, their colleague. They wanted to know how Wang Mingdao felt about his life imprisonment. Mr Zhang told Wang Mingdao that his sentence was flexible, and Wang

Mingdao understood by this that he could be released whenever the government saw fit. A lot would depend on his attitude. 'What do you want me to say?' he asked them.

'There is no hidden agenda – whatever you want to say,' came the reply.

With that Wang Mingdao began to retell his story, this time speaking the truth from beginning to end. He had come to the office at two in the afternoon and he did not leave until ten past five. For those three hours it was Wang Mingdao who was doing most of the speaking; Mr Zhang only interrupted a few times to clarify a point of information. Wang Mingdao spoke so much that his mouth dried up. When Mr Zhang offered him a drink, he said no, because although he was very thirsty he did not feel free to accept his offer. Mr Zhang asked Mr Liu to bring some hot tea anyway and, after having a drink, he became even more talkative.

When he had finished speaking, Mr Zhang gave him hundreds of sheets of writing paper, and asked him to write everything down. Wang Mingdao started writing that same day. The next day, Mr Zhang came to see him again to ask him if he had written anything yet. He said he had, and Mr Zhang wanted to read what he had written, but Wang Mingdao insisted that he would submit it only when he had finished one hundred pages. So he carried on writing day and night, stopping only when it was time for the curfew. On some days he wrote more than thirty pages. At the beginning, he admitted that everything he had confessed in the past was in fact lies. He had told these lies because he was afraid. He had never done anything to break the law. He retracted all his previous confessions, admitting that the only thing that was true was his opposition of the Three-Self Church. On and on he kept writing, page after page after page. He wrote so much that the top-quality pen his son had sent him from Shanghai wore out. After each hundred pages, he would staple them into a booklet, which he would submit it to Mr Zhang. He wrote dozens of booklets.

During this time, Mr Zhang came to visit him a few times, as did another prison director, Mr Duan. Wang Mingdao told him, too, that he had not committed the crimes he had once admitted and that he had lied because he was afraid of being shot. He was also afraid that his wife would die in prison. He had lied because he had been told by other inmates that the more he confessed, the quicker he would be released. So he had confessed many fabricated crimes he never committed. He had hoped that by co-operating with the government he would gain his release.

When Wang Mingdao took this step of retracting all his confessions, the government lost all hope for him. Wang Mingdao and his wife both knew what the government was trying to do. Whether they used a carrot or a stick, their only objective was to make them have a change of heart and repent. They used pressure, they used care – two tactics with one aim. The aim of the long sentence was not to keep him locked up for the rest of his life, but to exert pressure on him to facilitate the desired change. They understood how human psychology works. What they did not understand was that besides natural laws, the law of the Spirit works in Christians. Even their best efforts failed to produce the desired results.

Now Wang Mingdao's heart was full of peace. He had confessed not only before God but before the government. As God's Word promises: *'Though a righteous man falls seven times, he rises again'* (Proverbs 24:16). After eight years of failure, Wang Mingdao was able to stand up again. He was restored, and his spiritual life was completely revived. From then on, he set himself a high standard of absolute honesty and truthfulness, not tolerating even a trace of falsehood, as the Scriptures command: *'Let your "Yes" be yes and "No", no'* (James 5:12). For the next sixteen years (1963–79) he stayed faithful to this standard throughout his term of imprisonment. He resolved that it was better to die in prison than to lie.

After he stood up again, God gave him a special promise:

> *'You will go out in joy,*
> *and be led forth in peace;*
> *the mountains and the hills*
> *will burst into song before you,*

and all the trees of the field
  will clap their hands.
Instead of the thornbush will grow the pine tree,
  and instead of briers the myrtle will grow.
This will be for the LORD's renown,
  for an everlasting sign,
    which will not be destroyed.'   (Isaiah 55:12–13)

'*You will go out in joy*'. Go out from where? He was sentenced to life imprisonment. But God had promised. Surely he would 'go out'. Thanks and praise be to God! '*With man this is impossible, but with God all things are possible*' (Matthew 19:26). As Wang Mingdao's story continued to unfold, God perfectly fulfilled His promise.

Chapter 30

After Renewal

The work of writing his confessions to retract the lies he had made lasted for several months. When it was complete, he began writing down some suggestions for the government, which he hoped would be accepted. During this period, Wang Mingdao did little physical labour. At first, he went to political studies, but there was little content to the study. It was focused on nine editorials criticising Soviet Revisionism published at around that time by the *People's Daily*. Because Wang Mingdao was semi-deaf and it was difficult for him to study with others, the government allowed him to study on his own by reading the newspaper. Mrs Wang, however, had to do physical labour. Her job was to knit sweaters along with the other female inmates. This continued until the end of 1964.

When Wang Mingdao had nearly finished writing down his suggestions to the government, some other sick inmates moved in. Soon afterwards the government asked them to do some light work, such as polishing the edges of plastic shoes after they had been machine-pressed. One of the new inmates was a well-known political prisoner, Ge Peiqi. Another was a young man who was related to the woman chaplain of the Presbyterian Hospital and claimed to have been baptised at Wang Mingdao's church. Wang Mingdao did not remember him at all. One day this young man whispered to Wang Mingdao that there was a big room next door where inmates were locked up for days with nothing but porridge to eat until they starved to death.

After a few days of polishing shoes Wang Mingdao began to think that, since he had retracted his false confessions and was no longer a criminal, there was no reason why he should be doing such degrading work, and he began to refuse to work. Mr Zhang told him, 'The work of this prison is to execute prison sentences. The court has sentenced you, and we have to carry it out. We cannot decide what to do with you. There is no use complaining to us. If you have anything to say, you'd better write to the court.' So he wrote to the court. After a while, having received no reply, he became angry. Mr Xing asked him if he was afraid of physical labour. 'No,' he replied, 'I am not afraid of physical labour. I like it. I have always done hard physical work. But to force me to labour as a criminal is not right. I am not a criminal. I did not commit any crime.'

Mr Xing could see how bitter he was. He warned him that if he kept on refusing to work he would have to force him. 'I'll wait for you to force me then,' Wang Mingdao insisted. A few days later, Wang Mingdao was summoned to the office where some rather important-looking officials were waiting to speak to him. One of them asked him why he was refusing to work. 'I did not commit any crime,' he said, 'The only reason I was imprisoned was because of my beliefs. I can work, but I will not work with criminals.'

'If you refuse to work, I will place you in solitary confinement,' Mr Xing warned him.

'If you want to put me in solitary confinement, go ahead,' Wang Mingdao replied. 'No matter what you do, I won't change.' With that, Mr Xing told some of the inmates to move his things into the lock-up.

The lock-up was a horrible place. It was so small that inmates could not walk or move around at all. All the windows were boarded up and there was hardly any light coming in at all. To prevent inmates from committing suicide, there was an electrical light high up on the ceiling, far out of reach. The inmates were forced to use a toilet in the corner of the room which was emptied every morning. They were locked up permanently and not permitted to leave the cell. Wang Mingdao had heard about people starving to death and he thought he might die as well. Yet when the meal-time came, food was delivered through the small opening in the door.

That night as he lay in bed he remembered something that Confucius had taught: 'Judge oneself harshly but others kindly; in that way you will keep yourself far from complaints'. As he thought about these words he realised that his attitude towards Mr Xing had been wrong. The next morning he asked for some paper, with the intention of writing to confess his mistake. But his request was denied and he thought he would have to give up. But that night, someone came to ask him why he wanted paper. When he explained they brought him some paper and a pen. Wang Mingdao wrote: 'The other day when I spoke with Mr Xing my attitude was very bad. I was wrong. I have never spoken to anybody like that before, let alone to prison officer. I was wrong.' After realising his heart had softened, Mr Xing and the other prison officials changed their attitude towards Wang Mingdao and, as it was Sweet Dumpling Day, they even brought some sweet dumplings for him. But they did not release him from the lock-up cell immediately. They wanted to see first if he had really meant it.

Wang Mingdao was kept in the lock-up for four months. Before they let him out, one day Mr Xing came to tell him to change his clothes because he was to be escorted out of the prison to visit an exhibition. Wang Mingdao put on a new jacket and new shoes provided for the occasion and went to where the inmates had been told to gather. He was shocked to see Sister Guan Shuzheng who used to be a counsellor for Christian students in Beijing. Sister Guan had joined the Three-Self Church and, in fact, when he was released, she had already become the woman pastor at the Tabernacle. Even though she supported the Three-Self Movement and encouraged others to join, she too had been arrested. Wang Mingdao could only assume she had been arrested for keeping her own personal faith within the Three-Self Church, which would never be tolerated by the government.

The government had organised this trip so that the inmates could see a model of a house owned by a man called Liu Wencai, who was a rich landlord in Sichuan. Inside the house there was an underground cell filled with water which was supposedly used to punish peasants who could not pay their rent. The leader of the trip asked the presenter to speak louder so that Wang Mingdao could hear better. So he heard the story loudly and clearly twice.

After the visit, Wang Mingdao was returned to the lock-up, but a few days later he was transferred to a bigger prison near a place where he used to preach before liberation. At the time, Lao She, the famous playwright, and Chen Lingxiong, another writer, were imprisoned there as well. They knew Wang Mingdao and, after liberation, had been to his church to hear him preach.

In 1965 Wang Mingdao felt that the government might be thinking of releasing him and decided he wanted to give it a try. However, when he realised that, if he was released, he would still have to join the Three-Self Church, he decided to give up the idea. Had he been released, his experience during the Cultural Revolution would certainly have been even more miserable than that of the playwright Lao She's. In doing so, he followed the will of God. God actually used the prison to protect him from the storms of the Cultural Revolution, which were raging outside.

Chapter 31

Mrs Wang in Tongxian and Beijing Prisons

At the beginning of 1965, when Wang Mingdao finally gave up his efforts to seek release, Mrs Wang was still at the same prison as she had been when she had begun her fifteen-year prison term two years before. At around this time the government relocated the women inmates from that prison to a labour camp in Tongxian County east of Beijing. It was a good move. The labour camp was a much pleasanter environment than the prison, the food was much better – the cook there made delicious pancakes – and the inmates were even allowed to request fruit, sweets and other foods to be ordered in. This remained unchanged until the beginning of the Cultural Revolution.

At the labour camp Mrs Wang and Dr Chen, who had been sentenced to life imprisonment at the same time as the Wang Mingdao, were both assigned to work making paper-boxes. It was a task normally assigned to the relatives of the prison staff because it was the most profitable but once the women inmates arrived, it became their work.

Two women from the Christian Tabernacle who loved the Lord had been transferred to the labour camp before Mrs Wang. They were Shiwei Shulan and Li Rengzeng. The very next day after Mrs Wang and Dr Chen arrived, there was a visitors' day when inmates were allowed to receive visits from their families and relatives. Shiwei Shulan was visited by her husband, elder son, second son and his wife. Li Rengzeng received her good friend in the Lord Li Peizheng, and Dr Chen her two sons. Mrs Wang was the only one who did not have anyone to visit her. In order to be allowed to have visitors, the inmates had to get special permission from the manager. Mrs Wang thought, 'Why don't I ask for permission to see them as well?' So she went to the manager to ask for permission, and it was granted.

The next morning, all four of them sat together waiting for the visitors to arrive. Then they were ushered out to the reception room where the visitors and the visited were separated by a large table. Since they all knew one another, it was quite a reunion and everyone was overjoyed and full of smiles. This confused the manager of the camp, and he had to ask them who was visiting whom.

Soon after Mrs Wang arrived at Tongxian, she received a letter from her mother. Inside the envelope was a postcard, with the names and addresses of the sender and recipient both erased. Only the content of the message remained. When Mrs Wang saw the small characters she realised immediately that it was a postcard from Wang Mingdao to her mother. She learned that in 1964 when her mother was eighty-six years old, she had fallen and broken her rib, leaving her in agonising pain. She had written to Wang Mingdao, telling him that her suffering was good for her. She confessed that in God's hand she was much more precious than sparrows and told him that she knew God would not take her children's pain lightly. He had allowed it for some special purpose. With the letter she had included a money order for thirty yuan.

After Wang Mingdao had received the letter, he had written back on a postcard and said, 'I have received a letter from mother. Mother says that her suffering is good for her. I agree with her – it is also good for me. Mother also tells me she is more precious than many sparrows. I say I too am more precious than many sparrows. All things work together.' He left it there without writing the second half of the verse 'for the good of those who love God.' He went on to tell his mother-in-law, 'My heart is the same as it was forty years ago.' This referred to his visit to the south in the autumn of 1925 when he had met her for the first time. This postcard had been written when he was in good spirits after God had touched him and his faith had been renewed. Mrs Wang had no idea where her husband was, but she thought he must still be at the same prison because the inmates there were only allowed to write postcards.

Sister Shiwei Shulan and Mrs Wang would meet one another in the camp but they were not allowed to speak to one another. One day Sister Shi was washing some clothes in the yard and Mrs Wang walked past her humming a hymn quietly. In fact, it was a tune which was often broadcast on the radio not to praise God but to mock Christians. Someone heard Mrs Wang humming and reported her to the office, accusing her of using hymns to pass on information. The manager summoned Mrs Wang to the office to ask her if she had been singing hymns. Mrs Wang replied that she had only been humming, not singing. 'Every one hums that tune,' she said. The manager was quite interested, 'How do you sing it as a hymn?' he asked. 'Can you sing it for me?' The hymn she had been humming that day was Hymn 205, 'Singing praises to the Lord', so she began singing in the office:

'I lay my sins on Jesus,
The spotless Lamb of God;
He bears them all,
And frees us from the accursed load.
I bring my guilt to Jesus,
To wash my crimson stains,
White in His blood most precious,
Till not a spot remains.'

Even though this song was all about being a sinner, the manager did not say anything more about it.

When Mrs Wang arrived at Tongxian, Sister Yu was working in a nearby factory as part of her re-education. The gate of the camp was wide open and people could come in and go out freely. The moment Sister Yu saw Mrs Wang she asked about Sister Song Tianying. Mrs Wang told her that she had not seen her at all. A few months later, Mrs Wang heard someone playing different hymns on a harmonica outside the window. There were just tiny snatches of each tune so that no one could recognise they were hymns. Mrs Wang realised immediately that it was Sister Yu who was playing the hymns for her. In the summer of 1966, when Mrs Wang was transferred from Tongxian back to Beijing, Sister Yu stood and watched as the bus left, looking very sad.

Back in the Beijing camp, Mrs Wang met Sisters Xiao Yuzhong and Song Tianying. She realised that they were never transferred but had stayed at the same place for their stints of labour. Brother Lin Yunfeng was there too. They all worked on making plastic shoes. By then Xiao Yuzhong had been promoted to head worker collecting the finished products. For the first few months Mrs Wang was assigned to do odd jobs but later she became Xiao Yuzhong's workmate. One day they were sitting side by side as they worked and they said a few words to each other. Though this was the first time they had spoken to each other, someone sitting behind them saw them and reported them to the office. The manager asked Mrs Wang what they were talking about. She said Xiao Yuzhong had told her she had received a pen as a reward from the prison for her hard work. However, she had lost it and felt very sad about it. As Mrs Wang was telling the truth there was little the manager could say about it.

Between 1967 and 1968 Mrs Wang suffered from high blood pressure which meant she had a lot of headaches and had problems opening her eyes. Every day she had to take a green tablet to keep her blood pressure down. Later, when the inmates received their routine medical examination, she asked the doctor if her blood pressure was still high. 'Yes,' she was told, but she wanted to know if it was all right for her to stop taking the medication. 'Yes,' she was told again. From that point on she stopped taking the medication and her blood pressure returned to normal. Mrs Wang felt she had been healed.

Mrs Wang remained at Beijing prison for three years until, in 1969, she was transferred again, this time to Handan south of Beijing. When the government realised that Wang Mingdao was not even interested in trying to change, they finally gave up on him and in 1966 they transferred him with other inmates to Datong Mining Camp.

Chapter 32

Wang Mingdao in Datong

Wang Mingdao left Beijing just as the Great Proletarian Cultural Revolution was beginning. He was becoming increasingly deaf and could now hear very little. In Datong he was no longer required to join the political study group but was allowed to study by reading the newspapers on his own and writing down his thoughts and reflections, which he did, often adding his own suggestions.

Wang Mingdao had always been a very outspoken person – he could not keep silent in the face of injustice. Right from his student days, he was known to be uncompromising in his beliefs. As a preacher, this characteristic helped him to stand firm in the truth and in the battle against evil forces in the society and in the Church. But under Communism it brought him much pain.

At that time the country was in the throes of a political campaign to purge Liu Shaoqi, Peng Dehuai and Wu Han, all seen by Mao Zedong as his enemies. Had Wang Mingdao suppressed his opinions it would have been all right. But he wanted to seek justice for these people. This was bound to cause him trouble. As the President of China Liu Shaoqi took his wife Wang Guanmei with him on trips to Indonesia and Afghanistan. Watching Liu Shaoqi and Wang Guanmei receiving VIP honours as the Head of State, Mao's wife Jiang Qing was furious. Jiang thought her position was higher than that of Wang Guanmei and yet Mao would never take her with him on such important trips. So she had written articles accusing Wang Guanmei of being too ostentatious overseas. Wang Mingdao thought she was overstating the matter since she was almost inferring that Wang Guanmei was behaving like a prostitute. So he wrote in one report, 'To condemn the Head of State is to condemn the State itself.'

After Peng Dehuai, the Minister of Defence, and Wu Han, the Mayor of Beijing, were both purged as reactionaries, Wang Mingdao wrote to demand justice for them. He said that the Communist Party was not honouring its words. 'When Peng Dehuai was held in honour, he was said to be humble and friendly. Now he is in trouble, suddenly he was pretentious. What is false and what is truth? When Wu Han was respected, he was from a poor family where he had to borrow money to go to school. Now that he is dishonoured, his house suddenly is surrounded by private cars and his family full of money. What is the truth? If you want to condemn somebody, there is never a lack of excuses.' Wang Mingdao went so far as to say that the Communists were the most untrustworthy people in the world. He said, 'Even if you are as high as the Head of State, when you fall out of favour, you drop into the pit. How can a country function like that?' and he quoted Confucius' 'Dialogue on Politics', 'When a man is not trusted there is no way of knowing what he can do. It is like a vehicle with faulty wheels. How can you make a journey with it?' Wang Mingdao could not tolerate injustice and wrote many words in support of these fallen leaders. Because of this, public meetings were held at Datong Mining Camp to condemn him for defending leading reactionaries.

At one meeting a man asked him whether he liked Jiang Qing. Wang Mingdao replied, 'Jiang Qing is jealous of Wang Guangmei. Wang Guangmei accompanied Liu Shaoqi on his foreign trips and was warmly received by foreign governments and heads of state. Jiang Qing could not go overseas herself so she accused Wang Guangmei of showing off in Indonesia, inferring she was behaving like a prostitute. Wang Guangmei was the First Lady of the People's Republic of China. How can she accuse her of being a prostitute?' This statement was to have catastrophic consequences for Wang Mingdao. For over five months he was handcuffed at all times, even when he was eating and sleeping. Accusation meetings against him became more frequent and very vehement. At one, he became so angry that he even used the beheading of a young couple, John and Betty Stem, who were China Inland Mission missionaries in Anhui, to prove that the Communists were anti-God and anti-Christianity. Such open criticism of the Communist Party would never be tolerated by the government. Mr Xing was still trying to change him, but Wang Mingdao told him, 'Do not think that I can ever be re-educated. I cannot.'

After that Mr Xing selected nine inmates for the specific job of teaching Wang Mingdao. Wang Mingdao named them 'the Battalion of Nine'. These people included Wang Qi, Li Zhiyuan, Gong Changjing, who collaborated with the Japanese when they occupied East China, a Mr Wu, who served with the Air Force of the Nationalist Government, and Zhan Rugeng, who was a pastor from Beijing. Wu Qi, who was part-Japanese from Taiwan, had been arrested for helping the Japanese invade and occupy North China. He was the most brutal in his condemnation of Wang Mingdao and did everything he could to make sure he suffered. Li Zhiyuan was also part-Japanese but he was from Manchuria. Before he was enlisted by the Japanese to work against China he was one year short of graduating from Manchuria Institute of Technology. Gong Changjing had graduated from a Japanese Military Academy and had once served in the Japanese army. He made a paper hat for Wang Mingdao with the words, 'Wang Mingdao, the Counter-Revolutionary'. He never physically beat him, but insulted Wang Mingdao by drawing stinging cartoons. One of his cartoons had a woman holding a baby begging foreigners for help. This, of course, was supposed to be Wang Mingdao in his mother's arms. Another cartoon featured a man hanging himself on a tree, which was supposed to be Wang Mingdao's father.

Zhan Rugeng was a key person in the group. Between Japanese surrender and the return of Americans to China, he was sent to the US for theological training. There he spoke enthusiastically and frequently against the Communists but after his return to China he suddenly became very committed to his student ministries. After liberation, his words in America became known, and in 1958 he was arrested and sentenced to life imprisonment. He once said he was suffering for his faith, but this was not true: he was locked up for his anti-Communist words. Having been sentenced to life imprisonment, he wanted to find ways of currying favour to try and get his term reduced. Condemning Wang Mingdao was his great opportunity. Indeed, because of his diligence in this, his sentence was reduced many times and he was released earlier than Wang Mingdao. In the mid-1980s, he went overseas and gave many talks about his suffering in prison with Wang Mingdao. Everything he said was true, apart from the fact that he was one of the most active in condemning Wang Mingdao in prison.

In order to achieve the best results, the group planned their strategy and worked together well. The physical beatings were carried out by Wang Qi and Li Zhiyuan but Zhan Rugeng was the mastermind. Zhan Rugeng only talked; he never used his hands. Condemning meetings were often held at night. Wang Mingdao was forced to repeat statements made by Zhan Rugeng, such as that all preachers cared about was good food and they would go wherever they were paid the most. Wang Qi ordered Wang Mingdao to repeat Zhan Rugeng's words after him and, if he refused, he would tie a black rope onto his handcuff and force him to run around for hours with his back bent right over. As the tallest and strongest Li Zhiyuan's job was to shake Wang Mingdao's head. Every night he would shake Wang Mingdao's head dozens and dozens of times. In the end, Wang Mingdao's head was bent over so much that it almost touched the ground.

Earlier in his life, Wang Mingdao's back had been badly damaged when, after flooding had washed away the railway lines near Tanggu, he had become stuck on his way back to Beijing and had had to sleep on the ground for several nights. Since then he had always suffered from backache. He could hardly bear such abuse. Sometimes they would bang his head against the wall until Wang Mingdao literally fainted. When it was time for bed, they would make him write up his confession. After he had done this, they would make him rewrite it over and over again until the small hours of the morning. It was only when Wang Qi gave permission that they would allow him to go to bed. This persecution went on for over five months. During the day, they put the paper hat on Wang Mingdao and paraded him throughout the camp. Because of the handcuffs Wang Mingdao could not take it off with his hand so he would shake it off his head. But they would pick it up and put it back on him again. He went through a very hard time in Datong. But he understood that these people were being forced to treat him like this. It was their only way of getting their sentences reduced. It was a very sad situation indeed.

Most of the inmates at Datong were required to work underground in the mine, but. because Wang Mingdao was getting old, they did not make him. After the five months of torture, since he had little to do, he learned a bit of sewing. Once after washing his quilt he could not put it back together, and someone offered to teach him, but he still did not know if he should sew from the inside or the outside.

While he was at Datong, Wang Mingdao received a letter from a Christian lady in Hamburg, Germany. It was addressed to Beijing Municipal Prison and had been forwarded from there to Dajong. Wang Mingdao thought that his story must have been published in a German news-paper in order for her to know where he was. Mr Liu, the camp director, brought the letter him to him. Wang Mingdao translated the letter, which was written in English, and explained that the lady wanted him to write back to tell her if he and his wife were well. Two postal coupons were included with the letter to enable him to reply. Mr Liu agreed that Wang Mingdao should reply, but insisted it had to be in Chinese. Wang Mingdao disagreed, saying that he did not know how the address could be translated into Chinese. Months went by and Wang Mingdao never replied. In the end, Mr Liu took the letter away, saying that an inmate should not keep anything in a foreign language. Wang Mingdao never knew who the woman was that wrote the letter but he greatly appreciated such friendship in Christ. Had he been allowed to keep the letter, he would definitely have replied as soon as he left the prison.

Chapter 33

Mrs Wang in Handan

When Mrs Wang was moved back from Tongxian to Beijing, Wang Mingdao was also still in Beijing. However, within a month, many of the prison inmates were transferred. Many of the female inmates were taken back to their native province – such as Shanxi, Henan, Anhui and the North-east – for re-education. All the male inmates, including Wang Mingdao, were assigned to Datong Mining Camp. Mrs Wang stayed in Beijing until 1969 when she was transferred to Handan with Dr Chen Shanli.

Soon after Mrs Wang arrived in Handan, she developed a problem in her right eye. The prison doctor diagnosed the problem as glaucoma and prescribed some drops to release the pressure in her eye. Had the doctor's instruction to apply the medicine every hour been followed closely her eye would have been saved. However, prison regulations did not allow inmates to keep their own medicines and the group leader who held it on Mrs Wang's behalf refused to help her with the medicine every hour. As a result, the pressure in her eye worsened and the nerves were destroyed. Soon her right eye went blind completely.

In Handan, Mrs Wang went through a very difficult time. In 1970 orders were given that thieves and social manipulators among the inmates were to be purged publicly, so that it might be a lesson to everyone. With the constant transfer of prisoners between prisons the women were asked to reduce the number of possessions they took with them, and many sold off their belongings particularly their watches and suitcases. Mrs Wang had more possessions than anyone else, and just as she was thinking about what to do with them, someone reported her to a manager. The manager came up with the idea of holding a public exhibition of all her possessions. Mrs Wang thought he was joking, but he was not. The exhibition was held in a big tent with a big banner across the middle, which read: 'Liu Jingwen, Counter-Revolutionary with a religious coat'. All her dresses were hung out across the room for everyone to see. One of her silk dresses had been torn but they mended it especially for the exhibition. Every piece of garment was labelled 'bourgeois' and given its proper name. One cotton quilt was said to be of duck down. Mrs Wang was thoroughly humiliated.

As soon as the accusation meeting began, someone tried to strike her across her face. The manager prevented it and told them they could only use their mouths. Many inmates stood up to denounce her, including two sisters in the Lord. The first one was a Ms Zhang, who attacked her for wearing a ring. Someone had given the ring to her husband back in 1948 for their twentieth wedding anniversary when he was leading a service in Nanjing, and on his return to Beijing, he had presented it to her. She had been delighted as she had never had a wedding ring. When she was arrested, she had been wearing the ring. She never dreamt that one day it would be used to condemn her.

The other sister was a Mrs Chang. She said, 'How can anyone believe Jesus was really born of a virgin? When I married my husband, if I hadn't slept with him, there wouldn't have been a baby. A virgin can't give birth.' She also said, 'When Wang Mingdao preached, he always had one eye on the offering box. As soon as he finished, he would head straight for the box.' Mrs Wang thought, 'If we really were such awful people, why did you bother going to the meetings?' She was also condemned for being a university graduate. This was because only rich children could afford university education. In fact she had never been to university. Later she joked, 'I have been through the door of a university but I have never studied there.'

Although this sister had denounced her publicly, Mrs Wang understood. Mrs Chang had suffered a nervous breakdown after being arrested in 1960 for her faith and sentenced to thirteen years' imprisonment. While in prison, she had given up her faith but after her release she was restored to faith. Mrs Wang had been released soon after her and, hearing that Sister Chang was living a hard life in the countryside, she had mailed her twenty yuan to help. Some people could not understand why Mrs Wang helped her after all she had done but Mrs Wang did not think that way. Instead, she treated her with love. After their release Sister Chang had written to Mrs Wang to confess her sin of giving up her faith and, not long after that, she had died.

After the condemnation meeting in the afternoon, all the inmates gathered for supper and then in the evening they had political studies. A Catholic sister who had spoken against her at the meeting asked her, 'Liu Jingwen, do you think Jesus is real?' 'Yes,' she replied. When two other women heard this they started beating her up and then others joined in, kicking her and pulling her hair. Even the Catholic sister kicked her in the ribs. Mrs Wang screamed and yelled, hoping that someone would hear them and intervene. But nobody came to help her. Even though she was in a lot of pain she did not hate them. She learned later that these kinds of beating went on in every cell where there were believers.

While all this was going on, her group leader came to ask her if she was ready to give up. 'Do I have to take you to the Yellow River to make you give in?' she asked. Mrs Wang looked at her but said nothing. A few days before that, a Catholic believer, Zhang Antai, had been executed, and the group leader tried to scare her by telling her about it. Later, Mrs Wang went to read the public notice about his death and discovered he was shot because he had made contact with believers who had completed their sentences. Mrs Wang thought, 'He got caught doing something he should not have done. I have not done anything wrong. How does his case have anything to do with mine? I am fine.' She thought this because she had always obeyed prison regulations. At the time, all the inmates had to take turns on night duty. One night when Mrs Wang was on duty, she saw Sister Xiao Yuzhong in the toilets. Even though there was no one else around she did not speak to her because she did not want to break prison regulations.

The next evening, the beatings continued. Because she was screaming so much, the group leader put her hands over her mouth to stop her. She was a Muslim woman who was in prison for embezzlement, and she caused Mrs Wang much suffering. Not long after this beating, this group leader developed an infection on the back of her neck. But, despite what she had done, Mrs Wang was very loving towards her. After her release, she became a Christian because of Mrs Wang's witness and eagerly followed the Lord. On one occasion, on a visit to Beijing, she even went to see Sister Xiao Yuzhong and prayed with her.

During the beating an elderly lady who was a Catholic believer felt sorry for Mrs Wang and told her to confess that there was no God, no Jesus. 'Just say it so that they won't beat you any more,' she said. Mrs Wang knew she was telling her to say the words but keep believing in her heart, to avoid the beating – but how could she ever say such a thing? However, the Catholic woman received a reward for her efforts. That happened on 26 February 1970.

The next day, these women gathered together to discuss how they could make Mrs Wang suffer even more. Having decided that pulling her hair was the most painful way of attacking her, that night a young prostitute with a vicious streak, nicknamed 'Little Pepper', came over to her and started pulling her hair. Then the group leader joined in with a vicious slap across her head and another woman, who had beaten her own daughter to death, punched her face and nose. Then they all kept pulling at her hair. Mrs Wang was in so much pain that she tried to stop them grabbing her hair, but then they starting kicking her upper legs. When she tried to protect her legs, they went back to her head. They beat her all over her body many times. To their surprise, Mrs Wang was silent throughout the beating despite multiple wounds and severe pain, although astonishingly there was no bleeding. Many inmates were amazed to see her taking the beating with such peace and silence. After they completed their prison sentences, these women were forced to do more physical labour. Mrs Wang's three roommates, including a murderer who had killed her own husband, a woman street thief and an embezzler, asked her how she was able to bear so much beating. She told them about Jesus, and one of them believed.

After she was badly beaten up, Mrs Wang wrote a letter to the government, in which she said,

> 'Mao Zedong said in 1926, "We think peasants should be responsible for their own business." He meant by this that the government should not interfere but leave it to the peasants themselves. It is their business. Mao Zedong wrote in 1955, "Among us are good people who may not agree with Marxism and Leninism. We should leave such people alone and allow them to disagree. We should give them work to do. Such differences in ideology cannot be resolved with a few meetings." Mao Zedong also said, "Dr Sun Yatsun was one of those that did not share with us our world view." In 1926 and in 1955 Mao Zedong was saying the same thing. What he wrote confirms our constitution. There is freedom of belief in China. I don't want to be beaten by those who have beaten their own children to death.'

When she handed in her letter to the manager, she reported that they were planning to beat her again the next day, but she was reassured her that it would not happen again. Once the beatings were banned, her bullies seemed to have lost but they came up with a new form of intimidation. They told Mrs Wang, 'We have a new regulation. If you say Jesus exists you will not be allowed to eat. But if you say Jesus never existed you can eat.' Mrs Wang said nothing. She thought, 'If I don't eat, I will starve. If I starve, I will die.' So she went back to the person in charge to ask if indeed the government had brought in this new regulation. The manager told her to carry on eating. Dr Chen Shanli did not question the regulation and complied with its perpetrators' instructions. She already had high blood pressure and a heart condition. After not eating for a day, her condition deteriorated.

Mrs Wang was not the only one to be beaten up in those days. Dr Chen Shanli, Sister Song Tianying and Sister Xiao Yuzhong all suffered. Dr Chen was badly beaten about the head. When Sister Ying Lanyu refused to say Jesus did not exist they kept punching her in the teeth. When Mrs Wang got up one morning she saw Song Tianying in the toilets with a pale face and messy hair. She had been beaten up all over. Knowing Xiao Yuzhong had a bad back they concentrated their beating on her back.

While Mrs Wang was being beaten, the words of a song based on Isaiah 50:5-7 filled her mind:

> *'The Sovereign LORD has opened my ears,*
> *and I have not been rebellious,*
> *I have not drawn back.*
> *I offered my back to those who beat me,*
> *my cheeks to those that pulled out my beard:*
> *I did not hide my face*
> *from mocking and spitting.*
> *Because the Sovereign LORD helps me,*
> *I will not be disgraced:*
> *Therefore have I set my face like flint,*
> *and I know I will not be put to shame.'*

She had always loved this song and had often sung it at home. Now, after her experiences of being beaten, she thought Isaiah must really have been a saint. Beaten and spat at, he did not budge an inch. She felt there was no way she could be like him. She often sang this song silently while she was in prison to give herself strength and courage.

When Dr Chen's daughter saw how much her mother was beaten, her attitude towards the government started to change. Later, she came back to faith in Jesus and witnessed to Him. However, she too was then arrested for her faith. She was imprisoned with a sister from Grace Hospital, and she tried her best to love her, and do whatever she could do for her. She was also very open about her thoughts and feelings, having no idea that a person she had tried to help might report her to the government. Young as she was, she was handcuffed and pressurised to give up her faith. She was given many books to read and forced to write her reflections on what she had read. Eventually she caved in under the pressure. After her change of heart the government was very kind to her and she was allowed to see her mother, Dr Chen. When they met, she wanted to help her mother to change too but Dr Chen just sat there without saying anything. No matter how much she tried, her mother would not speak. It was very sad because they had not seen each other for many years and should have had much to share. In early 1969, when Mrs Wang and Dr Chen shared a cell in Beijing Prison, Dr Chen told her, 'She really hurt my heart. I feel so sad for her.' She could never understand why her daughter had given up her faith in Jesus, and, for the rest of her life, she never got over it.

After they both suffered the beatings, Mrs Wang and Dr Chen said less to one another. They were no longer in the same room and there were fewer opportunities to meet. One of Mrs Wang's fellow inmates Zeng Yuhua completed her sentence and went home for a visit before she was due to go to the labour camp. On her return she brought the bad news of the death of Dr Chen's husband, Zhang Zhouxin. Mr Zhang had been arrested at Grace Hospital in Hangzhou. After his release in 1957, he returned to Beijing and even visited Wang Mingdao in Sweet Rain Lane. They heard he had been rearrested in Tianjin and had died in prison around 1970. Mrs Wang felt she must somehow let Dr Chen know about her husband's death, but she could not find a way to speak to her. Later, Dr Chen learned about it through a letter from her son.

Dr Chen was very short, and as a result of her prolonged illness she seemed to have become even shorter. Now she could not even reach the washing line to hang out her clothes to dry. She was often heard to complain about herself, 'Oh, why am I so short, so short?' One day, Mrs Wang saw her trying in vain to hang her clothes on the line. When she saw Mrs Wang, she asked her, 'Can you please help me?' and Mrs Wang did.

Due to her high blood pressure and heart condition she could not eat salt or much of the food they were given, just some vegetables. As a result, she was losing weight. She often asked for sweets. Mrs Wang had some sweets but she never dared to give her any in case she was accused of trying to manipulate her. Later, both of them contracted a chest infection and were in the isolation unit of the hospital. During the Chinese New Year in 1971, Mrs Wang wanted to find a way to give some sweets to Dr Chen. One day when Dr Chen was out, she secretly filled her sweet jar. She thought if Dr Chen did not even know about it, she could not be accused of trying to manipulate her. With such an atmosphere of fear and suspicion, the love between the two sisters was much restricted.

Soon after that, Dr Chen's condition deteriorated. On 30 June 1971, the day before she passed away, Mrs Wang went to see her. Her eyes were closed. Mrs Wang did not feel free to speak to her, so she just said, 'Chen Shanli.' Her eyes moved slightly. The next day she left this world.

Chapter 34

Ten Years at Yingying

In April 1968, many of the prisoners from Datong Mining Camp, including Wang Mingdao and Zhan Rugeng, were transferred to Yingying Labour Camp. Datong is in the north of the Shanxi province while Yingying is a small town in Yangquan County in the centre. The prison was about ten miles from the railway station.

In Datong, Zhan Rugeng's efforts to condemn Wang Mingdao had been rewarded with a significant reduction in his prison term, and on their arrival at Yingying he continued to pursue him. One day, at a meeting in the camp yard where over a hundred people had gathered, Zhan spoke out once again against Wang Mingdao. Even though he did not mention his name or his church, everyone knew from his reference to 'a church in Beijing with a heating system donated by a wealthy capitalist' that he was talking about Wang Mingdao. One day, when Wang Mingdao was alone in the kitchen preparing cabbages, Zhan taunted him that all preachers were interested in was filling their mouths. Wang Mingdao told him that it was certainly not true of him, and reflected later: 'He may have preached to eat, but I preached for God's Kingdom. We were totally different.'

At Yingying certain prisoners were selected to be group leaders who were responsible for the day-to-day affairs of the group and reported important matters to the camp officials. Wang Mingdao was in Team 18. On one occasion, an inmate who lived next door to Wang Mingdao became so angry with his group leader that he planned to use the metal lid of the house stove to murder him. One night, having waited until everyone was asleep, he picked up the lid, intending to bring it down on the man's head – but his attempt was foiled. He had not realised it was connected to the stove by a metal chain which was not quite long enough. The group leader, who was alerted by the noise, started yelling, 'Murder! Murder!' and every one was roused. The incident was immediately reported to the camp director, and the man was handcuffed and led away.

One day, Wang Mingdao's group leader told him that the camp had a new director, and suggested he should write to him. Wang Mingdao had suffered much as a result of his efforts to seek justice for Liu Shaoqi and, after coming to Yingying, had determined not to write any more letters. But the group leader was in fact speaking on behalf of the new Director who wanted to know what Wang Mingdao was thinking, and kept on and on at him until eventually he did start to write again. The Director often came to talk with him and they got to know one another well. One day a parcel – a big box full of cans of meat – arrived from Wang Mingdao's son. Thinking it must have cost a lot of money to send it, the Director asked Wang Mingdao if his son made a lot of money from his work. In fact, Tianzhe and his wife had saved up their coupons to buy the cans of meat.

On another occasion, the Director came to show Wang Mingdao two of Mao Zedong's latest poems which had been printed in a newspaper. One of the poems contained the words 'Don't fart!' and he was interested to know what Wang Mingdao thought. Wang Mingdao said he would not wish to read them again. 'How can you use words like that in a poem?' he asked. 'I don't like words like that, and especially not in a poem.'

Despite the fact that Wang Mingdao's spiritual life had been fully restored, it was difficult for him to pray in prison. He could not kneel to pray, and even saying grace before meals was not permitted. He used to pray when he lay in bed at night, but he was not allowed to make any sound. He often experienced the Lord's protection. One day, Mr Xing from Datong was visiting Yingying. As he walked into Wang Mingdao's room, another inmate seized the opportunity to denounce Wang Mingdao once again. But Wang Mingdao was no longer afraid of him. Not long afterwards, the inmate had a stroke. In the morning he was going about his business as normal but by the afternoon Wang Mingdao was told that he had been taken to hospital.

At Yingying, all the inmates wore a uniform which had the name of the camp stamped on it. The Director told them that all of their own clothes must also be stamped before they could wear them and sent people round to stamp them. Wang Mingdao had two particular items of clothing that he liked very much and he didn't want them stamped, so he wrote to the Director to complain, 'I am not a criminal. I won't wear criminals' clothes. If you put a red stamp on my clothes, I will cover it up with a piece of cloth.' One day, Wang Mingdao was in the yard with everyone else watching some chess games when the Director pointed at the piece of cloth covering up the red stamp on Wang Mingdao's jacket and asked him about it. Wang Mingdao responded that he was only being truthful: 'If I were a criminal, it would be appropriate for my clothes to be stamped. But since I am not a criminal, I should not be labelled as one.' The Director asked him why he was imprisoned if he was not a criminal. Wang Mingdao replied that he was merely sitting in prison, just like Paul and Jeremiah. At that the Director laughed without saying any more. From then on, Wang Mingdao began to wear clothes that hadn't been stamped. On one occasion, when he was wearing one of the items with the stamp covered over, an inmate noticed and refused to let him use the toilet. However, when Wang Mingdao explained that he had already discussed it with the Director, he allowed him to go ahead. After that, no one troubled him about it any more. At Yingying, from that time until he left, Wang Mingdao was the only inmate who did not wear clothes with the prison stamp on them.

In April 1974, Mrs Wang had completed her fifteen-year prison sentence. Her son Tianzhe went to take her home. He thought that once the paper work was finished she would be able to go home with him. He did not realise that, whatever the length of their prison sentence, inmates who had completed their sentences were required by government regulations to work in a place designated for them outside the prison. They were permitted two weeks' holiday each year to visit their relatives. So Mrs Wang had to remain at Handan. After visiting his mother in Handan for a few days, Tianzhe went on to Yingying to see his father. Then on his way back to Shanghai, he stayed another few days with his mother.

In the same year, Mrs Wang was able to go to Shanghai to visit her mother who was now ninety-five years old. The Director told her to return before the Mid-autumn Festival, which in that year fell on a Sunday. Originally, the Sunday was included in Mrs Wang's holiday, which would have allowed her to stay in Shanghai one more day, but after what the Director had said to her, she felt she could not take that extra day off. As it turned out, she was glad she came back on time. The very next day after the festival, they were moved to Shijiazhuang. Had she stayed in Shanghai that extra day, she would have had too little time to pack her things. This experience taught her that it is always good to keep a promise. She remained in Shijiazhuang until the devastating earthquake in Tangshan in 1976. After Mao Zedong died later that year, she was transferred to Xingtai. In 1977, government regulations changed and all those who had completed their sentences were allowed to return home if they wished, and she was finally able to go home to Shanghai.

Tianzhe visited his father in Yingying three times. He went first on his own in the spring of 1973, then in 1974 he took his wife and daughter, and on the third occasion in 1975 he went with his mother.

In January 1974, Mrs Wang's mother passed away at the age of ninety-six. The letter which Tianzhe wrote to tell his father the sad news arrived in February. The Director summoned Wang Mingdao to the office to tell him. When Wang Mingdao heard the words, 'Sooner or later a person will die', he realised that his mother-in-law had died. When this was confirmed by the letter, he was overwhelmed with sorrow. She had loved him dearly, as if he were her own son. He managed to hold in his tears in the office but as soon as he was back in his room, he started to cry. Whatever he saw in his room, from his quilt to his clothes, if it was made or sent

by her, it would set him off. The Director asked his group
leader to comfort him and he really did try to help. The next
morning, when he woke up, he started crying again. The
more he thought about her, the more he cried. At first he
cried quietly but later he could not hold it in any more and
he began to weep loudly. This went on for two or three days.
After a while, however, he suddenly realised that he would
see her again in heaven and this thought comforted him.
Soon after this he stopped crying. His heart was comforted by
the Lord and he regained hope in the knowledge that they
would indeed meet again.

Wang Mingdao's reaction to his mother-in-law's death was
to have negative repercussions for him. When Mrs Wang
came to visit him in 1975 with Tianzhe, the Director told her
that Wang Mingdao had grieved very deeply after his
mother-in-law passed away. He told her that the government
had been trying to find a way of showing leniency to enable
the family to be reunited but, for some reason which
Mrs Wang could not understand, her husband's excessive
grief, as they saw it, had somehow prevented it. Mrs Wang
knew that Wang Mingdao had visited the model commune
at Dazhai some time before her mother had died and during
that time he had been quite progressive politically, which
may have prompted the government to consider leniency.

At Yingying Wang Mingdao had little to do and so he had
a lot of free time. Over the years Tianzhe sent him more than
500 books, including a number of classics. He spent the
whole day reading which damaged his eyes. Throughout his
time there the government officials were kind to him. Sometimes they even borrowed his books to read. God hid him at
Yingying where he was much safer than he would have been
in the outside world.

In 1975, a campaign against Lin Biao and Confucius swept
China, eventually reaching Yingying. At that time no one was
allowed to say anything good about Confucius. One day, four
or five officials met with Wang Mingdao to ask him what he
thought of the story of Confucius killing Shao Zhengmao.
Wang Mingdao replied, 'Confucius' killing of Shao Zhengmao
was absolutely right! Shao deserved it. Some people say

Confucius was brutal to kill a well-known gentleman. But it was not down to any brutality on Confucius' part, but simply to the nature of Shao Zhengmao himself. Such a person could only produce trouble for the Kingdom of Lu.' He then recited the story from the classics, explaining why Shao Zhengmao deserved his death because of the depravity of his heart, his wild conduct, hypocritical words and grave disobedience.

The leaders were amazed at how familiar Wang Mingdao was with the classics. Several of them came to speak to him about the campaign to condemn Confucius. Wang Mingdao told them Confucius should not be criticised, and that those who did so would live to regret it. 'Jesus is my Saviour and Confucius is my teacher,' he said. One day a meeting was held in the square attended by thousands of people. Because it was a Sunday most people were not at work. Two of the platform speakers vilified Confucius. There was no opportunity for anyone in the audience to speak, otherwise Wang Mingdao would have argued that to condemn Confucius was to insult the national saint of China. This was another reason why the government's softening attitude to Wang Mingdao did not last.

The prison directors continued to be very unhappy about the fact that Wang Mingdao did so much writing. After reading the newspaper each day he would write down his reflections, suggestions and advice. He wrote so much that they did not have time to read it all. And they did not know what to do about it either. If they did not turn it into the authorities, they would be in trouble. If they did, they were afraid of what the authorities might do. So they told him not to write anything. But Wang Mingdao carried on writing. In 1976 when Mrs Wang came to visit him with a relative, the leaders asked her to persuade him not to write. After she returned home, she wrote a letter specifically to urge him not to write, but it didn't do any good. In the end, they decided to punish him by refusing to buy writing paper for him. However, Wang Mingdao had a store of good quality paper from his days in Beijing Prison, which he had been saving specifically to write to Premier Zhou Enlai, but he had died before he could write. So he used the paper to write 'My last suggestion'. He wrote, 'Please do not worry about me committing suicide. My heart is rejoicing right now. The reason I am writing this is because I think the government must change course right now. If not, the government is merely covering up the facts and is being irresponsible. This will bring unimaginable consequences.'

After Mrs Wang returned home in 1977, she mailed nutritious food to her husband every month. Towards the end of this year, however, they changed their policy and refused to allow his family to mail him food directly. At the age of seventy-seven Wang Mingdao became very depressed and lost the will to live. He thought this was more evidence of pressure from the government who were still trying to make him give up his faith. So he wrote another report to the government which stated, 'I understand what the government is trying to do. You want to me to starve. Once I am starving, you think I will give up my faith. This is impossible! It is a small matter to starve to death but a huge problem to lose one's faith.' From then on he prepared to starve to death in prison.

One day in the autumn of 1978, ten months after this, Wang Mingdao became ill with an infection of his digestive system. One day he had to eat millet instead of rice but, because he had bad teeth and the millet was much harder to chew, he swallowed the food without chewing it properly. That night he was extremely ill with diarrhoea and vomiting. The next day, he could hardly get up and he stayed in bed for the whole day. Towards the evening, he was taken into hospital. After two days in hospital, the Director came to visit him. Wang Mingdao told him that the injection he had been given was helping him a lot. When the Director saw how weak he was he suggested that he write to his son. He replied, 'I don't want to write until I leave the hospital. If I die here . . . ' Later he did in fact write to his son, telling him he was very ill and had almost died. He told him he was in hospital but he did not say what was wrong with him. When Mrs Wang received the letter, she told her son, 'It's hard to tell if he is alive or dead. No matter what, we must go to see him. If he is still alive, maybe we can try and get him out for some medical treatment. If he is dead, at least we will know.'

By the time Tianzhe arrived, his father's sickness had subsided but the doctor informed him that his father was extremely weak. Tianzhe left him all the food he had brought with him, telling him there was more at the hotel in Yangquan. Wang Mingdao realised that he had not brought it all with him because he had not known if he was alive or dead. If he had been dead, there would have been no point in bringing it all. So Tianzhe went back to his hotel and got the extra food. After a few days', when Wang Mingdao received the food from the prison authorities, his health soon began to improve and it was not long before he was out of hospital.

When Tianzhe was visiting his father in hospital, he often saw the Director there and he asked him, in front of his father, why he had not been allowed to send in food. He was told that it was unfair if one or two of the prisoners received extra food while the others did not. However, from then on Tianzhe did not worry about permission and just sent the food anyway. With good food Wang Mingdao's health greatly improved. When Tianzhe had asked about taking his father out for medical treatment, he had been told that Wang Mingdao was sentenced to life imprisonment without any parole.

After his illness Wang Mingdao no longer worried about anything. In the past, he had dared not sing in prison but now he would walk around praising God. Even when the prison officials heard him singing, they pretended they didn't. They had finally realised he was not going to change.

After 16 December 1978, when the Sino-American Communiqué on establishing diplomatic relations was published, all organisations in China held meetings to study it. One day everyone was told to report to the yard for political study. As Wang Mingdao was just beginning to recover from his illness and it was the middle of winter, the duty officer said he could stay inside if he wanted to. He could just about hear from the loudspeaker that something important was going on but he could not tell what it was. Later, when someone told him China was establishing diplomatic relations with the United States, Wang Mingdao began to worry for the Church in

Taiwan. He thought that this would mean that the Communists would no longer be afraid of attacking Taiwan, which they had been in the past because of the American Air Force and Navy bases there, and the Taiwanese churches would be forced to align with the Three-Self Church.

One day there was a flurry of activity in the yard with many of the inmates making ropes out of their old clothes. Wang Mingdao couldn't understand what they were doing, but some of the inmates in his team were better informed. They told him that prisoners only made ropes whenever amnesty was about to be announced.

At the time when Wang Mingdao and his wife had been rearrested back in 1957, Tianzhe had taken his father's diary over ten years and his four photo albums back to Shanghai with him. However, when the government had asked for them, he had been forced to hand them over. Somehow – nobody knew how – the albums and diary had found their way to Datong. When Wang Mingdao had been transferred from Datong to Yingying, his luggage had been shipped by the government. When he had gone to claim it, he had seen his diary and albums tied up with mental wire among the pile of belongings. The camp officials had insisted that these things be kept in the store room rather than in his room. Later, when people were being released en masse, the Director told him to burn the albums as they were no longer any use but Wang Mingdao refused. 'They are my history. I must keep them,' he insisted. The Director told him he could not make a decision about them but would have to ask his superiors. A few days later, he was informed he could keep his diary and photos and, when he left the prison, they were all returned to him.

In February 1979, Wang Mingdao received a letter from his niece, Sister Liu Xiaoyu. In his reply he wrote about the importance of a child's upbringing. As he had personally suffered so much as a result of lies, he particularly emphasised telling the truth. He wrote,

'Above all, teach him to be honest, to speak the truth and act truthfully. All the sinful things of the world are connected with lies. Sin hides itself in lies. You and Yajun must provide a good example for your child in things big and small. It is far more important to teach with your actions than your words. Being honest means that sometimes you will suffer. But these short-term losses will be beneficial in the long term. Then they will not only be of temporary benefit but of eternal benefit. Most people are near-sighted. They only see what benefits them now. They do not take the consequences of their actions into consideration and they end up by harming themselves badly.'

This letter shows that even though he was in prison, he was still very concerned about the spiritual growth of the younger generations. He often used his own life experiences to speak to them from his heart, teaching them to walk the way of Jesus. In May, Liu Xiaoyu went to see Wang Mingdao in prison and they spoke together for over an hour. Because they were being watched, they could only talk about general things, such as their health and daily routines, but Wang Mingdao did mention his sufferings before 1963 and how his faith had been renewed after he had repented.

In the same month, a man called Dr Sheng Xianzhi from the US visited the prison with his son to see Wang Mingdao. He was following the teaching of Matthew 25 where believers are exhorted to visit fellow Christians in prison. Dr Sheng was the son of Sheng Xian, a Presbyterian pastor who was a good friend of Wang Mingdao and called Wang Mingdao 'Uncle'. Dr Sheng's visit was totally unexpected. Dr Sheng's brother had arranged his itinerary which had had to be submitted to the government. It was only due to God's grace that permission was granted to include the Labour Camp. Very few places in China were open to foreigners back then, and Yingying was certainly not one of them. Though they did not see Wang Mingdao, they hoped the camp would take notice of Wang Mingdao's foreign connections and perhaps treat him better, even release him. They left a letter, a pair of gloves and a flashlight for him.

After Dr Sheng's visit, the camp officials summoned Wang Mingdao to the office to ask him if he knew anything him. Wang Mingdao told them that the only Mr Sheng he knew was a Presbyterian pastor who was a good friend of his and whose four daughters and two sons all called him 'Uncle'. Wang Mingdao had no idea why they were asking about Dr Sheng and he felt deeply troubled. The next day, however, they asked for him again and told him Dr Sheng had left something for him. Seeing the letter with the gloves and the flashlight, he realised Dr Sheng must have tried to visit him. A few days later, they came to ask for the letter back, saying that they wanted to go to Beijing to investigate his relationship with Dr Sheng. Wang Mingdao's imprisonment had not only been reported in the German press but also by the American press. In fact, news about him had travelled far and wide and had aroused international attention.

In the months before he was released, Wang Mingdao knew a deep sense of peace and contentment which he expressed in this short poem:

> 'Prophets have died,
> disciples have passed away.
> Called to preach,
> I stand firm and strong.
> Knowing the Bible
> and understanding the truth
> nothing will bend me.
> I stand high and tall
> between heaven and earth.'

Chapter 35

Tricked

With the establishment of Sino-American diplomatic relations, China brought its closed-door policy to an end. Having now been embraced by the international family of nations it was more or less forced to subject itself to international laws and codes of conduct. A human rights organisation based in London began to campaign in over twenty countries for China to release all its political prisoners. When the government finally bowed to the pressure and decided to release its political prisoners, they included among them those who had been imprisoned for their faith. No distinction was made. However, Wang Mingdao was not willing to leave without his name being cleared. Just like Paul in Philippi he refused to allow himself to be released (Acts 16:35–40). When he refused their polite requests to leave, the government had to find another way round the problem.

In November 1979, Tianzhe received a telegram from Yingying saying, 'Come and take Wang Mingdao home as soon as possible.' Tianzhe did not know it was from the government: he thought it was sent by his father. At the time Mrs Wang was in Nanjing, not Shanghai, so Tianzhe wrote to her, telling her about the telegram and that he was on his way. He also contacted a relative in Shanxi to make arrangements for them to go together to meet his father. As soon as Mrs Wang received the letter, she returned to Shanghai, but Tianzhe had already left.

When Tianzhe arrived at Yingying prison, he was taken to the prison director's office, where he was joined by his father, who had been escorted there by some of his fellow inmates. When he walked in, he was surprised to see Tianzhe. 'Why are you here?' he asked.

'To take you home,' Tianzhe replied.

'I won't leave,' Wang Mingdao said. 'Go back and tell Mum that I am fine here.'

Before Tianzhe could say anything else, the Director told Wang Mingdao he should go home with his son. 'No,' Wang Mingdao insisted, 'my case is not settled yet. I have never committed any crime. I have been locked up for over twenty years for my faith.'

'Don't hold that against everybody any more,' the Director said. 'Go home. Prison is not a good place.'

'I have lived in prison for over twenty years. I should know whether it is a good place or not,' Wang Mingdao replied. 'I am used to it now. I regard the prison as my home now. I won't go.'

'You must go,' the Director insisted. 'You can't stay here any more.'

'Before I go, the government must admit three things. They must admit that they wrongly arrested me, that they wrongly sentenced me and that they have wrongly imprisoned for over twenty years. If they don't put this in writing, I won't leave.'

The government would never make any admission of this kind. So they argued for a whole morning. In the end, the Director told everyone including Wang Mingdao to go to lunch, promising that they would talk more in the afternoon. Another prison official came to speak to him after lunch, urging him to go home with his son. Wang Mingdao insisted that he would not leave. However, in the end, out of a desire not to disappoint Tianzhe, he changed his mind and said, ' OK, I will go home with you.' Tianzhe was delighted and told his father to pack up immediately. 'I have too much stuff to pack,' Wang Mingdao said. Tianzhe told him that he would take him to stay with him in the guesthouse that night.

Wang Mingdao returned to his room to pack. He gave his food to two prisoners with poor health and got out all his books, giving his cellmates the pick of whichever ones they wanted. He did not know that Tianzhe had brought quite a few big bags to pack them in. Later in the evening, someone came to tell him that Tianzhe was not coming until the morning, so he stayed in the prison for the night. The next morning, he put on some clothes that Tianzhe had brought for him to wear and waited in the yard for his son. A guard took him to the office, where Tianzhe and the relative were waiting. An official brought over a piece of paper, issued by the High Court of Shanxi Province, for him to sign. It said:

> The detained Wang Mingdao was sentenced to life-imprisonment for counter-revolutionary activities and is hereby released due to a change of sentence.

The official told him that as soon as he had signed the certificate he could go home with his son. 'I won't leave,' Wang Mingdao said. 'I will not admit that I am a counter-revolutionary. I have committed no crime. I was wrongly arrested, sentenced wrongly and wrongly locked up by the government. The government must investigate my case. Otherwise I won't leave the prison. I will stay here for ever.' Then he told Tianzhe, 'You can go back to Shanghai. I won't go.' The relative who was there saw how strongly Wang Mingdao felt about this and suggested, 'You do whatever your heart feels peaceful about.' With that, they set off on the journey home, leaving him with dozens of boiled eggs they had prepared for the trip.

As soon as Tianzhe got back, Mrs Wang asked him what had happened. Tianzhe told her how stubborn his father was. His arrival home was soon followed by a letter from Wang Mingdao, 'Unless you hear from me directly, don't come to pick me up. I won't leave.' He also wrote, 'Lying is the root of all crimes.' Because he had suffered terribly as a result of lies, he himself would never ever collude with lies in any way.

On 29 December Wang Mingdao was summoned to the office again where some of the prison officials were waiting for him. First, they asked him what the difference was between immersion and sprinkling. Wang Mingdao was very glad to be asked this question. He told them that immersion

involved submerging someone in water while sprinkling
derived from the Catholic practice of pouring water on
someone's head. He said sprinkling was very different from
the original meaning of baptism. He went on talking
about the subject for over an hour. In order to make him
happy they told him he spoke very well on the subject. Then
they began their real business. A Mr Li said, 'You told us you
didn't want to leave the prison. We can't force you to go. But
there are three empty rooms outside the prison that you can
live in. In a few days, the court in Beijing will send someone
to speak to you about your case. Once you leave the prison,
you are free. You can go wherever you want.'

Wang Mingdao believed that he was being told the truth.
He thought the official from Beijing would be able to clarify
his case so he accepted the offer and promised that he would
go and pack immediately, but Mr Li told him that his
belongings had already been packed. Wang Mingdao
insisted, however, on going back to have a look. There were
eighty-one steps up a hill to the block where his room was
and he barely had the strength to climb it – he had to be
supported by someone else.

When he arrived back at the block, he saw that his luggage
was already waiting for him outside his room. One of the
other inmates told him that he would walk him to his new
room and then bring his luggage. So he walked Wang
Mingdao through the first gate towards the second gate
where soldiers stood on guard with rifles. Before reaching
the second gate they turned and walked over a hill before
arriving at the place known as the Three Rooms. Since
everything was pre-arranged, they were allowed through all
the gates. There were two other rooms nearby where two
former inmates lived. Their job was to take care of the
residents in the Three Rooms. The rooms were surrounded
by an iron fence but the gate was kept open. As soon as he
stepped out of the prison, the prison officials' job was
completed.

The Three Rooms were not part of the prison. They were
places where those who had been released stayed temporar-
ily. They were fitted out with some basic kitchen

equipment such as stoves, chopping boards, and knives so the residents could cook their own meals. But Wang Mingdao's eyesight was now so bad that he dare not touch knives. Even though he could still have had meals in the dining hall, he would have had to cross the road and walk five hundred metres. With his poor sight, he could not see the road and could easily have been run over. Another problem was the toilets. After he had been sick in hospital, he could no longer squat. If he did, he could not get up again. In the prison toilets, there were some specially-made wooden boxes where he could sit but in the new accommodation there wasn't anything like that. The toilet was nothing more than a hole dug out of the ground with a bamboo fence around it. A wooden plank marked the place where he should stand or squat but, at his age, he could easily have lost his balance and fallen. He realised immediately that it had been a trick to get him out of the prison. He regretted that he had left, but there was no way of getting back. He had been forced out.

He asked the two former inmates who also lived there what he should do. They told him he could buy some sticky rice to make porridge. This was what he did – he ate porridge every day. There weren't any vegetables, not even pickled cabbage. How could he live like that?

On New Year's Eve 1979, everyone in the Three Rooms went to the cinema except Wang Mingdao and another resident from Hunan. The man told him he could not go on living there any longer. 'You are eighty years old. What will happen to you if you become sick? The prison hospital won't even admit you. You must go to Shanghai. But Shanghai is over a thousand miles away. You can't go there on your own. You'd better write to your son and ask him to come and take you home. Otherwise if you get sick, you will be in a real mess!' Wang Mingdao knew he was right. The next morning, he wrote a postcard with only twelve words, 'Tianzhe: Decided to go to Shanghai. Come to get me soon. Dad.' He asked one of the men to send it for him by registered post. As soon as he returned, the prison officials came to see him. 'So you decided to go back to Shanghai?' they asked.

'Yes,' Wang Mingdao replied.

'That is good then,' they said. 'We heard that you gave some of your books away to other inmates. Have you got any more that we can have?'

'Sure,' Wang Mingdao said. 'I just want to keep ten books of a history series and *The Chronicle of Three Kingdoms*. Otherwise you can pick what you like.'

After each choosing some, they left, adding that they might not be able to come to see him off. Wang Mingdao told them not to worry about formalities.

A plot had been used to force Wang Mingdao out of prison. The government wanted to release him, but he refused to leave. They would never have admitted to having made a mistake, so they plotted to force him out. They knew he would never be able to survive in the accommodation they had given him outside the prison. If they managed to get him to agree to go there, they knew he would have to return to Shanghai sooner or later. Wang Mingdao referred to it as 'the strategy of the end without an end' and said, 'I was not released but was forced out by deception.' Wang Mingdao always maintained that his case was a severe miscarriage of justice, just like the case of Yue Fei, the imperial general famous in China for having been gravely mistreated during the Song Dynasty.

Chapter 36

Leaving Yingying

When Tianzhe received his father's card at the beginning of January, he decided to leave immediately. On the 5th, he sent a telegraph to Zeng Pingdao, one of his father's oldest friends, to invite him to go with him. They decided to meet in Dezhou on the 6th and travel together. They arrived at Yangquan that evening and stayed there for the night. The next morning, after an hour's bus ride, they arrived at Yingying.

The labour camp was situated on a hill outside the small town. It was about one mile from the foot of the hill to the top. Halfway up the hill they could see the Three Rooms where Wang Mingdao was staying. There were very few people on the road, and hardly any strangers, and when people saw them walking up the hill, they all came out to watch. When they arrived, Wang Mingdao had no idea they were there as he was facing the other way. Tianzhe touched his shoulder and said, 'Dad, look who's here!' Wang Mingdao turned around and was surprised to see Mr Zeng. 'Pingdao!' he called out. They had not seen each other for over twenty years. They hugged one another with tears rolling down their faces. They were so overcome with emotion they didn't know what to say first!

When they had all calmed down, Tianzhe asked his father if he wanted to come with them to the guesthouse. Wang Mingdao replied he had too many bags to take, but as soon as his neighbours heard this, they all helped to carry his bags. From the Three Rooms to the guesthouse there were eighty-one steps. On the way Wang Mingdao saw a little girl of about ten years of age. He couldn't get over it, 'Look, a little girl!' Seeing Wang Mingdao's excitement at the sight of a little girl was a sad reminder to Mr Zeng of how many years his friend had been locked away.

The guesthouse, which had been built fairly recently, was just outside the prison. Tianzhe had stayed there before. There were four beds to a room, and each bed cost four yuan per night. The next day was a Sunday so they had to wait until Monday before they could get the appropriate papers. With nothing else to do, they spent the whole time talking in their room about the past twenty years. They studied the Bible, prayed, talked about how various brothers and sisters were, and recited poetry, taking turns to say all the verses. Wang Mingdao gave a perfect rendering of Wen Tianxiang's 'Song of Righteousness' all by himself without missing a word, which indicated that at that time his memory and thinking were still working well.

The next day they went to do the paper work. In normal situations they could have left on the same day, but because the prison was about ten miles from Yangquan and Wang Mingdao had a lot of luggage, it was not going to be an easy task to get to the station. Wang Mingdao sent Tianzhe to speak with prison officials about the possibility of using their truck to take his luggage to Yangquan. He was told it would be busy all day, but he did discover that they could take the prison bus the next morning to Yingying town and from there take the bus to Yangquan. So they stayed for another night. Before they left the next morning, they went to pay for their stay. The proprietor said there was no charge – they could just leave. Most people who came to collect their relatives from the labour camp stayed at the Three Rooms. Wang Mingdao's son and friend stayed in the guesthouse for free and they much appreciated the kindness of the prison officials who had arranged this.

When they got to the town of Yingying, they took a photo back up the hill with the prison in the background. From there they got on the bus for Yangquan. An hour later, they arrived at Yangquan bus station. Then Wang Mingdao stayed at the bus station and Mr Zeng stayed at the train station while Tianzhe rented a small cart to transport the luggage. It took him three trips to get it all the stuff over there. Then they checked all the bags in except the box with Wang Mingdao's diary. Wang Mingdao did not want that lost so he took it with him on the train. At Yangquan train station, they took more photos. The train taking them east arrived at noon. They decided to take a sleeping compartment, which had four beds, so that they could enjoy tea, food and conversation without being disturbed. The whole train had only one carriage with sleeping compartments and they were the only people in that carriage. They were very happy to have it all to themselves and had some excellent fellowship on the journey.

In the evening the train arrived at Dezhou, where Mr Zeng took his leave. The south-bound train did not arrive until midnight and it was so crowded that they could hardly get on. Mr Zeng made sure they got on the train before sending a telegraph to Tianzhe's wife asking her to meet them at Shanghai railway station. After a few more hours' wait, Mr Zeng was able to get on his train home.

When Wang Mingdao and Tianzhe arrived in Shanghai the next day, no one was there to meet them. They thought there must have been a problem with the telegram, but in fact it had arrived in time. Quite a few people had set out to the station to meet them, including Sister Xiao Yuping who had come to Shanghai from Beijing especially, but they had all followed the timetable. In fact, that day the train was early and that is why they missed one another. They got back soon after Wang Mingdao and Tianzhe.

As soon as Mr Zeng got home, he went to visit Mr Li Zaisheng and Wang Mingdao's old friends to let them know immediately about his release. They were all overwhelmed with joy and went around telling everyone the good news, which greatly encouraged his brothers and sisters in Christ.

Chapter 37

Days at Pingjiang Road

News of Wang Mingdao's release travelled like the spring wind. Soon it was blown all over China from the Great Wall to the Yangtze River, and many travelled long distances to visit him in his little room at No. 13 Pingjiang Road. They wanted to see this faithful servant of the Lord whom they had not met for twenty or more years because they loved and respected him. A few visitors had other motives too, but Wang Mingdao warmly welcomed and received all of them, freely speaking about his experiences and his faith.

The news soon travelled overseas, and many foreign and Chinese visitors came from abroad to see him. People came from all over the world, including Canada, the USA, Australia, New Zealand, Britain, West Germany, Denmark, Holland, Norway, Sweden, Switzerland, Finland and even Buddhist Japan. Wang Mingdao recounted to them the story of his life, in particular the eight years of failure in prison. He often quoted Proverbs 28:13:

> 'He who conceals his sins does not prosper,
>   but whosoever confesses them and renounces them finds
>   mercy.'

Whatever else they gained from their visits, people learned that because Wang Mingdao had not been afraid to confess his sins, he had received mercy.

The sheer volume of visitors Wang Mingdao was receiving made the public security officials nervous. They were worried about the impact his frank comments on his treatment by the Chinese government would have on both Chinese and foreign people. Soon after his arrival in Shanghai, he was visited by two policemen, Mr Kong and Mr Liu. The first time they came, it was obvious from their abrupt manner that they wanted to scare him. They asked him about the kind of people who were coming to visit him. Wang Mingdao told them that there was no reason why he should tell them. 'Don't forget you are still a counter-revolutionary,' Mr Liu warned.

'If I am a counter-revolutionary, why did you release me?' Wang Mingdao replied. 'I did not want to come out. You forced me out. If you think I am a counter-revolutionary, just send me back.'

'Those who come may be good or bad,' they argued, inferring that he should not associate with bad elements in society. They also recommended that he learn from his son to let the past go. Tianzhe had been locked up in a labour camp for a while but he never mentioned it.

They also discussed the subject of confession with Wang Mingdao, thinking that having spent over twenty years in prison he should understand it. Wang Mingdao was very happy to talk about confession but he would not admit to being a criminal. 'Before God, I am a dirty and broken sinner. But before the State, I have never broken any law. Ever since I was young, I have always been naturally shy and poker-faced. I would never have dared to break any regulation. In this country and society I am a law-abiding citizen. But you still arrested me. I have never committed any crime against the State. I was imprisoned for over twenty years all because of my faith,' Wang Mingdao told them. 'I was against the Three-Self Church. I am still against it.' Seeing that he was so firm in his position, they stopped trying to talk to him. After the first visit, when they returned to see him, they called him 'the elderly Mr Wang'.

They realised that dealing with Wang Mingdao was by no means easy. They had just released him. How could they send him back to prison again? Wang Mingdao was over eighty. How many more years did he have? If they arrested him again he was bound to die in prison, and the government would get the blame. On the other hand, they were becoming increasingly concerned about his growing influence. In the end, they decided to monitor those who came to visit him, investigate them and discourage them from seeing him. Once they isolated him, their purpose would have been achieved.

On one occasion Mr Kong and Mr Liu met Sister Pan Xiumei, the granddaughter of the late Zheng Shuying in Beijing. When she saw Mr Liu, she realised she knew him and asked him his name. At first he refused to answer her but when she insisted, he told her a name, but she did not think it was his real one. 'When you led the Red Guards in raiding our house, you saved our house with one word,' she reminded him. This exposed his real background. It was the police who led the Red Guards' raids on Christian homes. It was said that Mr Liu was in charge of monitoring Christians.

The two men would visit Wang Mingdao every two or three months. After a few times Mr Liu was replaced by another man. The person that they watched mostly closely was the son of Dr Yan Baotian. Every time he went to give Wang Mingdao food and water melon, they were there. Dr Yan, who came from Shanxi, had met Wang Mingdao as a young man in his twenties on a train and their friendship started from that very first meeting. He deeply loved Wang Mingdao and had always referred to him as his big brother. He said, 'Jesus is my Saviour and Wang Mingdao my big brother.' Every time Wang Mingdao went to preach in his town, if he heard about it he would be there.

One day, Mr Kong and Mr Liu were sitting in Wang Mingdao's room when Sister Wei Shulan came to visit. Mr Liu asked who she was. Mrs Wang said she was their relative. Hearing this he did not ask any more about her. Later he told Wang Mingdao not to associate with bad people, such as Yu Chongen and Yu Chenghua. How did he know the name Yu Chongen? He had seen it on Wang Mingdao's bookshelf. In fact, Yu Chenghua had passed away a long time ago, but Mr Liu had no idea. They said they were trying to help Wang Mingdao, but really they were trying to limit his social connections.

One day Mr Kong and Mr Liu came to ask for Wang Mingdao's help, saying they wanted to find out more about the Seventh Day Adventists. The leaders of the Three-Self Church was unhappy about the fact that the Seventh Day

Adventists opposed it. Mr Kong and Mr Liu wanted Wang Mingdao to write an article criticising them, but Wang Mingdao refused, saying, 'I don't write for others. Many years ago before I was imprisoned, I wrote an article about them entitled "Must Christians keep the Sabbath?" You can read that if you want. I only write out of my own conviction. I never write for others.'

Wang Mingdao and his wife did not want too many people to know that they were receiving copies of Wang Mingdao's books which were now being printed abroad. But the government knew what was going on. One day when Mr Kong and Mr Liu came, someone had just delivered two books. Mr Liu picked them up from the table and had a look at them before passing them to Mr Kong. He asked Wang Mingdao what he thought about his books being printed in Hong Kong. Wang Mingdao said he was very happy: 'After I was imprisoned, my books could no longer be published in Beijing. If they can be printed in Hong Kong that is very nice indeed. In these new editions of my books they even include my essays "Truth or Poison?" and "We Are for Faith". This is good because people will then know I went to prison for my faith.'

These visits from members of the Shanghai Public Security Bureau continued from 1980 to 1981, when they would always send two officials at a time to see him, but from 1982 they were discontinued.

The transfer of Wang Mingdao's police registration to Shanghai went very smoothly and within a few days of his arrival in Shanghai, he became an official Shanghai resident. Since he would not accept the Certificate of Release, Yingying Prison changed its name to the Certificate of Reference and deleted the sentence concerning his early release. Thus there were no irregularities in his paper work for the Shanghai police to pick up on. Tianzhe took the certificate to the police station and he was registered within a few days. Mrs Wang's registration, however, was not transferred to Shanghai as easily. It stayed in Tangzhuang for a long time. The re-education farm at Tangzhuang mailed her twenty-five yuan every month along with coupons for food and cooking oil. From 1977 to 1979, she accepted the money and coupons, thinking that even if she did not need them, someone else might find them useful. But Wang Mingdao thought differently about it and did not agree with her accepting the money. On one occasion when he opened the letter with the money and coupons he sent it back immediately with a note: 'Such rewards which do not come as the result of work make it hard for us to eat and sleep. Please stop sending money and coupons in the future.' In fact, Mrs Wang had retired from the farm where she worked after her release and the money was her retirement pension. She really had earned it.

The delay in Mrs Wang's registration was caused because the Shanghai police asked Tangzhuang Farm to produce two certificates, one to certify that Mrs Wang was no longer able to work and another to certify that Tianzhe was her only son. The farm was only able to certify the former. Tianzhe's workplace provided a certificate instead, but the police refused to accept it. So the matter was delayed for five years. Mr Liu agreed to help her, but he was never able to. The process dragged on until 1982 when another official at the police station helped her.

In 1980, Wang Mingdao was very upset when he heard that Miss Bei had told some people in Beijing that Wang Mingdao was still under surveillance. He wrote a letter to her, asking her where she had got that information from. He realised that it was fear that had made her join the Three-Self Church but she maintained that God had led her there. He was not happy with her at all.

That same winter Brother Meng Xianchao of Beijing Christian Assembly sent a letter to Wang Mingdao enclosing some money. He thought Tianzhe was the only one in Wang Mingdao's family with some income so life must be hard. Brother Meng owned a clock shop and was a leader of Broad Street Church. Because their preacher Pastor Yan had joined the Three-Self Church and had become its Deputy Chairman, their church was allowed to remain open. Meng had also joined the Three-Self Church. In 1980, when the Third National Christian Conference was held in Nanjing, Meng represented Beijing and was elected as a member of the

National Three-Self Standing Committee. Wang Mingdao wrote back to ask him about his relationship with the Three-Self Church. In his reply Meng admitted that he was a member. Once he knew that, Wang Mingdao returned the money with a letter saying, 'I am against your church. We do not have anything in common. I hereby return the money you sent me with my thanks.' After this, Meng wrote another letter, this time sharply reproaching Wang Mingdao.

For the first year Wang Mingdao was in Shanghai, he only travelled locally. Although he was in touch with quite a number of, only a few could travel to Shanghai to see him. People in Beijing were longing to see him and kept asking when he was coming. When the Wangs began to say that they planned to come in 1982, immediately preparations began to be made to welcome them. One person said, 'If Wang Mingdao comes to Beijing, all he has to do is to stand in front of the church at Rice Market Street and thousands of people would gather around to listen to him.' Tianzhe knew that if his father actually did go to Beijing, there was bound to be trouble and he became very concerned. He wrote a letter to Mr Li Zaisheng inviting him and Mr Zeng Pingdao to spend the Spring Festival holiday season in Shanghai. Mr Li's wife was sick and initially he felt he could not leave Beijing, but after giving the invitation some thought he decided to ask a sister to look after his wife while he went. So the two of them left for Shanghai on New Year's Eve arriving on New Year's Day. When Mr Li saw the man he loved and respected, he was filled with joy.

After a few days, Tianzhe spoke with Mr Zeng quietly about his concerns: 'One of the reasons we invited you here is because many people in Beijing are asking my parents to go and see them. Their hearts are kind but my parents are too old and weak to travel. We have to work and we can't go with them. So we are very concerned. Please do whatever you can to help my parents change their mind.' Mr Zeng said he would do his best. By the end of his month-long stay he had managed to dissuade them from making the trip.

At around that time Wang Mingdao suddenly remembered a song he used to sing as a boy. In all the years of their marriage Mrs Wang had never heard him sing it before. His grandmother, a God-fearing lady, had taught him the song when he was only four years old:

'I am a follower of Jesus,
And He is my Saviour.
Although I have many sins and pains,
The Lord has died for me to save me.
So I always rejoice.
Jesus can save me from all my sins,
Because His grace has reached me,
I will rejoice night and day,
Jesus has made me victorious over sin.'

Wang Mingdao had believed in Jesus at the age of fourteen and it had really changed his life. He readily admitted that he was a sinner but God's grace and mercy had rescued him. The knowledge that not only had his soul been saved but that his sins had been totally forgiven filled his life with joy. His failure over eight years in prison had been forgiven. God had lifted him up again and enabled him to stand, so he was just as joyful now as when he had first believed.

Mr Zhou Fuqing, an elder of Manna Church in Shanghai, often came to visit him and they became quite close friends. Sometimes Brother Luo Chunfang, a young man in charge of the youth work at the church, would come along with him and on the surface he was quite close to Wang Mingdao too. After a while, Mr Zhou's began to have problems with his legs and he could no longer visit, but Luo Chunfang continued to come on his own. When Wang Mingdao came to realise that he was part of the Three-Self Church he said to him, 'You belong to the Three-Self Church. It is not right for you to come here so often.' He replied, 'That's not a problem, nobody knows anything about it.' The next time he came, he brought a box of cakes but Wang Mingdao insisted that he take them away again. Mrs Wang was too polite to let that happen so she accepted them, but after that Luo never came again. Wang Mingdao had a heart-felt hatred for the Three-Self Church.

In 1982 the Flying Doctors came to Guangzhou. They were a medical team made up of many foreign doctors who flew all over the world carrying out eye operations. It was hoped that something might be able to be done to improve Wang Mingdao's eyesight and he had registered for treatment. On 20 September he went to Guangzhou with his daughter-in-law for an eye operation. His own eye doctor, Dr Wang, followed them later. Unfortunately, the operation was not successful – nobody knew why. Some thought it was because of a comment Wang Mingdao had made – 'Such crystals once damaged would not be easily replaced in China' – which had upset the doctor and made him not want to carry out the operation. Others claimed it was because his daughter-in-law had spoken with foreign doctors without the permission of the Chinese doctors. Whatever the reason, they returned disappointed on 28 September. Dr Wang tried to comfort them by saying he would try again once they were back.

A second operation, carried out by Dr Wang, took place on 11 November at Rengji Hospital. When Wang Mingdao left the hospital on the 26th he could see better with the new glasses he had been given. However, because he had been in hospital for over twenty days with hardly any exercise, he was very weak and was no longer able to take care of himself, requiring help with the most basic tasks like dressing and eating. After a while, he became more like his old self. In September 1983, he returned to the hospital for an operation on his right eye. Again, the lengthy stay in hospital considerably weakened his health. Immediately after the operation, he could see but the improvement was short lived: eventually his eyesight failed completely and he could no longer read or write. Although the operations did not prove successful, Wang Mingdao felt it was all under God's control. The Wangs knew much blessing and good will as they quietly went about their day-to-day lives.

Between 1980 and 1982, Sister Zhou Yuan was mainly responsible for looking after Wang Mingdao and Mrs Wang and then, from 1983, for the next ten years, Brother Zhang Guanying took care of them.

Chapter 38

Years in Wukang Road

The house in Pingjiang Road had only one room which served as a bedroom as well as a sitting room. When they received a lot of visitors, as they did sometimes, it was much too small. On one occasion a group of more than ten Americans came to see Wang Mingdao. Some neighbours lent them some extra chairs and an electric fan, as it was extremely hot, but it was extremely crowded. On another occasion, a Japanese guest came. Before he left he asked if he could bring some people to see them. The next day ten Japanese men came, only one of whom could understand Chinese. All they wanted was to meet Wang Mingdao.

After a while, Tianzhe's workplace assigned him an apartment with two bedrooms and one sitting room. Tianzhe decided to give this apartment to his parents so that they would have more room. They moved into No. 69 Wukang Road in the autumn of 1983.

When he was talking to his foreign visitors, Wang Mingdao was always frank about his failures; he wanted to show them that even if a believer fell God could raise him up again. He often quoted Mencius to encourage himself,

'Dwell as widely as the world,
Stand as straight as heaven,
Act as justly as God,
You will win support from the people.
If you are not winning people's hearts,
You must be walking your own way.
No matter how rich you are,
Do not become adulterous;
No matter how poor you are,

Do not shift your position.
No matter how strong you are,
Do not bend to pressure.
This is a true gentleman.'

Wang Mingdao said he had learnt some of these lessons before he was fifty but it was only after that age that he had learned how not to yield to pressure. He said that one of the most important things he had learned in prison was to forgive others. Even if people sold him out, condemned him and opposed him, he was able to forgive them with the love of Jesus. Speaking about Matthew 6:14–15 he said we do not forgive in a sort of exchange in order to receive God's forgiveness: we forgive as a result of God's forgiving us. Forgiveness is not a condition but a consequence of our salvation.

Wang Mingdao still could not give up his desire for justice. He felt that if he could only present the facts of his case, reason would prevail and the wrongs he had suffered could be righted. He was concerned to do this not just for himself but for the sake of the Chinese government and the Chinese Church. He believed in absolute truth and thought it could be achieved. So he spent a lot of time gathering information to present to the government. Mrs Wang did not agree with what he was trying to do. She said, 'If you want to do this, take yourself out of the equation. If any part of this is to get justice for yourself, drop it. Don't even talk about it any more. If there is anything of you in it, you are merely arguing for own benefit and that is not right.'

Like many elderly people Wang Mingdao became extremely stubborn in his old age. Mrs Wang told him, 'You told lies. That was where you failed. But now, if you continue trying to achieve redress by arguing your case, that would be an even bigger failure. You must leave this failure behind. You think you were treated unfairly. I think I was mistreated too. You went to prison, so did I. Fifteen years in prison plus four years of hard labour. Nineteen years all together. There is nothing to complain about. Everything was permitted by our Heavenly Father. If He allowed it to happen, there must have been some reason for it. Even if we cannot understand it today, we will one day. I think it was all right. I don't feel bitter about it at all.' When Mrs Wang reasoned with him in this way, he could see the truth in what she was saying, and called her his wise wife, but it did not last and soon he would go back to it. In the end Mrs Wang had to give up trying to talk to him about it and just concentrate on praying for him. She was definitely a wife full of wisdom, knowledge and support.

Before his eye operation, Wang Mingdao had composed the beginning of a letter to the Chief Justice of the Supreme Court of the People, which he showed to some of his friends. Hardly anyone supported him in pursuing this. Not only was it unhelpful, it was potentially harmful. But Wang Mingdao insisted that he should write, and so others could only pray for him. Later, when he began to lose his sight and could no longer write letters, they felt his plan was being blocked by the Lord. However, when he could not see any more, he resorted to tapes instead. He made one tape after another to present his case. His thinking was still quite clear at that time. Sometimes, when he got the facts wrong, Mrs Wang would gently remind him and he would accept her correction. But sometimes when he was really concentrating on what he was saying and she interrupted him, he would get really angry at her. He never finished this work. There was simply too much to say. Even these tapes he made with much hard work disappeared.

In late 1983, before leaving China, Brother Wang Chang-xin went to see Wang Mingdao. Pastor Wang Zheng had just passed away in Beijing and the two men talked about him. Wang felt a great deal of sympathy for him as he had faced a lot of difficulties after his release. Wang Zheng's wife, who had been a faithful servant of God, had died before his release and, as his children were far away from the Lord, he had had to move to the countryside to live with his 77-year-old blind brother. When the Three-Self Church in Beijing heard about his misery, they sent some money to him every month. At first he did not realise where the money had come from and, when he eventually did realise, it was too late to return it all.

In this way he was dragged into the Three-Self Church. When Wang Mingdao prayed that day, he gave special thanks to God for taking Brother Wang Zheng home before he could fall even deeper. Wang Mingdao spoke of how important it was to remain faithful to God in old age. Many people seemed to be able to remain strong when they were young but lost faith as they grew older.

In his life Pastor Wang Zheng had been greatly used by God. He was arrested in 1955 and did not return home until 1979. In 1980, after hearing of Wang Mingdao's release, he had written a letter to him, from which it was obvious that he was enjoying a close walk with the Lord. He said he was weak and asked Wang Mingdao to pray for him. He was confident that the Lord knew exactly what lay ahead. It was such a pity that he later fell into the Three-Self Church's trap. After that, he publicly said, 'Today's Three-Self is no longer the same as the old Three-Self. Today's Wang Zheng is no longer the same as the old Wang Zheng.'

In 1983, Sister Liu and Sister Li went to visit him. Sister Li did not say a word during the whole visit, but as they were saying goodbye at the door, she said, 'Today I came to be Balaam's ass' (Numbers 22). Pastor Wang did not say anything in reply but later he wrote to Sister Liu, telling her that if her friend had anything against him she should say so. Sister Li did not want to reply because she knew he had a heart condition and she did not want to make him angry. Later, other sisters heard about it and told her she should tell Pastor Wang the truth. She then wrote to him saying: 'Balaam was a prophet of God who was sent to meet Balak. Balak told him to curse Israel, but he started singing praises. But later Balaam and Balak worked together to plot against the Israelites. You were once a prophet. Yet today you work with unbelievers to lead the people of God astray (Revelation 2:14).' She concluded by saying, 'If I have said anything wrong, may the Lord discipline me.'

Pastor Wang Zheng wrote a letter to respond to her. He ended by saying, 'If I'm wrong, may the Lord's discipline of you fall onto me.' Sister Li was very surprised to read this because God takes prophets' words very seriously. Within a week, news arrived that Pastor Wang Zheng had died and his death had occurred in a very strange and scary way.

After Wang Mingdao moved to Wukang Road, he began to hold a meeting every Sunday morning in his apartment. Forty or fifty people crowded into the room. The sitting room could hold about thirty people, and others would sit or stand outside in the hallway. At first Wang Mingdao would speak. Later he started reading his old articles, followed by some comments. After 1989, his speech became very repetitive. He would say something and then, having forgotten what he had just said, would say the same thing again. The meeting, which was open to public, was never stopped or interrupted by the government, and he was never even questioned about it.

In 1985, it was suggested that he reprint his translation of 'Building Virtue' first published in his *Spiritual Food Quarterly* more than thirty years earlier. This book had thirty-two chapters, eight of which (Chapters 3, 26–32) had never been translated. When Sister Lu Mingru went to Canada, Wang Mingdao asked her to enlist the help of Brother Wang Changxin to finish the translation. Wang Changxin agreed and completed it in the winter of 1986. The complete Chinese translation was published in June 1987 by Morning Star Publishing House in Hong Kong.

Before Wang Mingdao became ill in 1987, a Mr Lin from the Seventh Day Adventist Church came to see him with a theology student. Lin, who attended the Tabernacle with his mother, had been baptised by Wang Mingdao when he was young. Later he had gone to the USA to study at a Seventh Day Adventist college. After graduation he had been ordained and had returned to China to be the chief of staff of the Seventh Day Adventist Church in Shanghai. After liberation, he had been imprisoned for many years. That day he said to Wang Mingdao, 'In fact you would make a better leader of the Three-Self Church than Wu Yaozong. Your church genuinely was Three-Self. Many believers all over the country know you. You would be a much more suitable leader.' Wang Mingdao replied to him with these simple words, 'I changed my name to Wang Mingdao when I was twenty. I am not prepared to change it to Wang Judas when I am eighty.' Lin did not understand what he meant by this so he asked him what the connection was with Judas. This indicates that despite many years in prison some people still did not clearly understand the truth.

In the winter of 1987, Wang Mingdao caught a bad cold. His fever soon subsided and after two days' rest he was much better. Two weeks later, however, the fever returned and he was too weak to leave his bed. In December, he caught another cold. Doctors were afraid that the cold would trigger other problems and prescribed rest. After these bouts of illness his health deteriorated rapidly. He had problems walking, and by 1988, even though he was not sick, he became almost immobile. In the past when visitors left he would always get up to see them off, but now he was no longer able to do so. He felt weak and lost most of his energy. He also suffered from incontinence. By the winter of 1989, he seemed to have regained a measure of health and was able to walk a bit too. For over a year he did not catch any colds. He became very talkative and would often tell jokes. To clear his throat, he would often sing funny rhymes in his bed, such as:

> 'It's hard to be old,
> It's hard to be old.
> There's always stuff in the throat.
> Joan has become Jane,
> And Jane has become Joan.'

In 1988, Dr Billy Graham, the well-known American evangelist, visited China accompanied by Pastor Teng Jinghui. There were two things he particularly wanted to do on this visit: the first was to see his father-in-law's former home and the second was to meet Wang Mingdao. The Chinese Ministry of Foreign Affairs was informed of his intentions and permission was granted, but because Dr Graham was a religious man, he had to receive an invitation to visit China from the official Three-Self Church. This connection immediately made him unwelcome at Wang Mingdao's home. Dr Graham's senior advisors tried to mediate, but both Wang

Mingdao and his wife conveyed the message by different channels that he should not go. But despite the fact that Wang Mingdao did not welcome his visit, Billy Graham went anyway.

At about 10 a.m. on Saturday 23 April, Wang Mingdao had just finished his breakfast and was being given some physiotherapy by his doctor, when Dr Graham arrived, accompanied by his wife Ruth, Pastor Teng and an Englishman. Pastor Teng translated his questions. In describing his experiences of suffering Wang Mingdao quoted Revelation 2:10 *'be faithful, even to the point of death'*. He said, 'It is easy to be faithful for a short time. But it is far from easy to remain faithful unto death. Being faithful unto death is very precious.' The visit was very short, but Wang Mingdao found Dr Graham pleasant in many ways but he remained unhappy about his connection with the Three-Self Church.

In September 1989, Wang Weifan, Associate Professor at Jinlin United Seminary published an article in *Tianfeng* entitled 'Wu Yaozong and Wang Mingdao'. Wang Weifan had played an active role in the condemnation of Wang Mingdao in the 1950s and this had impressed the government, leading to his promotion from a student to a professor. After thirty or forty years of silence, he started to replay his old tune – no doubt prompted by the political situation in Jinlin Seminary after the student demonstrations in Tiananmen Square in spring 1989. He wrote:

'The first thing that caught people's attention was counter-revolutionary propaganda from overseas to the effect that Wang Mingdao had been sentenced to death by the people's government. All Wang Mingdao had to do was to speak out and make it known publicly that he was still alive. Yet he refused to destroy the lie. At the time there were peace-loving campaigns against the development of atom bombs. He refused to sign. Those who knew these things were not happy with him at all.

In 1936 when the Japanese expansionists came to Beijing, Wang Mingdao preached, "If our enemies are hungry, feed them. If they are thirsty, give them a drink." He also said, "Bless those who curse us and pray for those who insult us." He asked people to "bear with unjustified and unfair treatment from others." In 1947, he taught his congregation to "obey the law" and "obey authorities." Yet after 1949 he asked them to "risk and sacrifice their lives to fight, fight, fight, to stand up boldly in the face of death with no fear." Such comparison was like what Wang Mingdao told a group of students in 1948, "The Nationalist Party are our mothers, the Communists are our step-mothers."

Attacking someone as "unbelieving," or opposing or disagreeing with a Christian movement or organisation is not counter-revolutionary. Some people in Hong Kong and overseas tried hard to argue that Wang Mingdao was arrested because he opposed the Three-Self Movement. This was not true.'

At eighty-nine years of age, when Wang Mingdao heard about this article, he was extremely upset. He said,

'This is a complete reversal of the truth. I fought the Japanese for seven or eight years, but according to him, I was liked by the Japanese. I taught my people to love their enemies and to obey state laws. He said I was surrendering to the Japanese. I spent eight years in Beijing during the occupation resisting the Japanese. I was ready to be shot. But he still maintains that I was liked by the Japanese. As for the rumours, I had no idea they even existed overseas at the time. Not one person from the government or the Three-Self Church ever asked me to help clear up these rumours. My supposed words to students in 1948 about the Nationalists and Communists were totally fabricated. Regarding the notion that attacking someone as "unbelieving" and opposing or disagreeing with a Christian movement or organisation not constituting counter-revolutionary crimes, such talk is based on no evidence whatsoever. During my interrogation, I was told many times that "it is a crime to oppose the Three-Self Church."''

In April 1990, Wang Changxin and his wife came to Shanghai and stayed with Wang Mingdao for three weeks. Every day they talked about his life from 1950 onwards, and the detailed notes taken from the conversations form the basis of this book. Though Wang Mingdao was in his nineties, he could still retell clearly his experiences over the past forty years. His long-term memory was surprisingly good, although he did repeat himself quite a lot. He could recall things from a long time ago more clearly than he could more recent events.

From 1991, Wang Mingdao no longer enjoyed talking about the past and he became quite confused. In 1990 the Lord granted him a golden year. He was not sick even once, and he had a lot of energy to recall vividly his past. In the year before or after 1990, this would have been impossible. The fact that this book was completed and published shows God's special timing at work.

Chapter 39

'I Was Blind, But Now I See'

Mrs Wang had been blind for some years, having lost the sight in one eye over thirty years ago in prison and then later the sight in the second eye. But she never worried about the fact that she could not see. She had a wonderful peace from the Lord. Every morning when she woke she gave thanks and praise to God. She rejoiced in the sunshine on her face and in all the daily blessings she received from God's hand. However, many brothers and sisters in the Body of Christ prayed that her sight would be restored. Christian doctors in Beijing and Suzhou offered to come down to Shanghai to operate on her eyes and various other offers of help were made, but somehow Mrs Wang's heart was never troubled by her blindness. She trusted God and waited for whatever He might have in store.

In 1990, one of the brothers heard that an eye doctor from Seattle, Dr David McIntyre, had started working in conjunction with the hospital in Shanghai and every year came over to carry out a number of operations. This brother had no way of contacting the doctor but he did mention it to an elderly Christian he knew in America, who regretted there was nothing he could do either. However, a Christian woman overheard the conversation and felt led to try and help. She tried various avenues without success, but just as it was beginning to seem hopeless she discovered that Billy Graham's wife, Ruth, had had some contact with Dr McIntyre because he had operated on her son. When Ruth Graham heard about Mrs Wang she agreed to bring her case to Dr McIntyre's attention. The specialist agreed to examine Mrs Wang's eyes on his next trip to Shanghai.

When the news reached Shanghai, Brother Zhang Guanying, who was looking after Wang Mingdao and his wife, went to the hospital and learned that Dr McIntyre was due to arrive in Shanghai on 25 May 1991. Mrs Wang was still quite reticent about having the operation, insisting that she only wanted to follow God's will. This was a lesson for Brother Zhang, too, as he had to learn to surrender the matter to God, trusting that if it was God's will, it would happen. As it turned out, God led every step of the way.

The day after Dr McIntyre arrived, the hospital telephoned to ask Mrs Wang to come in to be examined. On examining her, he decided on the spot to keep Mrs Wang in the hospital. That meant that very few people knew she was in the hospital, which saved a lot of trouble.

God's hand was clearly in all that happened. Mrs Wang had been suffering from a persistent cough, which was particularly bad in the mornings. It would have made undergoing the operation very difficult. Yet two days before she went to the examination, her coughing stopped, and from that time on she hardly coughed very much at all. While Mrs Wang was in hospital, there would have to be somebody at home to take care of Wang Mingdao. Tianzhe was out of town on a business trip and his wife had to work every day. However, shortly before Mrs Wang was due to go to hospital, Sister Zhang Shuzeng came to visit them from Beijing. Since she had just retired she was able to stay on and help Brother Zhang Guanying and Sister Qian, who did the cooking, to look after Wang Mingdao. Then Zu Xingyan arrived as well from Anhui, so between the four of them they were able to make sure that everything went smoothly both at home and at the hospital, and Mrs Wang didn't have to worry about a thing. The way God made these supernatural arrangements was amazing.

Mrs Wang's operation took place on 28 May. Under the skilful hands of Dr McIntyre, within an hour the operation was over. Mrs Wang could not tolerate pain and was not very good at suffering in silence, but throughout the whole operation, the only time she felt any discomfort was when she was being anaesthetised. In the operation, Dr McIntyre

implanted a new lens into her eye. The advances in technology meant that she did not have to wear glasses, as Wang
Mingdao had done. In a letter to her friend Mrs Wang wrote:
'We really did not know how to pray about this but the Spirit
prayed for us with unspeakable words. We are showered by
grace and blessings upon blessings.'

On only the second day after the operation, Mrs Wang's
vision showed a significant improvement. She was filled with
joy and thanked God with all her heart. After twenty years
she was able to see herself in the mirror again. Wang
Mingdao was brought to the hospital in a wheelchair pushed
by Tianzhe's wife. After Tianzhe returned from his trip, he
took all the family photo albums into the hospital to show
her. She was amazed at how much everyone – including
herself – had changed. The fact that she had been blind for
over twenty had protected the other parts of her eye from
deterioration and so she recovered quickly. She was able to
see everything, but, because only one eye had been operated
on, she had problems judging distance.

On his trip to China eight operations had been scheduled
for Dr McIntyre and Mrs Wang's name had not been
included on the list. It was only as a result of Dr McIntyre's
personal request that her name was added by the hospital.
Mrs Wang wrote two letters herself to tell others about God's
healing touch on her body:

> '"Thanks be to God for his indescribable gift" (2 Cor-
> inthians 9:15). "From the fullness of his grace we have all
> received one blessing after another" (John 1:16). After the
> operation at 1:30 p.m. on 28 May, my left eye which had
> been blind for thirty-four years could see again! I left the
> hospital on 4 June. Before the operation, Brother Zhang
> Guanying said this was like water flowing where it
> wished. He followed God's guidance and completed all
> the preparations which needed to be made. On 26 May I
> received the notification asking me to go to the hospital
> the next day. Dr McIntyre who was to operate on my
> eyes carried out the examination. Before he finished, he
> decided to keep me in hospital. At 1.30 p.m. on 28 May, I

felt a bit of pain during the anaesthetic. About an hour later, when doctors put a bandage on my eye, I could see through the small holes! Now I can sing John 9:25, *"One thing I do know. I was blind but now I see."* Before I came into the hospital, I was prepared to pay the fees. But a sister volunteered to be responsible for all the costs. Because the doctor used crystal, I do not even need to use spectacles. It is so convenient. I do have to wear the bandage for some time but it is very comfortable. This operation was so much easier than Wang Mingdao's two operations in 1982 and 1983. The doctor did not tell me to be careful with this and that. All he said was to stay in bed and rest. God has richly blessed me. I know that many of you have been praying for me. All the glory belongs to God Himself! (14 June 1991)'

'"In the same way, the Spirit helps us in our weakness. We do not know what we ought to pray for, but the Spirit himself intercedes for us with groans that words cannot express ... And we know that in all things God works for the good of those that love him, who have been called according to his purpose" (Romans 8:26, 28). Without a doubt God prepared the way. Sister Shuzeng came from Beijing to look after Mingdao. Brother Xingyan unexpectedly came to Shanghai on 22 May. Thus with Sister Qian cooking, two brothers and two sisters were able to look after everything inside and outside. Tianzhe was in Beijing on business, his wife had to teach. Everything was better taken care of than I would have been able to. The second day after the operation, my vision had improved to 0.4. After leaving the hospital, it became 0.6 and 0.8. But since it was only one eye things were two-dimensional. The colours are very rich but it is hard to judge distances. For protection I have to wear bandage over my eye, which is full of little holes through which I can see everything around me. I know you have been praying for me. Now you can rest assured and give Him thanks. May our Lord give you strength and energy. May He make you love Him more. May He help you to please His heart.

The days that remain are not many. Strength is lacking. But guided by the Lord let us finish every step of our road. May God bless you and your family! (15 June 1991)'

God works in ways that are truly wonderful, far beyond our expectations. He knows the days allotted both to us and to our beloved in the world. He is not too early and not too late. Mrs Wang was given back her sight just before God took Wang Mingdao home All we can do is bow down before God in thanks and praise.

Chapter 40

They Rested
from Their Labour

In late May, when Mrs Wang had her operation, Wang Mingdao was still able to visit her in hospital. No one could have guessed that within two months Wang Mingdao would have left this world.

Throughout June everything was normal, and there was nothing to indicate his rapidly deteriorating health. The Sunday meetings went on as usual. His last messages were 'Waiting on the Lord', 'Misunderstanding' and 'He who honours Me I will honour, he who disowns Me I will disown'. After reading his sermon on 'Waiting on the Lord', he said, 'Waiting on God is an important lesson which believers must learn. It is one of the hardest lessons too.' At this meeting Mrs Wang shared the testimony of her operation to illustrate how she had discovered this truth in her own life. Because she had not done her own will but had waited on the Lord with all her heart, she had been blessed. On 16 June, after reading 'Misunderstanding', he added, 'Seeing me so joyful and happy, few people can imagine the terrible misunderstandings I have had to bear. From the age of fourteen, the person I loved more than anyone else in the whole world was my mother. My mother loved me to the best of her ability. But she was also the person that spoiled me the most.'

Based on his decades of experience, Wang Mingdao's sermons in his last years focused on knowing God, depending on Him and waiting on Him. It is only when we know God that we will truly be able to depend on Him and wait on Him. In these sermons he used his own experiences of success and failure to teach how true and trustworthy God's word is, and this made his messages even more inspiring.

On 25 and 26 June, he was still able to talk about the past with Mr Zeng Pingdao who came to Shanghai to see him. They reminisced about the days after Japanese surrender when Wang Mingdao preached in Yanjing and Huaxi Universities in Chengdu. Wang Mingdao remembered a story about Wu Yaozong who was a pro-Soviet and pro-Communist lecturer who taught at Huaxi University. In order to mock him, those who opposed him had replaced some words in the Lord's Prayer: 'Our father in the North [Stalin], may your will be done in China as it is in Russia. Give us today our daily rouble...' The fact that he could clearly remember anecdotes such as these from over forty years ago show that he was still very alert.

Only God knows what He has in store for us each day. On 2 July when he got up, Wang Mingdao had trouble speaking. He felt sick and as if his mouth was distorted. He thought it was because he was not wearing his dentures. But even after he had put them in, it did not improve. There was obviously something wrong. In the afternoon when Tianzhe came to see him, he told his son he felt unwell. Though he could still speak clearly, his speech was somehow abnormal. Mrs Wang did not feel it was necessary to go to the hospital but Tianzhe asked an old classmate who was a doctor for some advice. He was told there were three possibilities: a stroke, a blood clot, or not enough blood being pumped around the body due to a weakened heart. Since Wang Mingdao's blood pressure tended to be low, it was unlikely to have been a stroke. It was most likely to be a blood clot in the brain, which would need medical attention.

That night, Wang Mingdao asked his wife to read him the article 'God is absolutely right in His dealings with me' and he was able to understand everything. Before he went to sleep, his temperature was 37.4°C, but towards midnight he developed a fever and by the early morning he was hardly able to speak. He was rushed to Huashan Hospital's Emergency Department where a CT scan revealed a number of blood clots and damage to his brain. It was the blood clots which had affected his speech.

He was sent home after lunch where he was made comfortable on a bed in the sitting room. Various brothers and sisters took turns to tend him day and night, including the head nurse of Huashan Hospital who had just retired. She took charge of all the treatment and medication. They obtained antibiotics and supplies of liquid nutrition from the hospital. By this time he had lost his speech and his vision, and his right side had become paralysed. Two days later, he was no longer able to swallow and he had to be fed directly into his stomach. A few days after that, he had to be given oxygen. The various procedures added to the pain he was already experiencing and sometimes he would try to pull out the tubes. But his carers would whisper reassurance into his ears and then he would stop – showing that he still understood what was going on. Sometimes he would call his wife, 'Wen, Wen.' Now and then he had fever and shortness of breath, but his temperature never went beyond 39°C. Whenever he became conscious, Mrs Wang would sing songs of praises into his ears. On his ninety-first birthday (25 July), his tongue was so misshapen that he could not even say one word. Mrs Wang kept singing 'Forever with the Lord', hoping that the knowledge that he was getting closer to the Lord would bring him comfort. From his facial expressions it was clear that he had total peace.

> 'To dwell forever with the Lord,
> This is the desire of my heart;
> The time will come when I am resurrected,
> To enjoy blessing for ever.
> Today I have not put off my old clothes,
> Far away from the Lord there is much pain.
> In His blessing I set up my tent every night,
> And day by day I am closer to home.
> Nearer, nearer, I am closer to home.

My Father's home is in heaven,
My heart often misses it.
Sometimes faith helps me see it right before me,
There it is the golden gate.
I pray for the blessings of my Heavenly Father,
That He will fulfil His promises.
May His grace enrich my heart,
So that I can dwell in the Lord today.
Dwell in the Lord, dwell in the Lord,
I can dwell in the Lord today.

Between my breath,
Between life and death,
Only by dying can death be overcome,
Then there is life eternal.
In heaven I will gain better understanding,
Just like the Lord knows me.
Before His seat I will offer my praises,
To dwell with Him for ever.
Dwell in heaven, dwell in heaven,
Dwell with the Lord for ever.'

On Sunday 28 July, when Brother Dai Shaozeng woke up, he had a deep sense that Wang Mingdao would soon be going home. At 7.00 a.m. he called Mrs Wang from Hong Kong and learned that, just as he had expected, Wang Mingdao was in a critical condition. Sunday worship was just about to start at Wang Mingdao's home and Brother Dai, hearing the singing of the choir in the background, quickly ended the call. But he had no idea that within an hour Wang Mingdao would leave the world to be with the Lord.

At 9.00 a.m., as believers gathered at his home to worship, Wang Mingdao took his last breath and entered his rest. The joyful singing of angels in heaven was echoed by the praises of the believers on earth, taking this faithful servant of God before the Lord whom he had loyally served all his life.

After his body had been taken to the chapel of rest, a commemoration service was held at his home. There were readings from 1 Corinthians 15 and 1 Thessalonians 4 and the choir sang 'One day the silver chain will be severed', 'Forever with the Lord' and 'Meet again'. When the brothers and sisters were reminded that they would soon meet again in heaven, they were much comforted. This was a genuine service of farewell so there was no further service at the funeral home.

Mrs Wang was very aware of the presence of the Lord and felt a tremendous sense of peace. She understood this was the will of the Lord. Three months later, she wrote, 'Thanks be to the Lord; many people touched by the love of the Lord sustained me with their prayers. In fact, I did not know sorrow, because his suffering had ceased. This was what we hoped for the most. He fell sick on 2 July. On 3 July he was no longer able to speak. Half of his body was paralysed. He had difficulty breathing. Even respiratory apparatus could not help him. He is now totally released. I am only nine years younger. Soon I will follow him. Then we will meet again.'

Mrs Wang mourned deeply the loss of her life-long spouse, but she did not despair. The grace of the Lord sustained and comforted her. Her heart was so full of concern for her brothers and sisters that she had hardly any time for herself. On 25 July, in the very last days of Wang Mingdao's life, she had written to send some money to a sister in West Germany. She always said, 'To give is much more blessed than to receive!' Those who are always thinking of others are the most joyful and happy of people!

Mrs Wang was right when she said she would soon follow her husband. Only nine months after Wang Mingdao passed away, she became sick. On the evening of 15 April, 1992, she had hardly anything to eat. The next day, she felt weak and again had no appetite. She rested for the whole afternoon just getting up for supper, when she ate a few red dates and some noodles. In the morning of 17 April, she started to vomit yellow liquid from her liver. The same head nurse who had tended Wang Mingdao for four weeks came to see her. She told her the hard lump discovered two months ago at the lower right side of her belly had grown to the size of an egg. Recently she had felt severe pain there but, not wanting to worry anyone, she had not spoken about it. They wanted her to go to hospital immediately but she felt too weak to go. By the afternoon, when a doctor friend came to the home to examine her, she had a fever of 39.1°C. Fearing the possibility of cancer along with pneumonia and flu the doctor advised urgent hospital treatment, and by this time Mrs Wang was ready to consent.

At five in the afternoon, she arrived at Sun Yatsun Hospital's emergency department where doctors quickly diagnosed stomach cancer and pneumonia. But as there was no vacant bed they had to put her on a trolley in the corridor. Because it was noisy and crowded in the emergency department and they did not want her to catch cold there, they decided to take her home and treat her with antibiotics and liquid nutrition. They tried to control the fever, hoping to be able to bring her back to hospital for more tests the next day. At 11.00 p.m., she started to throw up again, and her hands and face began to shake. Her words became confused, except when answering simple questions. Her temperature rose to 39.5°C: her forehead and hands were burning hot, she was sweating badly and suffering from shortness of breath. They tried to bring her temperature down with cold towels.

At 3:20 a.m. on 18 April, Mrs Wang's face became pale and her lips lost colour. An ambulance was called to take her to the hospital. Her heartbeat was 120 per minute. The doctors realised the seriousness of her condition and gave her oxygen immediately. They thought the cancer must have spread, and the pneumonia worsened. They sent her for an X-ray but her breathing was so weak that they could not do it. On the way back to the ward she stopped breathing and her pulse disappeared. As the heart monitor still indicated a weak heartbeat, the medical staff administered emergency treatment and gave her an injection to strengthen her heart, but they were not able to save her. She died at 5:45 in the morning.

Mrs Wang's illness had only lasted thirteen hours, from being admitted to hospital to her death. Many people were shocked at how fast the onset of the disease had been. She had only suffered for a short time – it was only during the last two days that she felt intense pain. This was the mercy of the

Lord. Because her health had deteriorated so rapidly, few people had had the opportunity to visit her in hospital. So a remembrance service was held at Longhua Crematorium on 26 April, conducted by Brother Cheng Bowei. There were prayers, singing and speeches from a few brothers and sisters. The ceremony lasted for two hours.

Thus Wang Mingdao and his wife were both taken to be with the Lord. 'They rested from their labour, their fruit with them.'

Chapter 41

Temporary Home by Taihu Lake

After China's Reform and Open Door policy began in 1988, peasants in Suzhou began to cultivate a hill by Taihu Lake as a cemetery which they named 'Dongshan (East Mountain) Overseas Chinese Cemetery' and then sold off the land for burial plots. At the time Mrs Wang happened to see an advertisement for the new cemetery in one of the flower shops in Shanghai and she sent for more information. She decided to buy four plots, thinking that whoever needed them could make use of them. For years they were not needed and no further thought was given to the matter.

At the end of 1989, Mrs Wang's niece, Sister Liu Xiaoyu, came to Shanghai to stay with them for almost three weeks and, in the course of their conversation, Mrs Wang happened to mention the cemetery plots she had bought, and added, 'I was thinking that since your parents and we were married on the same day maybe the four of us ... ' But she had to stop there because it was too hard a subject to talk about. Throughout her life Mrs Wang never imposed her will on others, and was always willing to accept other people's decisions, but on this occasion she happened to let her niece know what she would like to happen.

When Wang Mingdao died in 1991, nobody mentioned this, but the year after Mrs Wang passed away, the family began to think about where their ashes should be buried. Remembering her aunt's words Sister Xiaoyu mentioned the wishes she had expressed and everybody agreed that they should be respected.

In the spring of 1994, Tianzhe discussed the arrangements for the burial of his parents' ashes with friends and relatives in Beijing, Shanghai, Tianjin and Nanjing. They all agreed that it would be good if there was a site where those who loved Wang Mingdao could go to pay their respects. Tianzhe composed the wording for the tombstone, which Brother Wang then engraved. It read:

Born on 25 July 1900
Gone to his rest on 28 July 1991

**Temporary Resting Place of Wang Mingdao
and Liu Jingwen**

Born on 29 March 1909
Gone to her rest on 18 April 1992

Son Wang Tianzhe
Daughter-in-law Ying Weizang
Granddaughter Wang Qingying

On 30 June Tianzhe and his wife went to the cemetery to make the final arrangements for the burial which was to take place in early October. On Sunday 9 October, over thirty close friends and relatives of Wang Mingdao and Mrs Wang made their way in two mini buses to Dongshan, which was situated about 45 kilometres south-west of Suzhou. When they set out it was raining but, because of road works, it took them over four hours to get there and by the time they arrived at the beautiful cemetery overlooking the lake, the rain had stopped. Thanks be to God.

Brother Zhang Guanying conducted the simple burial ceremony. After singing and prayer, Brother Wang Changxin, who had travelled many miles to be there, gave the message and then Brother Zeng Pingdao gave an overview of Wang Mingdao's life. The ceremony lasted for about an hour.

The brothers and sisters of Beijing Christian Tabernacle had sent a beautiful basket of flowers to express their love and respect for their beloved Mr and Mrs Wang Mingdao whose memory they deeply revered. The dedication card read, 'Uncle and Aunt: Rest in the arms of the Lord.' Although Wang Mingdao and his wife no longer lived on this earth and Beijing Christian Tabernacle had been closed for many years, they had preached God's truth which lives for ever. Their work was continuing to bear fruit in the lives of the younger generations of faithful Christians whom God was raising up to continue the spiritual fight against the evil one. Mr and Mrs Wang Mingdao were resting but one day, when the trumpets sound for the last time, they will be resurrected and raised up in the clouds to be with the Lord Jesus. Then they will hear the Lord say, *'Well done, my good and faithful servants. Come and share your master's happiness.'*

Chapter 42

Some Words of Advice

In 1985, at the request of his friends, Wang Mingdao gave some words of advice to Christian believers, especially those who teach the Word of God, urging them to study the Scriptures conscientiously and memorise carefully the principal promises and teachings of the Bible. Drawing on his own life experiences, he encouraged God's people to seek the truth of God's word with all their heart and then to expound it faithfully. He concluded with a direct warning to all Christians living in this world not to forget that they are involved in a spiritual battle, which they are well advised not to take lightly.

In particular, Wang Mingdao recommended three passages from the Bible which had deeply impacted his life.

The first passage is 1 Corinthians 10:13:

> 'No temptation has seized you except what is common to man. And God is faithful; he will not let you be tempted beyond what you can bear. But when you are tempted, he will also provide a way out so that you can stand up under it.'

Wang Mingdao told the following story:

> 'In the spring of 1921, I was expelled from school for getting baptised. I thought my decision would at least meet with the approval of my mother and sister at home but even they did not understand. Later, as news of my expulsion from school spread, many thought I had simply gone insane. It was an agonising time. I was upset even more by the thought that I had given up the hope of a good career and promising future in order to obey

God, but God did not seem to have prepared the way for me or to be opening any doors. Instead, He had led me into all this turmoil. I felt God was unkind, unfaithful, and unloving, and so I decided to abandon my commitment to serve Him.

That night, I thought I would pray and read His Word again. By now I had made up my mind not to be His close friend and servant any more. I did not know which passage I should turn to, since at that time I was still unfamiliar with the Bible so I randomly flipped it open and found myself in 1 Corinthians 10. As I went through the chapter, the verses delighted my heart with the light of truth. By the time I reached verse 13, I realised that the temptation I was facing was far from unbearable, however heavy it might appear. Nobody was holding a knife against my throat. So what was it that I could not stand any more? The passage showed me that I was being tempted by Satan. He wanted me to doubt God's faith and love. Immediately I prayed to the Lord, "God, please have mercy on me, because sinful desires have stirred my heart. Please take them away so that my faith for You becomes firm and strong." Thanks to God, He has made me victorious.'

The second passage is 1 John 2:15–17:

'Do not love the world or anything in the world ... For everything in the world – the cravings of sinful man, the lust of his eyes and the boasting of what he has and does – comes not from the Father but from the world. The world and its desires pass away, but the man who does the will of God lives forever.'

Wang Mingdao testified:

'One day, a few months after this, I went to Wangfujing Street.[1] On the west side there used to be a shop which was called "151" because most of the items for sale only cost one *mao*,[2] five *mao*, or one yuan. As I walked by the shop, I saw the many items on display in the windows. There were nice treats to eat, pretty garments to wear, fancy things to use. It suddenly occurred to me, "All these are good things that God has prepared for people. If they can enjoy them, why can't I? Because of my faith, I have been expelled by the school and have no job, no future. That's it. I will go back to my old school. I will confess that my baptism was indeed a mistake. The London Mission Society will help me to go to university and study overseas. I will turn back to seek all the riches and fun of the world." These thoughts grieved my spirit and made my heart very heavy.

Then, suddenly, I remembered 1 John 2:15–17. The passage reminded me that even the highest honour we could possibly receive, the best fun we could possibly have, and the most money we could possibly make, would all pass away. Obedience to God is the only thing that can and will last forever. These powerful verses effectively delivered me from temptation and restored peace in my heart. When I got home, I had the strength to carry on bearing the cross of my suffering and hard work. I had the peace to continue with my Bible studies.'

The third passage is Micah 7:7–9:

> 'But as for me, I watch in hope for the LORD,
>   I wait for God my Saviour;
>   my God will hear me.
> Do not gloat over me, my enemy!
>   Though I have fallen, I will rise.
> Though I sit in darkness,
>   the LORD will be my light.
> Because I have sinned against him,
>   I will bear the LORD's wrath,
> until he pleads my case
>   and establishes my right.
> He will bring me out into the light;
>   I will see his righteousness.'

As Wang Mingdao expounded the meaning of this passage, he alluded to his darkest hours behind bars:

'In September 1963, after receiving my sentence of life imprisonment with my political rights permanently revoked, my heart sank into total despair. I felt it was all over, everything. Had it been ten years or even twenty years, there would still have been hope of being released one day. With a life sentence, I knew I would never leave the prison again. A sinful urge again stirred my heart: I had had to suffer so many blows because of my faith to God, because of my obedience to Him and work for Him. How could this God still be loving and kind? I did not deny God, but I began to doubt His love and righteousness.

Years ago I had memorised Micah 7:7–9, and through this passage God helped me to remember His love and righteousness. It says, *"as for me, I watch in hope for the* Lord, *I wait for God my Saviour; my God will hear me."* Then it says, *"Do not gloat over me, my enemy! Though I have fallen, I will rise. Though I sit in darkness, the* Lord *will be my light."* His words brought me hope and comfort.

The passage goes on to say, *"Because I have sinned against him, I will bear the* Lord's *wrath"*. I immediately realised that the reason I had had to suffer was because I had sinned against God. On 7 August 1955, with a gun pointed at me, a sinful thought had come into my heart and I had told the first lie. I had thought that after I had spoken, my problems would be over. I would be allowed to go home. But it wasn't as simple as that. My first lie quickly led to the second, then to the third, fifth, tenth, hundredth. I have no idea how many lies I told over the years. And not only did I tell lies, I wrote them down as well. I piled on my head crimes that I had never committed. My original intention was to get out of prison as early as possible, to avoid a severe sentence. I did not realise that my lies would bring me no benefit whatsoever but would in fact do me much more harm, even resulting in a sentence of "life imprisonment, with all political rights permanently revoked."

The passage revealed to me that I had committed terrible sins against God. I began to confess before Him. I also asked Him for an opportunity and sufficient time to retract my false confessions. God showed me His mercy and heard my cry. By the end of 1963, the Southern Prison transferred me to the rehabilitation centre of Beijing Prison Hospital. I was given all the ink and writing paper I needed and ten months to write down my reflections and retract all my false crimes that did not really exist at all. During those ten months, my heart was filled with peace, joy and power which God richly bestowed upon me. Finally I was able to stand up again, from lies to truth, from weakness to strength, from failure to victory.'

Wang Mingdao emphasised the importance of studying the Bible and memorising God's promises and teachings. He said,

'For over twenty years in prison, I could not read the Bible. There was no possibility of having one. But the verses and passages I had memorised years before gave me a lot of strength, comfort, and hope. That is why it is imperative to memorise key promises and teachings in the Bible, to keep them in our hearts. There may be times when it is impossible to have a Bible with us. But if we have learned the verses by heart, they will produce a great effect in our lives. We do not need to memorise all the chapters and verses of the Bible. The historical records, for example, do not need to be memorised. But God's promises and teachings must be remembered well. Whenever we are tempted, when-ever our faith is shaky, as soon as we remember these verses from the Bible, we can defeat the enemy.

In 1 Samuel, we read about Saul's "armour bearer". Whenever Saul went out to fight a battle, there was always a man following him with his armour. Those who used the armour were not the ones who carried it. It was used by the generals. Ephesians 6 teaches us about the *"sword of the Spirit, which is the word of God."* Only the Spirit of God can use it. Our responsibility is to bear it. When the time comes for the Spirit of God to use the armour, we need to have it ready so He can take it from our hands and use it against the enemy to win victory. However, if the armour bearer has left the armour behind, if he hasn't got it with him, and when the battle comes and the general wants it, he says, "I left it at home," or "I lost it on the way." How can the general fight the enemy without his armour? Hence, it is very important always to *"take the sword of the Spirit."* '

On truthfully interpreting the Bible, Wang Mingdao said:

'In recent years I have come across many people in China who have misinterpreted the Word of God. While their mistakes were not deliberate, they have often used a few words from the Bible to justify their actions. Many of them have gone seriously astray and ended up in dire straits. I heard of a man who, after reading the story of Abraham's sacrifice of Isaac, decided to sacrifice his own son to God. He killed his son to show his faith in God. Killing one's own son is just as murderous as killing anybody else, if not more. He committed murder and was sentenced to death. The man came to this disastrous end because he abused the Word of God. All he remembered was that Abraham was prepared to kill Isaac as a sacrifice to God. He failed to understand that God was testing Abraham with the situation. Before Abraham plunged the knife into his son, God stopped him, *"Abraham, Abraham ... Do not lay a hand on the boy ... do not do anything to him"* [Genesis 22:11–12]. God provided a ram to take Isaac's place. So Abraham did not really kill his son. This man killed his own son. He was not obeying God's command at all but was violating the law. It was a disastrous consequence of utterly misinterpreting the Bible. We must be very careful. Not only do some believers misinterpret the Bible, but some teachers do so as well. This has caused much harm. It has dishonoured God's name and impaired people's understanding of the Bible. When Paul wrote to Timothy, he taught him to be *"a workman who does not need to be ashamed and who correctly handles the word of truth"* [2 Timothy 2:15].

The Church in China today is in dire need. Since the policy of "freedom of belief" was re-introduced in recent years, many foolhardy people, with the help of their churches, began to teach the Word the way they liked after reading merely a few verses and short passages. I would not be hasty in matters such as teaching others without carefully considering if I have correctly interpreted the passages and thoroughly understood them. Without correct interpretation and thorough understanding, I would not be able to handle the Word of God properly. I would not be qualified to teach others. It is because of this that people who hear me are not led astray.'

Finally, Wang Mingdao talked about spiritual warfare. He said,

'Since the origin of man, there has been a war, a war between Christ and Satan. In this war, we can only march forward. We must not lose ground. Once we lose one inch, we lose two inches, then one foot, three feet, one mile, five miles, ten miles ..., until we are completely defeated. My big mistake in August 1955 was to give up truth. I have always told others, "Say yes when you mean yes and no when you mean no; say white when it's white and black when it's black. There is no middle ground in between." I even used to carry a piece of white paper with me, and ask people, "What colour is it?" They would say, "It's white." Then I would insist, "Since it's white we must always say it's white. We must never say it's black, no matter how dangerous our situation becomes." Yet in 1955, I went against this principle myself. Because I was afraid, I called what was black white. As a result I was completely confused and frustrated. Had it been just left up to me, I would have failed all the time. But God for His glory and His name did not allow me to keep on failing. That was why He gave me victory after eight years of defeat. Now, is the war over? Not at all! As long as we live in this world, there is a war. We must therefore be alert all the time. There must be no carelessness, not even a suggestion of it.

For that matter, there is another passage that must be memorised, 1 Corinthians 10:12: *"So, if you think you are standing firm, be careful that you don't fall!"* Whenever we think we can stand firm, we are in danger of falling. I was defeated like that in 1955 because I took it for granted that I was still fighting a war. I forgot this warning. The battles during that year were bitter and fierce. But I thought I could stand firm on my own. Because of this, I was not careful. I did not stay alert and keep praying. As a result, I experienced a terrible defeat.

A while ago a brother who came to visit me, told me, "You must be careful about yourself. Many people in China and abroad see you as a banner of truth now. You must not become weak and fail again. If you fail again, many will fail with you." He was right. Since his reminder I have become even more careful. We must remember this important warning: *"So, if you think you are standing firm, be careful that you don't fall!"'*

Notes

1. Wangfujing, the 'Well of the Prince's Palace', has been one of the best known shopping streets in downtown Beijing.
2. One *mao* is ten cents in Chinese currency.

Open Doors Addresses

Open Doors
PO Box 53
Seaforth
New South Wales 2092
AUSTRALIA

Missao Portas Abertas
CP 45371
Vila Mariana
CEP 04010-970
São Paulo
BRAZIL

Open Doors
PO Box 597
Streetsville, ON
L5M 2C1
CANADA

Åbne Døre
PO Box 171
DK-6900 Skjern
DENMARK

Portes Ouvertes
BP 139
67833 TANNERIES
cedex (Strasbourg)
FRANCE

Åpne Dører
Boks 4698 Grim
N-4673 Kristiansand
NORWAY

Open Doors
PO Box 1573-1155
QCCPO Main
1100 Quezon City
PHILIPPINES

Open Doors
Raffles City Post Office
PO Box 150
Singapore 911705
REPUBLIC OF SINGAPORE

Open Doors
Box 990099
Kibler Park 2053
Johannesburg
SOUTH AFRICA

Offene Grenzen
Postfach 2010
D-38718 Seesen
GERMANY

Porte Aperte
CP45
37063 Isola Della Scala, VR
ITALY

Open Doors
Hyerim Presbyterian Church
Street No. 403
Sungne 3-dong
Kandong-gu #134-033
Seoul
KOREA

Open Doors
PO Box 47
3850 AA Ermelo
THE NETHERLANDS

Open Doors
PO Box 27-630
Mt Roskill
Auckland 1030
NEW ZEALAND

Puertas Abiertas
Apartado 578
28850 Torrejon de Ardoz
Madrid
SPAIN

Portes Ouvertes
Case Postale 267
CH-1008 Prilly
Lausanne
SWITZERLAND

Open Doors
PO Box 6
Witney
Oxon OX29 7SP
UNITED KINGDOM

Open Doors
PO Box 27001
Santa Ana, CA 92799
USA
Santa

If you have enjoyed this book and would like to help us to send a copy of it and many other titles to needy pastors in the **Third World**, please write for further information or send your gift to:

Sovereign World Trust
PO Box 777, Tonbridge
Kent TN11 0ZS
United Kingdom

or to the **'Sovereign World'** distributor in your country.

Visit our website at www.sovereign-world.org for a full range of Sovereign World books.